40-

Elusive development

The oil boom prompted a massive inflow of capital into the Arab region. But whilst the investment this facilitated clearly had benefits for the region, the developmental achievements of the boom decade are demonstrably unable to match the magnitude of the resources directed to development and the reasonable expectations invested in it. Professor Yusif Sayigh draws a powerful and painful lesson from this experience applicable to other areas: you cannot buy development; it must be soundly orientated and sought with resolve by society's leaderships and a people enjoying a large measure of freedom and political participation.

Sayigh begins by examining the historical factors which still affect Third World countries – colonial legacies and heavy dependence on the developed world for assets, technology, and thought. Whilst rejecting some aspects of dependency theory, he goes on to outline a powerful alternative – collective self-reliance. In conclusion he discusses the conditions necessary for self-reliance to be feasible, and the dynamics and machinery essential for it to be successful.

Yusif Sayigh studied at the American University of Beirut and did his doctoral work at the Johns Hopkins University in the United States. He taught for many years at the AUB and worked for a few years as a visiting scholar at Harvard, Princeton and Oxford universities. Since 1974 he has served as economic adviser to some international commissions as well as the League of Arab States and its major organizations. His numerous publications include *The Economies of the Arab World: Development Since 1945* and *The Determinants of Arab Economic Development* (both published by Croom Helm, 1978), and *The Arab Economy: Past Performance and Future Prospects* (Oxford University Press, 1982).

Elusive development

From dependence to self-reliance in the Arab region

Yusif A. Sayigh

ROUTLEDGE

London and New York

First published 1991
by Routledge
11 New Fetter Lane, London EC4P 4EE

Simultaneously published in the USA and Canada
by Routledge
a division of Routledge, Chapman and Hall, Inc.
29 West 35th Street, New York, NY 10001

Typeset in English Times
by Pat and Anne Murphy, Highcliffe-on-Sea, Dorset
Printed in Great Britain by
Biddles Ltd, Guildford and King's Lynn

British Library Cataloguing in Publication Data
Sayigh, Yusif A. (Yusif Abdalla)
Elusive development: from dependence to self-reliance in the Arab world.
1. Arab countries. Economic conditions
I. Title
330.9174927

ISBN 0–415–06258–6

Library of Congress Cataloging in Publication Data
Ṣā'igh, Yūsuf 'Abd Allāh, 1916–
Elusive development: from dependence to self-reliance in the Arab region/Yusif A. Sayigh.
p. cm.
Includes bibliographical references and index.
ISBN 0–415–06258–6
1. Arab countries – Economic conditions. 2. Arab countries – Economic policy. 3. Arab countries – Dependency on foreign countries. 4. Autarchy. I. Title.
HC498.S234 1991 91–2491
338.9′00917′4927–dc20 CIP

To Rosemary

Contents

Tables

Acknowledgements

I would like to express my thanks to the Arab Banking Corporation, Manama, Bahrain, whose President and Chief Executive, Mr Abdulla A. Saudi, and Board of Directors made available to me a research grant which enabled me to devote the time needed to prepare this book, and for the complete freedom I enjoyed in writing it. However, I alone bear the responsibility for the views expressed and the judgements made.

In addition, I would like to thank the Oxford Institute for Energy Studies which extended to me its facilities as a Research Scholar during the academic year 1984/85, and to St Antony's College, also of Oxford University, which invited me simultaneously to be a Senior Associate Member. The help extended by the Institute and the College, and the vast library resources of several other colleges in the University, enabled me to conduct extensive research on dependence and self-reliance, which are at the centre of the concern of this book.

Y.A.S.
Beirut, Lebanon

Introduction

The urge to write this book gripped me a few years ago, when it became obvious, from 1982 onwards, that the Arab oil industry was heading for a deep crisis that would last for several years – a crisis which was to be expressed in severe shrinkage in the world demand for Arab crude oil, and which was to result in substantial contraction in oil exports, oil prices and oil revenues accruing to the Arab oil-exporting countries. The 'loss' to these countries by 1985 of over half of their earnings as they had stood in 1980 was deeply bemoaned not only by the oil exporters, but also by the other Arab countries, owing to the far-reaching ripples which the oil revenues had activated in the Arab economy as a whole.

Paradoxically, however, it was not so much the crisis which was the motive force behind the urge, but more so the oil boom in the decade 1973–82, which had preceded the crisis. This was not merely because I assessed the nature and the implications of the crisis quite differently from the mainstream assessment made by Arab officialdom, and by the contractors, merchants and middlemen for whom the oil boom had opened the doors to financial opulence and, in many instances, to virtually astronomic riches, but essentially because I had assessed the nature of the boom itself quite differently. In my view, certain aspects of the boom had a grim side in urgent need of examination.

These aspects included irresponsible over-production and depletion of a most valuable resource; short-sightedness in market expectations; inflow of easy money and the resultant separation (if not divorce) between effort and reward, and serious damage to the work ethic; gross misspending both in consumption and investment, private and public alike; and, on balance, development which in some basic aspects was patchy, misdirected, distorted, and sustainable only because of and during the inflow of substantial oil revenues. Needless to say, these revenues did not derive from a renewable resource and, to that extent, were no more than the proceeds of a sale of a scarce asset rather than income from a self-generating and sustainable activity. But, above all, the boom generated the dangerously erroneous view – implicit if not openly stated – that money, and the open flow of foreign imports, together could 'buy' development as well as national security.

The preceding paragraphs thus point to the reason why it was the boom which betrayed the basic weaknesses in the perception and process of Arab development, essentially because the boom contained great promise. On the other hand, the crisis has emphasized the weaknesses, and to that extent its impact on development comes as no surprise.

Admittedly, what I have just said with regard to the grim aspects of the boom caricatures these aspects deliberately, in order to bring out and emphasize the 'social cost of oil revenues' (as I had referred to the aspects in a paper given at the First Arab Energy conference, see Sayigh 1979b). Undoubtedly, the oil boom generated certain undeniable benefits – economic, social and political – for the oil-exporting countries themselves, and for the rest of the Arab region. And it conferred some benefits on the world economy as well. The latter included the sharpening of awareness of the need for discipline in the use of energy, the urgency of the search for and development of alternative sources of energy, the intensification of world trade, and the outflow of substantial financial aid from the Arab oil countries to a number of Third World countries in need.

But this balance sheet of benefits did not succeed in muting serious misgivings in my mind with regard to the quality, direction, meaningfulness and sustainability of the 'development' which the oil boom activated. This is not to deny the impact of the energized drive for development. This impact was visible in the extremely brisk construction activity, the setting up of many factories and the broadening of the industrial base, the expansion and improvement of transport and communications, the fast development of banking, infrastructure and public utilities, and, above all, the improvement in the general level of living and the vast expansion in education and health services. Yet, deep down, the cumulative developmental achievements of the decades of political independence before the boom, and of the boom decade itself, are demonstrably unable to match the magnitude of the resources directed to development and the reasonable expectations invested in it.

The serious shortfall can be discerned in several major areas, which I will only list here without elaboration. They are: the painful underdevelopment of the two basic productive sectors, namely agriculture and manufacturing industry; insufficient rationality and far-sightedness in the formulation and implementation of oil and gas policies; the underutilization and/or faulty utilization of a large part of the land and water resources available; the quantitative expansion of educational facilities without parallel improvement in the quality of education; glaring slowness in the building of a base of science and research for the acquisition and implantation of effective technological capability, and this in spite of the availability of large numbers of well-educated men and women, as well as the loss of many of these through emigration; the widening gap in income and wealth distribution among individuals, classes and regions, in spite of the rise in the floor of income and wealth; and the fast adoption of a 'consumerist culture' (as one aspect of cultural alienation) which is not sustained by the prevailing levels of production and income.

In addition, two areas which are more pointedly political in nature can be noted. The first is the unduly slow movement towards effective political and economic complementarity and integration among the countries of the region, or some groupings among them, even though such movement is manifestly in the interest of the individual countries as well as that of the region as a whole. The second glaring shortcoming is the continued curtailment of freedom, encroachment on human rights, and the severe limitation of political participation as an index of democracy. It can be strongly argued that freedom, human rights and democracy are essential not only for the regeneration of society, but also for the drive for development if it is to enjoy broad-based commitment and to mobilize a national resolve behind it.

The overall assessment which can sum up all the ailments listed is the vast reach and entrenchment of the state of dependence of the Arab region on the advanced industrial countries, but particularly on the West and most heavily on the United States. This dependence, which had already been prevalent in the few decades following the Second World War, became much more pressing during the decade of the oil boom. It is manifest not only in the economic area, but also in those of technology, culture, information, politics and security.

This has come to seem to many Arab observers like a baffling paradox. However, on deeper scrutiny, it must be seen to be a logical result of the philosophy, outlook and positions adopted by those Arabs who influence the shaping of behaviour and policies. Their influence derives from their pre-eminence as politicians, intellectuals, businessmen or other actors within the structure of power and privilege. Furthermore, this influence can be seen with respect to political, cultural, social and economic issues. These actors constitute the major social forces in the 'internal factor' which largely determines the directions and content of the development being pursued. But they are not the only actors of relevance. The 'external factor' – the powerful forces and interests in the industrial world – is also of strong and close relevance. This external factor has changed its tactics and instruments in recent decades, but not its aims and strategy in its dealings with the Arab region, whether in the political or economic areas of life. The external factor and the internal factor, in their action and interaction, have made Arab society and economy sink deeper into dependence and distorted development. It is the abortion of much of the promise of the oil boom because of the interplay of these two factors, and the urgency of the search for a course of action that could vitalize the promise and give it credibility, that have together served as the central urge behind the writing of this book.

The essence of what I have ventured to say in the last few paragraphs should not be understood as the presentation of the Arab countries and region as a special case. I have focused on the Arab region so far because of my feeling that I stand on firmer ground of conviction here than with respect to any other Third World region. Nevertheless, there is considerable evidence to suggest that all the Third World regions suffer more or less the same distortion in their development as the Arab region, and more or less the same state of dependence, even though there are differences in degree and in the causes that lie behind them. Because of this conviction, the first and second chapters of this book deal, respectively, with frustrated expectations owing to a defective internal understanding and pursuit of development, and with dependence as a major cause of the poor harvest of development efforts in the Third World in general.

A word of explanation is called for at this point, with respect to Chapter 2 which deals with the paradigm of dependency. This chapter is not meant to be a treatise on dependence; nor is it justified on the grounds that dependence is the sole cause of *present-day* underdevelopment. It is rather meant essentially to provide a justification for the claim that self-reliance (as the antidote to dependence), carefully and gradually approached, could lead to meaningful development. To this extent, an examination of the paradigm of dependency is no more than the use of 'dependence' as an input in the search for meaningful development via the strategy of self-reliance. This examination will consider the value of the paradigm as an explanatory concept in the understanding of the state of underdevelopment and its origins, its limitations in the context of the realities of the last decade of the twentieth century, and the qualifications that necessarily have to be introduced into its content.

As the reader will see, I do not load all the blame for this harvest on dependence as a prominent external factor. Indeed, political independence, which is now almost universally achieved, together with developments involving radical restructuring in the socio-economic system in most of the European socialist countries and in China, and the emergence of the many organizations of the United Nations system as a broad forum for debate, challenge and interaction have together created a new situation that could be effectively utilized by the Third World in an attempt to free itself of gripping dependence. Thus it can be maintained that today many Third World countries – especially if groupings of them were to act collectively – could generate new internal dynamics which would enable them to face the state of dependence, even if slowly, and to seek development through recourse to the strategy of self-reliance, as an antidote to dependence. The third chapter of the book tries to defend this thesis.

With Chapter 4 I turn to focus more narrowly on the Arab region as a test case, by moving on to a discussion of the feasibility of Arab self-reliant development. The conclusions which I reach after an assessment of feasibility through the application of a number of specific criteria are conditional and rather heavily qualified. But they are reassuring enough to permit me to move on in the fifth and final chapter to an exploration of the dynamics and machinery which could make a determined drive for Arab self-reliant development operational and promising. However, here again the drive must be expected to produce not speedy and dramatic results, but a slow and graduated achievement. Hopefully, the test case chosen can be of value in the attempt to assess the feasibility of self-reliance in other regions of the world, with the necessary qualifications to take account of special characteristics and circumstances.

Yet, in the final analysis, I cannot shake away the fear that meaningful development, whether under socialism or under progressive nationalism, will remain elusive, unless it is sustained by a number of critical and tough prerequisites. Above all, these must include the resolve of a free people determined to rely on their vision and capabilities to the utmost possible, and to capture and safeguard their democratic rights, in launching the drive for self-reliant development.

N.B. I have provided both an English and an Arabic bibliography at the end of this book. Some authors appear in both, and so to aid readers in sourcing a work I have given a reference in roman type when the work is in English, and in italic type when the work is in Arabic.

1 Expectations and the frustrated pursuit of development

Carried on the wings of euphoria as a result of their newly-gained political independence in the years following the Second World War, most of the countries in what is today known as the Third World entertained wild hopes of swift and far-reaching economic development. To the vast majority among them, development, however understood or defined, seemed an essential supplement to political independence – indeed, they viewed it as the second leg on which their sovereignty could stand, proud and firm.

The feeling of euphoria was strengthened by a combination of factors. Foremost among these was the formal disappearance of colonial power from the land of the new nations – 'new' mostly in the sense of having newly-acquired statehood after generations or centuries of foreign domination. Associated with political liberation was the capacity for independent decision-making which was considered vital to the process of national reconstruction and development, through the seemingly unfettered control and use of national resources and conduct of economic activity. Furthermore, a number of the new nations in Asia and Africa found themselves with relatively large foreign exchange reserves as a result of war-time spending in their territories by England and France, the main former colonial powers, for goods and services purchased during the Second World War. These reserves were seen as a timely facility for the importation of capital goods needed for development, and as backing for the associated expenditure in local currencies.

The rosy expectations of economic development were in no small measure encouraged by the example of the prosperity and high levels of living witnessed in the Western industrial countries which Third World countries were not slow to set up as a reference group to emulate, in spite of (one might even say because of) the bitter recollections vividly held of the still fresh colonial connection. The desire for emulation was not solely internally-generated or auto-suggested within the Third World countries; it was also in no small measure externally promoted or suggested by the erstwhile colonial powers themselves. The interplay of the internal and the external pressures was intensified through widening contacts at various levels by politicians, traders and travellers, as well as large number of students from the underdeveloped countries training abroad.

One factor of great promotive force which helped inculcate and deepen the belief in Third World countries that the process of their development would in effect be the mirror image of its counterpart in the developed countries, though with a certain time lag, was the development literature pouring out at a quick rate from the West. This was strongly supplemented by the vast intellectual influence of the education and training in the West of substantially growing numbers of Third World university students, as well as by the active role of the colonial powers in the shaping and operation of the educational systems even after independence. This cultural factor represented one major aspect of dependence by the former colonial territories on their former rulers – a dependence which constituted an implicit (but sometimes even an explicit) admission of inferiority, helplessness and awe towards the Western country or countries concerned, and a belief that the West had the answers to the problems and questions which weighed heavily on the Third World. These answers were believed to come via conceptions and perceptions transmitted through the flow of ideas and the example of experience. More specifically in the context of development, the answers came through the teachings of economics and sociology.

These two disciplines, in their mainstream Western content and methodology predominating in the post-war years – say, at least down to the 1960s – provided the Third World peoples with the explanation they sought of underdevelopment, and with the mapping of the avenues to be followed in the pursuit of development. Though no attempt will be made here to identify more precisely the broad economic and sociological ideas and methodologies of relevance, it is necessary to emphasize three special interrelated features of the cultural factor that in large measure shaped the diagnosis of underdevelopment as well as the prescription for development.

The first of these was the neglect of the historical experience and perspective as a determinant of underdevelopment: specifically, silence about the direct responsibility of the Western capitalist colonial powers in the generation of circumstances that had brought about the underdevelopment of most colonized countries, or at least had blocked the way to development. Essentially, colonialism was 'achieved' through a process of dispossession, which was undertaken over generations – centuries in some instances – and took many forms. The basic form from which all others derived was the suppression of political independence and therefore the usurpation of the right and power of national decision-making in the colonized country. The economic expressions of dispossession, which were made possible by political dispossession, ranged from primitive appropriation of national resources and of economic surplus, and the takeover and exploitation of opportunities in mining, finance, manufacturing, agriculture, and transport and communication, down to economic legislation and the determination of the direction and composition of foreign trade and of the terms of trade – all in a manner essentially and glaringly favourable to the colonial powers.

Dispossession reached into the social and cultural spheres as well, involving the promotion of social organization suitable and subservient to the interests of the colonial power, and the blocking of such organization as would suit and serve the interests of the colonized. Cultural alienation was also promoted through the implantation of those of the occupiers' values, modes of thought and systems of education which were thought appropriate to the conditions of the colonized societies, at the expense of the national cultures of these societies and the scope for their healthy development. The combined result of the varied expressions of dispossession was the pauperization and the warping of the societies and economies under occupation, the severe dwarfing of their capacities and the long-term limitation of their potential. Understandably, this result went far beyond the economic sphere.

However, two qualifications – even if partial – are necessary here. The first is that colonialism did not fail to develop those sectors or subsectors in the countries under domination where its impact fell most heavily and strongly. Nor did it fail in many instances to transplant some more modern or more efficient political, social and economic institutions, or yet to provide the opportunity for the acquisition of some limited technical and administrative training and proficiency. But the prevailing characterization of such positive impact was that it was merely a by-product of the self-serving policies and activities of the colonial power, not a result of ones purposely pursued in the interests of the colonized. Furthermore, the resulting 'development' was invariably fragmentary and distorted, leading to dualism in the economy (and the society) and the dislocation of the patterns of social and economic organization and performance desirable to, or wanted by, the occupied. No wonder that this development, outward-orientated as it was, intensified the dependence of the colonized (peripheral) countries on the colonial (centre) countries in the world capitalist system.

The second qualification is that the colonized dependent countries suffered from internal structural defects and weaknesses, and in many instances were characterized by political and social organization and economic features and levels of performance distinctly inimical to an active and healthy process of development. The extent to which external forces and influences had brought about the internal defects and forces hostile to development need not be investigated here, although a strong case can be made to establish this as a historical fact. It is sufficient for present purposes to indicate that the external factors originating in the process of colonialism further capitalized on and consolidated the internal factors, as these blocked the emergence or operation of corrective inward-directed policies and measures. Furthermore, external forces and interests most frequently entered into collusion with particularistic forces and interest groups in the colonized country, to frustrate corrective tendencies. However, though the colonial connection had mainly determined the course of events in the manner just described in very broad terms, the mainstream development literature of the Western countries, both economic and sociological, failed to reflect the causal relationship between Western colonialism and underdevelopment, except marginally and patchily. The omission could not but be deliberate, considering the magnitude and force and the transparency of the external factors involved.

The two disciplines concerned together produced the second special feature of the cultural factor which shaped the nature of the diagnosis of underdevelopment and of the prescription for development. This was the ethnocentrism of social scientists in the West which led them instead to place the blame for underdevelopment totally on the Third World itself, through the attribution to its countries of a long list of deficiencies and shortcomings of political, economic and socio-cultural nature. In fact, reading the development literature of the first fifteen or twenty post-war years was like reading an inventory or a catalogue of woes, where the attempted explanation of underdevelopment was concerned and, by implication, how the cure leading to development was to be pursued.

The sociological and economic works identifying the handicaps to development contained long lists. These almost invariably included items like: illiteracy; the weakness of the work ethic; the low level of economic motivation; cohesiveness within the extended family as a value predominating over consideration of efficiency and purely economic criteria; social hierarchy on the basis of inherited status or sectarian grounds rather than personal achievement; insufficient mobilization of the financial resources available and therefore insufficient capital accumulation; rigidities in market structure; low level of technical skill prevailing; an antiquated and inefficient land tenure system; conspicuous consumption especially by the wealthy and the general weakness of the propensity to save; clogged social and economic mobility, and so on.

That Third World countries suffered from these ailments in varying degrees cannot be denied, although several of the presumed ailments called for a second probing look to determine the authenticity and the relevance of the accusation directed at them. But my criticism in the present context is directed at the self-righteousness of most European and North American scholars which permitted or generated no self-criticism and allowed no admission of Western responsibility for the emergence and/or sustenance of the negative features just enumerated, and therefore for the underdevelopment which they were in part to bring about or at least to preserve.

It ought to be added here that the kind of catalogue of social and economic woes just referred to was mechanistically drawn up. No doubt in some instances the catalogue was in part the result of some independent field research. But in the majority of cases it seems to have been the product of an inward look at the societies of developed countries. The socio-economic features or traits of these countries were thus labelled by Western scholars, and designations representing the opposite of the labels were attached to the counterpart features and traits – seen but also expected or imagined – in Third World countries. In fact, some of the features and traits became formalized in the literature (especially in comparative sociological works containing 'modern–traditional' sociological typologies) into pairs of attributes or labels,[1] or pattern variables, with the praiseworthy item in each pair applying to advanced countries and the blameworthy item to underdeveloped countries.

Such characterization was generally taken as a starting point in time, with no indication of its historical depth or genesis and no attempt at an investigation of the factors or forces structurally behind it, generating, intensifying or sustaining it.[2] But the central point that concerns us now is the fact that it was the Western socio-economic experience and wisdom that was set up as the necessary and sufficient model for the Third World to learn from, both in the search for an explanation of underdevelopment, and in that for a prescription for development. This matter will be discussed at greater length in the next chapter; at the present I need not go any further except to point to the implications of this ethnocentrism (essentially Eurocentrism, whether emanating from Western Europe directly or from the United States which, in the present context, constitutes an extension of Europe).

The foremost implication was the adoption, of necessity, of a universalistic approach to development,[3] which also saw it as inevitable and unilinear – therefore relatively easily accessible. Perhaps the most explicit post-war specimen of this approach in the literature was Rostow's 'stages of growth' (Rostow 1960). According to his view of development, the countries of the world moved as though in a caravan, some ahead of others, but all on the same track that would ultimately lead to the target of development, once they satisfied certain conditions or requirements that qualified each of them for promotion from one stage to the next.

It would be unfair to deny that Rostow's system recognized the differences in background and social and economic conditions among countries. But it oversimplified in associating the differences mainly with the stage of growth in question, and in laying exceptional emphasis on a minimal rate of investment to be achieved as the key to the motion towards the take-off stage and beyond, thus overlooking the differences between what we now call developed and underdeveloped countries – elusive and even misleading as these terms are. But what is much more serious than these differences as they appear today is the objective, historical process behind them which essentially brought them into being. Colonialism, as an integral product of the development of the capitalist system, and the expansion of the Western capitalist countries within the process of imperialism has no place in Rostow's scheme of things. And in this Rostow is far from being alone among Western social thinkers concerned with underdevelopment and development. It is no wonder that there was only one model in the repertoire of mainstream Western literature on the subject to offer to the Third World – the one that grew out of Western experience which had largely shaped Western thinking.

The third of the special features of the cultural factor – the influence of Western economics and sociology in the study of underdevelopment and development – is the confusion between growth and development, or the non-differentiation between them, historically, conceptually, schematically and operationally. While clear differentiation had been attempted early on in the twentieth century by Schumpeter (1949: Ch. II, Sec. 1), the bulk of the post-war literature used the two terms nearly interchangeably. The reader today is not in need of an elaborate or rigorous definition of growth and of development to be sensitized to the basic differences between them. Most readers now at least realize that the first term is the product of a positivist position and it relates to a narrow, quantitative, measureable concept connected with changes over time in the volume of national product or national income, in the aggregate or per capita. Although this change has economic as well as non-economic factors behind it, in itself it remains a purely economic concept. The actual growth is achievable without substantial change occurring in the structure and locus of social and political power, values, organization or technology – in short, without radical change in the non-economic forces of relevance to the operation of the economy.

On the other hand, development is generally characterized as a normative concept which requires and signifies cumulatively important transformation in the forces or areas just enumerated, leading to further transformation in them and in economic performance as well. The cumulative effect of development is not mere growth: in Schumpeter's terms it is not something merely achievable within the 'circular flow' of the given factors in the economy (Schumpeter 1949: Ch. I). Instead, it is a widely spread and profound transformation – even if gradual – in the capability and performance of the economy and in the attitudes and skills of the operators in it, thanks to the cumulatively significant changes in the political, socio-cultural and technological environment within which the economy functions. Whether the non-economic changes precede or occur simultaneously with the economic changes need not detain us here. Furthermore, development is not meant merely to bridge some income gap between the group of 'developed' and that of 'underdeveloped' countries, but essentially to improve the quality of life of individuals and to promote the socio-economic liberation of society.

There can be little doubt that contemporary Western social thinkers, who did not draw the basic distinctions between growth and development, committed this oversight not because of non-awareness, nor because of their underestimation of the significance of such distinctions. The reason probably lies in the fact that Western societies and economies had already achieved notable transformation of the type referred to, and had already built a substantial political, social and economic infrastructure and a well-equipped capital and technology base, that together are potent determinants (as well as indicators) of development. Social thinkers, being the product of their own developed environment, quite naturally emphasized narrowly defined economic growth as the critical objective to seek – for their own economies and, by extension, for Third World economies as well.

However, if no blame could attach to this attitude as far as the needs of the developed world were concerned, it certainly was blameworthy as far as the needs of the Third World were concerned. Such mechanistic extension of the experience of the advanced countries to the Third World came on top of the failure – no matter how generated or motivated – to explore and unmask the historical causes for the delayed and hesitant start in the multifaceted transformation vital for the process of development in the Third World, and to draw the lessons and heed the implications of such exploration.

Coming on top of their silence on the major responsibility of capitalism/colonialism for underdevelopment in the Third World, and of their offer of one model only for development moulded out of the experience of their societies and their ethnocentric intellectual orientation, the non-differentiation between growth and development by Western social thinkers has very strongly influenced development thinking in the Third World. Under this influence, and for at least two decades after the end of the Second World War, the Third World at large was trying hard to design and seek development along the guidelines of the Western model and the conceptualization behind it – including an overdose of confusion between growth and development – in disregard of the inappropriateness of that model for Third World conditions, irrespective of its merits for the advanced industrial countries. This has had serious policy, methodological and operational implications for the underdeveloped countries. These range all the way over the choice of development concepts, objectives and priorities, the design of strategies, the drawing up of plans and programmes, and the formulation of implementation policies and measures.

Without going into detailed or specific implications, we can say that the diagnosis of underdevelopment and the prescription for development, coming out of the conventional wisdom of Western academics and politicians addressing the problem of poverty in the Third World, have been characterized by two prominent features. These are the isolation of this poverty from the historical depth behind it, and oversimplification in prescribing for development. The prescription varied over time, focusing on technical assistance by the industrial world in one phase, shifting to investment capital inflows in another phase, on to entrepreneurship and the managerial factor in yet another. But in all instances the treatment prescribed remained skin deep, hardly ever deviating from the 'manual' in hand, whatever the treatment it offered at the time.

This approach involved grave sins of omission and of commission whose bitter harvest to a considerable extent explains why development efforts in most Third World countries are in a mess today. I single out and use the experience of the countries of the Arab region for much of the support for this judgement, without, however, pretending or implying that this region has had a unique or atypical experience among Third World regions. My references to the Arab region, here and elsewhere in the book, are essentially justified by my wider and deeper familiarity with its conditions and experience.[4] However, it is my contention that these references are also illustrative of Third World experience in general.

The mainstream development thinking and observation in the Third World, under the influence of contemporary Western thinking and experience, has in turn generated expectations in the Arab region, and in other Third World regions, that for most of the post-war period were on the whole fanciful and ill-conveived, especially as they were fattened on generous promises by politicians – well-meaning and machiavellian alike. As a logical result, the expectations have largely ended in frustration as well as in a vast waste of efforts, time and resources. I need not go into a detailed survey of the development experience of the Third World, covering nearly half a century now since the end of the Second World War, to show that the harvest has fallen far short of the targets set.

The shortfall is a matter of common knowledge and observation, and is well reflected in relevant statistics and qualitative analysis. It is also a matter for common observation and complaint in underdeveloped countries. The evidence can be brought together from many indicators. These include hunger among considerable proportions of the populations of many Third World countries, while statistics show rising levels of average income and in many instances respectable rates of growth; gross and widening maldistribution of wealth and income; poorly spread health services and the persistence of a number of endemic diseases; shabby and insufficient housing; shortage of clean piped water and sanitary facilities; insufficient and faulty formal education and technical training; shoddy and inadequate clothing; high rates of persistent unemployment; sluggishness in the acquisition of appropriate technological capability – and all this on a vast scale in every region of the underdeveloped world.[5] This statement can be better appreciated if read against the enormity of the problem of underdevelopment on the one hand, and against the time and vast resources directed to the developmental effort since the middle of the present century on the other.

This is not to say that there are not many bright spots in the record, or to deny that development is a very long process that cannot be, and must not be expected to be, compressed tightly in time. The creditable performance in many Third World countries, and certainly in the majority of Arab countries, can be readily seen in the expansion and improved quality of the basic amenities of life: food, health services, rising life expectancy, housing, educational and training facilities, reading material and other cultural and artistic output, the widening range of goods manufactured within the Arab region, roads, means of communication and transport, irrigation and drainage networks, electricity and piped water, well-equipped public buildings – to name the most obvious or striking indicators.

But the bright spots are discontinuous and not infrequently far between, often overtaken by relapses, failures or serious 'side-effects'. To restate the point differently, the islands of failure loom large beside the islands of success. Though both are generally real and involve the broad masses, the successes are often optical or statistical illusions and, where real, not infrequently benefit the influential and those already well-off. On balance, now in the last decade of the twentieth century, large portions of the populations of underdeveloped countries are still left in cruel need of many basic physical and social amenities. To this extent, it is as though the transmission or conveyor belt between economic and social performance and achievements and the masses for whom the achievements are, or should have been, primarily targeted is defective. And, in the international context, the underdeveloped countries are still in a state of painful, wide-ranging dependence on the industrial world, and more specifically on its transnational corporations, and are at the receiving end of a very inequitable and harsh world system of distribution of costs and returns.

To all this must be added the fact that internally, the countries of the Third World, with few exceptions, have seen their already limited political participation seriously eroded and their freedoms severely curtailed by their rulers over the past few decades. This has resulted in shrinkage in the people's say in the choice and design of the development they need and want, along with increase in the burdens – economic as well as social and political – which they are asked to shoulder. In short, there is no doubt that development is in deep crisis.

At the root of this crisis is an intricate interweaving of colonialist/historical, structural/political, conceptual/analytical and policy/operational factors. These factors, which essentially in their genesis derived from the influence of the colonial past as well as the external cultural factors operating in the underdeveloped countries, are becoming increasingly internalized as well. This is true as these countries become more and more used to their independence, the exercise of sovereignty, the freedom to generate their own concepts and undertake their own analysis of development, and to choose and design their own institutions, policies and measures for implementation.

The internal agents involved are many, but can be classified under four groups: development economists, sociologists, political scientists and social thinkers at large, as the providers of intellectual input; politicians, as the decision-makers who formulate policies and are supposed to lead the people and to reflect and respond to their needs and expectations; planners, as the designers and architects of development work; and the execution agencies and private business, as the down-to-earth interpreters of the development effort into concrete fact. There is enough evidence to show that the fault basically starts with these agents through the process by which they internalize Western development thought and experience – a manifestation of the cultural factor already referred to. This has made for a partial and distorted understanding of underdevelopment and its genesis and complications, and therefore of development and how its process can and should be put in motion. But this problem is compounded by the operation of internal forces and factors. The interplay of external and internal forces and factors acquires its own dynamics and becomes self-perpetuating, unless somehow the process is broken and its direction is changed.

So far, the Third World has by and large failed to bring about a reversal of the process. A number of its social thinkers have generated their own ideas with respect to development, and identified the quality and content of the development appropriate for their history, present conditions and future aspirations, and more in harmony with their culture and resource endowments. In spite of this, their societies have on the whole failed to generate their dynamics for greater self-reliance and more independent experience in a forceful and sustained manner. The allocation of responsibility for this failure between the external and the internal factors is not an easy matter. This is not only because of the intricate intermeshing of the two groups of factors, but also because we do not deal with simple arithmetic which lends itself to clear-cut calculation of shares. But there can perhaps be little disagreement with the statement that the pattern of allocation varies from one country to another, depending on the historical experience of each country, its internal structure, the attitudes and influence of its power groups, its social vitality, its resource endowments and economic performance, and its determination to reduce the degree of its dependence and to enhance self-reliant development.

How dependence and underdevelopment have been understood and explained, and how they relate to each other, is the focus of Chapter 2. But, more importantly, the *problématique* which it is the central task of this book to explore is how self-reliant development can be understood and sought. Thus the book attempts to assess the feasibility of transition from dependence to self-reliance. However, in the present chapter I concentrate on a more immediate task. This is a brief identification of the misunderstanding of the real nature and significance of development, and the wrong and distorted perceptions held about it; the misallocation of the tasks and burdens associated with its pursuit; the misdirection of its rewards; the confusion of its basic determinants and the insufficient involvement by the population at large in the development process at all crucial stages. In all these areas serious mistakes have been committed in the underdeveloped countries. These lie in the setting of the objectives, priorities, strategies and plans of development; in the definition of its agencies and their tasks; in the formulation of the political and social frameworks essential to its pursuit and in the policy and operational instruments designed and utilized in its service.

In consequence, other mistakes have been committed which are the outcome of faulty emphasis and, in many instances, can be considered derivative or technical. These relate to such matters as the pattern of investment resource allocation among sectors, particularly between manufacturing and agriculture; permissiveness not only in consumption but also in investment, with the result that considerable 'conspicuous investment' has been undertaken no less than 'conspicuous consumption'; the neglect of the countryside and rural areas compared with urban centres, though the cities themselves have their own sores of dire poverty, shoddiness, congestion, unemployment and insufficiency of public services; confusion in the delineation of the frontiers of the private and the public sector; the faulty choice of education philosophies and systems; and the weakness of notions and mechanisms of accountability in public life, owing largely to the narrowness of the base of political participation by the people, and the severe limitation of their freedom, plus the usurpation by the executive of the role and powers of the legislative and judiciary branches of government.

This is a long, though incomplete, bill of charges. Perhaps it can have better focus if the substance of the charges were looked at in the context of a discussion of four basic, organically related questions which the agents of development ought to address. Implicit in these questions is the need for purposeful and sound orientation of the drive for development, if the societies of underdeveloped countries are determined to exert sincere and energetic efforts to pull development out of its current deep crisis. The questions are:

- Why develop?
- For whose benefit is development?
- What kind of development is needed?
- How can development be undertaken?

These outwardly and deceptively simple questions in fact contain pointers to the four central and complex dimensions of development: its justification and purpose; its orientation and rightful beneficiaries; its quality and specifications; and its dynamism and machinery. To address them is to provide the rationale for the substance of the first two chapters of the book which trace the main intellectual currents of post-war years in the search for an explanation of underdevelopment. It is also to provide purpose and focus to the pursuit of development whose course this book sets out to explore in the remaining three chapters.

However, in spite of their central place in the developmental enterprise, and their complex content, the questions will be addressed in as simple and operational terms as possible, for two reasons. The first is a disclaimer: that it is essentially not in protest against rigorous, academic discussion (with or without mathematics, modelling and diagrams), or in underestimation of its effectiveness and value. Instead, it is to confirm my belief that there have been many complex academic works on development which are far beyond the grasp of the educated reader who is not a trained economist, and few works that bring the question of development within the reach of the general reader, to the point where he or she can identify with the purpose and problems of development and with the need to participate in the development effort – in its burdens and rewards alike. If development is a matter for the people at large to think about, to seek and to enjoy, then it must primarily be a matter for them to understand and to voice their preferences about.

The second reason for the approach adopted in the book is in protest against the prevailing tendency among today's writers on underdevelopment, many of whom are from the Third World, to be overly polemical, and to branch off into many schools and sub-schools of thought in disagreement over relatively small or obscure points of difference, or ones only mildly relevant to the burning issues of underdevelopment and development. As an economist from an underdeveloped region who is deeply concerned with the poverty and associated ailments prevailing, I find that the literature on underdevelopment – particularly the outpouring of works on the dependency paradigm which was initially of great relevance and explanatory usefulness – has become, since the 1970s, of more limited explanatory and operational value, and is rather confusing.

This has occurred because the literature has become more polemical, excessively tending towards purism, and narrowly focused on debating points, rather than attempting to achieve more synthesis of core issues around which a broad agreement can be discerned. Furthermore, by emphasizing the need for the search for openings that could possibly lead to development through the constraining wall of underdevelopment, I attempt to avoid the straitjacket of dogma which often severely curtails flexibility in the search, and narrows the options of action. Reality often allows more manoeuvrability than theory, and much more than ideology. And now back to the four questions.

WHY DEVELOP?

This is not a rhetorical question. It is necessary to pose and examine it in order to determine whether the need to develop is merely a notion in the heads of economists which they try to project to the minds and policies of political decision-makers, to the message of the managers and shapers of public opinion, and to the awareness of the population at large. The advocates of a simple or even primitive life, to be lived in happy austerity and in harmony with the environment and the resources available, have a strong case to make against the race for acquisitiveness, the drive to 'keep up with the Joneses', the submission to the appeal of consumerism and superfluous gadgetry promoted relentlessly by the media, the pace-setters, and the large multinational producers of the goods and services that these advocates rebel against.

Yet there is another side to the matter. It may not be true – indeed it probably is not true – that the masses who are the declared targeted beneficiary of development seek development either in an explicit, articulated manner, or as an abstraction. The vast majority of people do not understand development and articulate it in the formal way used by economists and other social thinkers and activists. Who has heard or read of demonstrators marching behind the banner of development, or mobilized behind one development plan as against another, or yet behind the demand for a 4 per cent rate of growth per capita as against 2 per cent? Nevertheless, the vast majority of the population in every underdeveloped country continually ask and press, march and demonstrate, and often rise in violent action for many of the very things which make the substance of development. They do this for jobs and income, for food, medical care, adequate housing and clothing; for cheap and efficient transport; for more and better schools; for security and a better future for the children; and for the right to unionize and have a say in the issues that concern them closely and concretely.

It is true that almost all the demands just enumerated are components of what is now placed under the rubric of 'basic human needs' (see Streeton 1979; Streeton *et al.* 1981; Stewart 1985, and International Labour Office 1976), but they leave out much of what is considered part of the substance of development in formal development thought or in formal development plans. However, the statement calls for some explanation and qualification. Economists and planners defining or characterizing development in a rather formal way would generally agree that it involves changes in values, motivation, work attitudes, social organization and technological capability, which together lead to expansion, improvement and sophistication in the productive power of the economy. These changes constitute part of the wide-ranging and profound transformation which, as I had indicated earlier, differentiates narrowly defined growth from broad development. Such a position is consistent with the development economist's understanding and definition or characterization of development, if his or her social vision is wide and reaches far beyond the purely economic conceptualization.

That the position of the population does not fully coincide with the economist's or the social thinker's invalidates neither. The public at large characterizes development, and seeks it, in practical terms via its manifestations which are of direct and close meaning to itself. It is an awareness and a view of development that is perception-specific and society-specific, which relates to highly desired needs that belong to the day-to-day and, beyond that, to the future pursuit of welfare and socio-economic security in a particular country or even one community in a country.

On the other hand, the development economist, as a social thinker, has of necessity to have a wider horizon within which to place his view of development. This horizon will, of necessity, comprise not only the content of development expressed in the components of 'basic human needs' which loom large in the perception of the general public, but also those other goods and services which the earners of higher income in the middle- and upper-income strata of the population want and for which they generate an effective demand, and the improvement and sophistication in the productive capacity of the economy to cope with all branches and aspects of production and distribution. Such capacity will naturally have to include factories, road networks, irrigation and drainage systems, banks, and all the other parts of a complex, national productive machine.

Consequently the horizon of the development economist, especially if his or her intellectual interest is wide and explorative enough, has to comprise the political, socio-cultural, organizational, institutional and technological components of the transformation that he considers essential for the improvement and widening of the performance of the economy. This condition will have to be satisfied for the economy to ensure first the ability to produce the wide range of goods and services, demanded primarily with articulation and insistence by the general public, but also by the well-off and rich strata of the population, and second the ability to distribute the social output and economic opportunities as equitably as possible. Hence the greater role that conception plays in the understanding or definition of development, and of the need for it, seen by development economists (and other social thinkers) than in that of the down-to-earth general public.

FOR WHOSE BENEFIT IS DEVELOPMENT?

The attempt to answer the first question has led in a natural way to the question presently addressed. Here it is necessary to try to combine the rationale of the general public and that of the development economist and planner, in their desire for development and the identification of the beneficiaries who should be targeted. To do so in direct and simple terms, we can say that the drive for development for the satisfaction of basic human needs – a concrete critical necessity for the bulk of any population in a developing country – is no mean ambition and objective, if it is borne in mind that basic needs ought to be understood dynamically.

By this I mean that the satisfaction of each 'generation' of basic needs opens the door and creates the pressure for another generation characterized by greater abundance, a wider variety, and better quality of goods and services. In other words, the satisfaction of basic human needs creates the appetite for what looked before like less-basic needs. A society setting this dynamic objective for itself can be sure, first, to remain occupied with the tasks of development for a long time, and second, to have to acquire many of the capabilities (technological, organizational, educational, vocational, and so on) without which the production of the goods and services involved cannot be assured efficiently and adequately, and their distribution as equitably as reasonable and possible.

However, to satisfy basic human needs in this dynamic sense, through the efforts of a society in the Third World, would represent the realization of a major component of the ambitious conception of development of the economist or social thinker. This is necessarily so since the ability to exert the effort required would call for the translation of a considerable part of the society's and economy's potential into concrete reality. And such translation is the core substance of development as the development economist has to see it, if he is truly concerned with the welfare of the bulk of the population. Indeed, at this point one can raise the distinction between the *needs* of the poor, the underprivileged and the disenfranchised masses, and the *wants* of the better-off and rich minority in any population.

The former truly and literally need what they explicitly ask or even agitate for; the latter wish to have the semi-luxury or luxury items they want to possess, though these cannot be considered truly crucial in their life. In the case of the former group, it is the aggregate demand of the underprivileged which largely draws forth the supply. In the case of the latter, it is usually the supply (supported by the force of the media and advertising) which largely creates, or stimulates, the demand. And here lies a central distinction between development ignited and activated by the pull of basic needs demand, and that largely ignited and activated by the push of the multinational producers (and their powerful salesmanship), that is, by the supply of not-so-essential (or less essential) goods and services which the strong effective demand of the well-off and the rich can eventually clear off the market.

Supposedly, the developers/planners in most Third World countries have the basic needs of the majority of the population in mind when they set out to plan the development of their economy. This can be read in plan documents and heard in the rhetoric of politicians all over the media. And, in many instances, the programmes and projects that are included in the plans, and to a certain extent are fortunate enough to come to their fruition wholly or in part, coincide with the pressure by the poor majority for basic human needs. To this extent, the concrete perception of this majority of what development means (and why it should be pursued) merges or blends with the more abstract conception or vision of the developmentalists: in other words, to this extent development moves from the realm of abstraction to the world of real people.

But the sights of the developers – who can be thought of as forming a network which includes politicians, economists, planners, executing agencies (including private businesses) – in fact never stay focused for long on the needs of the poor majority. They soon shift to the conception of development as a broad abstraction (even if expressed in quantitative terms as aggregates, averages, or percentage points). And these sights are then raised to reach the further horizon: to scan the areas of production well beyond the contents of the basket of basic needs, and therefore to build the production capacity able to cope with the more varied, more sophisticated, better-quality semi-luxury and luxury goods and services that the well-off and the rich want to have. Indeed, even with their initial concern to satisfy these non-basic wants, the developers often fight a losing battle against the importation of foreign counterparts of the coveted goods and services, which usually enjoy greater status and prestige appeal and promise a fuller satisfaction of the urge for conspicuous consumption.

It is here in the shift of focus and emphasis from the needs of the masses to the wants of the better-off and the rich that scarce resources and efforts move away from the more urgent, but less powerful, need-orientated economic activity to the less urgent but more powerful want-orientated activity. Thus, the experience of the Third World over the past decades since the end of the Second World War has revealed that the interests of the majority of virtually every population have rarely ever remained for long at the centre of the purpose and concern of the power elite, or even of the developers who presumably ought to be essentially concerned with this majority.

It can be strongly argued that development must target the whole of society: the middle- and upper-income groups in the population, along with the lower-income groups, and should therefore aim at building the productive capacity to satisfy the combined effective demand of all these groups. This is not out of line with social systems based on and structured along capitalist principles, whether they are dominated by private enterprise or state capitalism, or a mixture of both. As only a handful of Third World countries have adopted socialism as a social system and adhered to it consistently – apart from paying it lip service – it can safely be said that the developers in the societies structured along the lines of private enterprise and state capitalism are consistent in their choice of development philosophy and policy options. It may also be suggested in apology that they ought to be judged against such philosophy and options, not against some 'idealistic', utopian or populist philosophy or social system not predominant in their society.[6]

But such arguments amount to no more than an escape from the central issue: that development ought essentially to be concerned with the interests of the underprivileged majority, the powerless, the disenfranchised, not in spite of their handicap but because of it. However, in the real world, development is not so orientated in practice and in its final results. The rhetoric of the apologists can be met by the counter-question: why should the main developmental effort, and the bulk of investment resources, not be so allocated as to serve, first and foremost, the interests and the needs of the majority of the population? What principle or system of true democracy can rightly justify that the majority should receive, proportionately, little concern, attention, effort and resources in the pattern of priorities translated in the developmental enterprise?

The answer to the question 'For whose benefit is development?' would then simply be: primarily for the majority, which is to be provided with what it needs and deserves, with the goods and services that satisfy its basic human needs in a dynamic sense. The productive capacity of society should be designed and built to this end. And for this to happen, the wide-ranging economic and non-economic transformation (referred to earlier) ought to be energetically promoted and sought, so that society as a whole, and individual citizens, can experience self-fulfilment to the utmost of their potential. This is a tall order. But to the extent that human, natural, and man-made resources allow, the development effort ought in addition to attend to the wants/demands of the better-off and the rich among the population, also along an order of priority elaborated by the politico-social system under which the poorer majority should occupy their rightful place. But to define the system to be asked to order priorities in this fashion would take us to a discussion of the machinery of development, which will only be undertaken later on in the present chapter, when the fourth question will be addressed.

The last few paragraphs contain a basic distinction between two types of development, and not a marginal or superficial difference in emphasis. The first, 'mainstream' type is the widely predominant one under the influence of capitalism and a market economy, where the basic orientation of the developmental efforts is to produce what the market is willing and able to pay for. This is a value-free, positivist orientation – indeed, a 'non-orientation orientation'.

In contrast to the mainstream type of development, which is the product of the largely prevailing conventional wisdom, there is the second, 'counterpoint' development philosophy and orientation.[7] This is value laden and has an explicit normative orientation, with its primary emphasis on development for the people and by the people –

that is, essentially on the powerless, underprivileged majority. As indicated further above, this orientation does not exclude the wants of the well-off and the rich, but it starts from the explicit and non-apologetic position that the basic human needs of the poor should occupy top priority in the concern of society, and, more specifically, of what I designate as the 'development network'. That the under-privileged majority does not command a purchasing power immense and influential enough to determine the direction of production is not accepted, by those upholding the normative orientation, as enough justification for the (not so benign) neglect this majority receives.

Although the view of development of the second type is currently espoused by a relatively large number of development economists in the Third World, it remains in actual practice a minority view, judging by the approaches to development adopted: from the philosophy underlying these approaches, to the objectives and priorities set for development and the plans formulated to embody them, all the way down to the policies and execution measures, and the programmes, laid down and implemented. The second type under discussion is embodied in the systems of thought now known under such labels as 'another' or 'alternative development', 'basic human needs satisfaction', 'self-reliant development' and 'populism or populist development'. That these have some common features or emanate from very much the same concerns and values does not negate the fact that they are conceptually distinguishable from each other. I will be referring to them at greater length when I come to examine the third question in due course, and need go no further here into their content and implications.

However, it is necessary to register a brief comment here on the development experience of most developing countries in the post-war period, with respect to the manner in which the question under examination now has in practice been answered. In most of the Third World, and certainly in most Arab countries, the answer has so far contained a great deal of ambivalence, if not outright 'double-talk'. Thus, the politicians, economists, development planners and executing agencies, and even the leaders of the business community, have consistently and loudly declared themselves to be believers in and seekers of the second, that is the normative, orientation of development. But in fact, the same elements of the development network just enumerated have in practice mainly promoted a development of the first, positivist orientation which submits to and reflects the power of market forces and the wants and purchasing power of the better-off and the rich. This is what, by and large, the concrete answer to the question under examination has been in practice.

It is necessary to make a few qualifications to the response of the economic performance of the society to the aggregate demand of all strata of the population – poor, middle-income and rich alike – apart from the social considerations brought up earlier. The first qualification is that the beneficiary of development must not be seen as merely the consuming public, even if insistence is placed on the expansion and the variety and improvement of the quality of the goods and services targeted for production, and therefore on the expansion and the improvement of the productive capability of the economy.

The deep changes just referred to cannot be realized unless a number of social, cultural and political objectives of value to society are also sought. These partly precede development, partly overlap it, and partly are served by the unfolding of the development process; but the time association need not detain us here. They include education and the acquisition of effective and appropriate technological capability; promotion of the arts; the encouragement of horizontal association at the local, subnational and national levels among people with like or similar interests and occupations; and wider-ranging political participation and freedom – just to list a limited number of prominent objectives. In brief, the fulfilment or realization of society's and the individual's potential ought to be the ultimate beneficiary.

Needless to say, society must also devote attention and resources to its security, in order to shield its developmental achievements against external attack and internal attrition. In this context, security must be understood in a broad sense that goes beyond the military aspect. It includes economic security involving the ability of the economy to provide much of what the society needs by way of goods and services, for consumption and investment, and for export in exchange for imports.

Of particular significance in this matter is food security, seriously and dangerously exposed in most Third World countries, dependent as they are for a substantial part of their food requirements on imports that can only be obtained against the outlay of scarce foreign exchange resources. (The Arab region, for instance, imported more than half of its food requirements, to the tune of about $23 billion annually in the first half of the 1980s, but about $14 billion for 1987.) Closely associated with economic security is technological security, which involves a tangible reduction in the degree of dependence on the advanced industrial countries and their transnational corporations for excessively much of the hardware and software of technology. To reduce dependence, a society must build a sound science and technology base, and gradually move into greater self-reliance and the adaptation of available imported technology to become more appropriate to its human and resource endowments, and its culture and values. Undoubtedly, the ultimate objective would be the acquisition and implantation of considerable technological capability within society itself and through its own inventiveness and problem-solving ability.

Other aspects of security involve information, cultural alienation, and political vulnerability, but it would take us far outside the scope of the present chapter to discuss them. However, it must be emphasized here that these aspects are probably the most serious and most in need of curative and preventive attention. This is so because excessive dependence on the advanced industrial countries is essentially a matter of socio-cultural attitudes and political alignments of power elites in Third World countries. Many of these elites are externally orientated rather than concerned with the society's identity and its own interests and internal sources of cultural richness, political self-reliance and self-respect.

Two final points must be made in connection with the notion of security. The first relates to the military aspects of security, and here it is undeniable that Third World countries in the aggregate are devoting excessively large portions of their domestic product to the acquisition of arms and technical military aid, away from development. According to a recent IMF study, the proportion is 2.8 per cent of aggregate gross domestic product, on average.[8] In the Arab region alone, the outlay on arms imports and related imported services has been absorbing about 4 per cent of aggregate gross domestic product per annum, on average, since the early 1970s.[9] This outlay does not include purchases of locally-produced military equipment and services for which payment is made in local currency, though many of the inputs used in the local production of arms are also imported against foreign exchange.

The defence of national territory and interests is certainly legitimate. But what can be witnessed is the obsession with defence to the point of the creation of imaginary enemies or the exaggeration of the menace of real ones, and the submission to the attraction which modern and ever-changing weapon systems have for governments (and certainly for arms dealers or middlemen eager for their fat commissions from suppliers). The irony is that often the arms imported at exorbitant prices are not used against the enemy – real or presumed – and often deteriorate or go rusty while in storage. In fact, in many Third World countries, even the proper maintenance of the modern, complicated and sophisticated arms remains for years beyond the capability of the national armies, to say nothing of the effective use of these arms in the field. Often, the weapon arsenals and the armies are essentially meant for the internal security of the ruling juntas or regimes, or as a warning to neighbours often referred to as 'sister countries', not in reality for a genuine external enemy. But in any case, an unduly large portion of the military hardware acquired becomes obsolete before it is ever used or is likely to be used, and adds to the heaps of scrap.

The second point relates to what should be understood by the concept of security itself. If it is necessary to emphasize here that what should realistically and properly be sought is not absolute security, that is, total non-vulnerability, whether to military or political incursion or danger, or to dependence on external suppliers of technology and food imports, or yet to cultural and informational interaction and exchanges. It would be not only unrealistic to seek or expect such absolute or total security – that is, complete absence of dependence and complete self-reliance – but absurd as well, even if such absoluteness were possible.

There is no need to go any further in the discussion of dependence and self-reliance in the present context, since these are issues that will be dealt with at greater length in the following chapters of the book. What I want to emphasize here is the urgency for Third World countries to seek self-reliance seriously, that is, realistically and intelligently, and to design development so that security in the measured sense used here will be served. Finally, with respect to the qualification now being discussed, the seriousness of the pursuit of security-focused self-reliance derives from the fact that interdependence, which is widely hailed in the industrial world as a healthy relationship between the developed and the developing worlds, can be meaningful only if a large measure of security is achieved through the pursuit of self-reliant development. Otherwise, interdependence would remain a euphemism for dependence, or a polite and more attractive way of retaining the reality of dependence by outside countries while changing the obnoxious label.

Yet another qualificatioan to the identification of the beneficiaries of development suggested earlier on is the need for proper and adequate consideration to be given to harmony between man and environment. Such harmony must be targeted as a critical objective and beneficiary of development. It involves not only the fight against pollution and the wasteful use of resources, but also the understanding of the nature, potential and limits of natural endowments; the search for the optimal ways of realizing the potential and further developing it; and the enjoyment of the endowments through a harmonious mix between human effort and the environment's resources and possibilities.

The last qualification to suggest is the targeting of other societies and countries as beneficiaries of national development. This is not meant as a utopian or idealistic objective, but as a hard-headed, down-to-earth one. The objective would be particularly realistic and feasible if it were sought in the context of regional co-operation, co-ordination, complementarity and collective self-reliance among countries that have a common cultural heritage, a shared history and/or future outlook and demonstrable common interests. The countries of the Arab region provide one such striking instance. Other instances exist elsewhere in the Caribbean area, Central America, Latin America, West Africa and Southeast Asia.

It is also demonstrable in these cases that the process of development can be promoted further and can benefit from a regional approach. Such an approach can supplement and intermesh with a national approach, given the existence of significant common interests, similarity of outlook, an honest intention to achieve co-operation and complementarity, and a sizeable measure of co-ordination of development policies within the framework of collective self-reliance. Again, much more will be said about the promotive power of the regional dimension of development in the Arab context, and it is hoped that the analysis will also prove relevant to other regions in the Third World. Finally, it is to be pointed out that a well thought-out and designed, and a seriously sought, regional approach to development not only benefits from the national effort in each of the political entities within the region concerned, but it also in turn bestows benefits on the individual entities.

WHAT KIND OF DEVELOPMENT IS NEEDED?

The attempt just made to identify the social groups that ought to be urgently targeted as the primary beneficiary of development has already pointed to the basic and critical specifications of the development that ought to be sought if the announced objective is to be reached. Such development will, of necessity, first require the adherence by the decision-makers at the various rungs, and in the various circles, of the process of decision-making, and obviously by society at large through the various channels and means whereby society's awareness is made sharper and clearer, to a conceptualization of development appropriate to the choice of the objective stated earlier on as top priority. For this to happen, an appropriate 'development climate' and 'development machinery' ought to take shape, as I will try to show during the examination of the fourth and last question on pp. 31–9.

However, at this point it is sufficient to say that the choice of the satisfaction of basic human needs, dynamically defined as primary objective, ought at least to be accompanied, if not already preceded, by acceptance and institutionalization of the primacy of the objective. This involves movement towards and acceptance of those socio-political and structural aspects of the transformation of society which are appropriate for the establishment of this primacy. Furthermore, the productive machine must also be so transformed – in capital structure and composition, in technology, in infrastructure and in training – as to meet the requirements of the production of basic human needs.

Consequently, it will be essential to allocate manpower, entrepreneurial and managerial talent, investment finance, physical input and service inputs so as to suit the social objectives of the development sought. But above all, the population at large will have to be made aware of and sensitized to the justification of the disciplined prioritization that will be necessary in the use of resources in the process of production.

Necessarily, such prioritization has serious implications. These will reach far into consumption habits and pressures, saving attitudes, acceptance of tax obligations, and other relevant limitations and burdens. The response of the better-off and the rich will no doubt be less than welcoming, but their hostility will be less obstructive the more convincing the political system is in its explanation of the rationale of the prioritization and discipline required, and the more reassuring the system is that the wants of the better-off and the rich will be attended to on a phased, gradually increasing scale, as the resource and other bottlenecks are gradually widened and the productive machine is gradually readied to cope with an expanding flow of goods and services beyond those included in basic needs.

The preceding few paragraphs will, hopefully, have made it clear that development is nothing less than a civilizational enterprise involving the whole of society in virtually all aspects of its life, and to that extent it involves radical, deeply penetrating re-education or socialization of the population along a very wide front. Necessarily, such socialization will require enormous effort by society, and will need decades if not generations to proceed to a point where it can leave its marks on values, mental attitudes, economic expectations, social behaviour, institutions, the forms of socio-economic organization, and the work ethic. There is hardly any need to remind ourselves of the large distance that separates this conceptualization of development from the concept of economic growth, with its purely economic components, its quantifiability, the close time horizon within which it can be achieved, and the narrowness of the scope of social change within which it is possible for growth to be engineered – a scope which remains imprisoned within the 'given' economic factors, the 'circular flow' of the economy in Schumpeter's words referred to earlier on in this chapter.

If the specifications so far suggested refer to the quality of development appropriate to the objective stated as of paramount importance and top priority to Third World societies, what is it that needs to be said about the economic content of such development? It will be difficult to identify this content without involvement in details that would sound like the presentation of the components or programmes of a conventional development plan. This is not intended here. Furthermore, development plans will necessarily have to differ from one country to another, because of the different identity and intensity of problems which the plans are presumably drawn to solve or alleviate, and the objectives they are meant to achieve. Therefore what is considered of relevance here, and of general applicability to underdeveloped countries except a small minority with very scanty agricultural resources, is the need for especially strong initial emphasis on those areas the development of which makes possible the production and distribution of the many goods and services that satisfy the basic human needs. Underlying these needs will be the need for income-generating jobs which will put in the hands of the workforce the income and purchasing power with which to buy the goods and services in question.

Obviously, the provision of such goods and services calls for prior emphasis on the development of certain specific sectors, sub-sectors and activities that are capable of producing them. Agriculture, within the broader area of rural development, emerges in this context as deserving top and most urgent consideration. The reasons for this are many, and they are well known and generally accepted. They include: the large proportion of the population living in rural areas and engaged in agriculture and other ancillary activities; the concern with food security from within the national economy to the extent possible; the fact that the rural population constitutes a potentially large and significant market for manufactured goods, which makes rural development closely complementary to industrial development; the importance of the rural population as a main contributing tributary to the reservoir of industrial labour; and the ability of a well-developed agricultural sector within a balanced development of the countryside, first to earn foreign exchange through the substitution of imports, second to protect the environment and use its resources wisely, and third to make the countryside more attractive (and rewarding) to live in, and thus reduce the enormous outflow to the urban centres which drains the countryside and chokes the cities at the same time.

We need not go into a listing of all the political and institutional/structural changes, especially in land tenure, that all this would require. They include, among others: rural-orientated schooling and training; more and better housing; the irrigation and drainage, transportation, storage, and other networks and facilities that rural regeneration calls for; the appropriate technology that will need to be chosen and inculcated; and – perhaps above all – the possession by the rural population of much greater weight in the political system through the enjoyment of true participation, if half or more of the population is to escape the neglect which is its lot in most Third World countries. As one author put it in a convincing and moving way, far-reaching and meaningful rural development means 'putting the last first' (Chambers 1984).

As the discussion in the last two paragraphs has shown, there is strong interdependence between the development of agriculture and the rural areas, and that of manufacturing industry. This in itself points to the need for serious concern with the latter, apart from the significance of the contribution of manufacturing to the provision of many of the goods needed for the satisfaction of basic human needs. Again, here we need only say that these primary goods and services – food and other agro-industries; housing and the hundreds of individual inputs required by the building industry; clothing and the numerous branches of textile, leather and other industries; means of transport and the many related facilities and inputs; school books, stationery, laboratories and equipment in general – all call for an energetic and growing manufacturing industry, and all cater to basic human needs.

In turn, manufacturing industry as well as agriculture, with their wide scope of production and the inputs they need for their activities, will of necessity require the development of many other commodity and service industries. Reference has already been made to the building industry and to transport. In addition, the sector of electricity and/or other energy, urban housing, public utilities in towns and cities, banking – to name only a few – will all have to be developed in order for them to provide their own output for final consumption, as well as for use as input in other sectors and activities. However, special emphasis needs to be placed on education, training and research, as on the acquisition by the working population of effective, appropriate technology. This requirement is crucial for the wide gamut of areas of economic activity: indeed, it is crucial for modern society in all aspects of its activity. But of particular significance here is the contribution that education, research and technological capability make to the formation and sharpening of man's scientific outlook and problem understanding and solving.

Even though the choice of the satisfaction of basic human needs may at first glance seem to be one embodying a modest social objective, the discussion undertaken around the content of appropriate development must have reflected the enormity of the tasks involved, and the time, efforts and resources that of necessity would have to be put into the shouldering of these tasks. The tasks will be heavier and draw much more on society's capabilities, endowments, imagination and patience, for the gradual transition from the primary objective of the satisfaction of basic needs, to the provision of a wider range of less basic but no less desired goods and services, which will become increasingly attractive to the erstwhile beneficiaries of the primary concern with basic human needs. And the tasks will get yet heavier and more demanding, both on the economy and the society, as the transition is continued, over and beyond, into the realm of semi-luxury and luxury goods and services, along with what these require by way of capital goods, manpower, physical resources, infrastructure and services.

The pressure for this transition to be effected will be great, though most probably premature and unrealistic in most Third World countries. Hence the difficulty and unpopularity of serious resistance to it. It will take all the comprehension, intelligence, skill and determination of political decision-makers, of educators and opinion-makers, and of the leaderships of trade unions and professional associations – assuming they all had the desire to do so – to preach the need for moderation, patience and realism by the consuming public and by vested interests in the business community.

What has been witnessed time and again in many developing countries in the post-war years has been the outdistancing of the productive capability and the resources of economies by the explosion of consumption expectations and pressures. The sad result has often been the intractable problems of massive foreign indebtedness, socio-political tension and unrest, frustration, and finally lethargy in the face of the need for discipline and drastic corrective policies. Yet it is ironic that the response of most Third World governments has been not a clear and patient explanation of the inescapable need for proper prioritization and restraint in the allocation of resources between basic and less basic uses (both for consumption and capital goods and services), but the application of force against the poorer masses when these have risen in protest against food shortages, the gross insufficiency of other basic goods and services, and soaring inflation. (This has been the case in half a dozen Arab countries in the years 1977–89.)

If the attrition of public morale and determination is to be stopped and reversed, society will have to resort to the principles and policies of self-reliant development. This is crucial, as continued heavy dependence on the resources and skills of external sources will lead only to continued lethargy, further submersion in foreign debt, and a false sense of satisfaction that the problem is manageable and is even being solved. Self-reliant development of the type advocated here – namely with social emphasis and a humanitarian dimension – has far-reaching implications for the vision of development and its objectives, priorities, strategies, policies and plans and programmes. Indeed, it has significant healthy implications for the world outlook as well as the inner strength and resourcefulness of a society, which go well beyond the realm of economics. Self-reliance as a strategy for development will receive extensive examination further on in this book. At this point we need only stress that self-reliant development can embody the quality and content capable of providing satisfactory and reassuring answers to the questions which we are in the process of examining in the present chapter.

Self-reliance is not incompatible with the contemporary socialist approach to development – indeed, many of the advocates of self-reliant development maintain that it can be sought by Third World countries only via socialist transformation.[10] This view is held by economists who are labelled 'neo-Marxists', or who are described as 'socialistic' in outlook. These argue that conventional (orthodox) Marxism, and even Leninism, contain a view of development that is at variance both with that held today by many leftist social scientists, and with the reality of contemporary capitalism and the world economic system it has come to dominate after its many generations of maturing and expansion. The main points of variance will be considered in greater detail later in this book.

There will also be occasion further on to look into the origins of the notion of self-reliance in development. It will be seen then that this notion was put into a theoretical framework and applied in practice on a large scale in communist China three decades ago. On the other hand, the term 'another development' has received its widest circulation through the work of the Dag Hammarskjöld Foundation (1975), in its report entitled *What Now?* and through the much fuller publication which appeared subsequently under the title *Another Development: Approaches and Strategies* (Nerfin 1977). The designation 'alternative development', which was coined at about the same time, is mainly used by the International Foundation for Development Alternatives (IFDA), especially in its periodical *Dossier*.[11]

In his introduction to *Another Development*, Marc Nerfin sums up the specifications or features of this development as those who advocate it see it. According to them it would be: need-orientated, endogenous, self-reliant, ecologically sound, and based on structural transformations. He considers that these five points are

> organically linked. Taken in isolation from each other, they would not bring about the desired result. For development is seen as a whole, as an integral, cultural process, as the development of every man and woman and the whole of man and woman. Another development means liberation.
>
> (Nerfin 1977: 10–11)

IFDA, in its turn, adopts the same definition which it considers as hinging 'on five interrelated pillars'. In the words of a recent publication, these are:

> satisfaction of all human needs; self-reliance; endogeneity; harmony with nature and ecological sustainability; and people-empowering structural transformations. It is a systemic process, personal and social, cultural and political, technological and economic. It offers a *project* to every society, be it in the North or in the South.
>
> (IFDA 1986)

Without elaboration on this definition, it can be seen that the concept of alternative/another development is extremely broad. Furthermore, in a sense it also incorporates certain actions and principles of populism and, more so, neo-populism (see Kitching 1985).

It must be admitted that another development even more than self-reliant development sounds both eclectic and utopian. It could be argued that any society that has a comprehensive enough conception of development to embrace all the components identified above, and the will to seek such development in all its richness, must already be developed in its vision, intellectual capability, resolve and moral concern. Perhaps it is this generosity with which another development *and* self-reliance have both been characterized in the relevant literature (see Galtung 1980: 26–34; and Nerfin 1977: 9–17) that has made a careful analyst of development thinking conclude that 'self-reliance . . . is in the context of the present world-system the strategy which is most unlikely to succeed. This is indeed bad news for the development theorists of the Alternative school'.[12]

However, I will not attempt at this point to explore the degree of realism and practicality in the pursuit of self-reliant (or another) development and its chances of success, as the third and fourth chapters of the book will undertake such exploration. It is therefore necessary now to examine the last of the four questions that this chapter is addressing which, in one basic respect, is of direct relevance to an assessment of the feasibility of self-reliant development.

HOW CAN DEVELOPMENT BE UNDERTAKEN?

This question is concerned not only with the dynamics and machinery of self-reliant development but, underlying that, also with the socio-economic system within which it is sought and expected to unfold. The question must be posed for two reasons: first, because it is essential to explore how such development can possibly (or at least hopefully) be approached and pursued, if its characterization is to have any practical and useful purpose – in other words, if it is at all to be relevant to the real world; and second, because it is essential to see if the avenue to self-reliant development has been followed in the Third World in general, but particularly in the Arab region. The consideration of the present question, along with that of the three preceding ones, is meant to explain the central enquiry in this chapter – namely the reason why the performance of the developmental effort in most Third World countries has fallen far short of the expectations both of developers and of the presumed and advertised beneficiaries of development.

The shortfall can be seen to a far greater extent in the quality and content of development, which were discussed under the last question examined. In this respect it might be said that it was the very tough specifications set for satisfactory achievement which were responsible for what seems to be the shortfall in the record, and ought not therefore to be applied as a test of commendable performance. However, the shortfall is seen even in the quantity and range of the goods and services produced when set against the targets of the developers themselves, as well as in the insufficient reach of development which has left behind, almost untouched, large segments of the population of virtually every developing country. In addition, only a handful of these countries have succeeded in implanting in their society an effective and appropriate technological capability, and remarkably few have managed to reduce tangibly the degree and intensity of their many-sided dependence on the advanced industrial countries. These generalizations are true both of the vast majority of Third World countries that have sought development through the capitalist avenue, and of the smaller number that have sought it (or at least claim to have done so) via the socialist avenue.

The fact that many or perhaps most developing countries started with exaggerated ambitions and expectations and have shown insufficient awareness or realization that development is of necessity a very long and demanding process, explains the shortfall only in part. Misguided convictions and serious oversights provide another part of the explanation. As an example of the former, there is the wide belief that money can buy development – a belief that can best be seen in the behaviour of most of the oil-producing and -exporting countries' members of OPEC during the decade of the oil 'boom' 1973–82. On a more modest scale, this is a general conviction of Third World countries with few exceptions. To illustrate the oversights it is appropriate to quote from the 'Cocoyoc Declaration (1974)' which set out to widen the angle of vision from which development ought to be considered. Thus it should include many other objectives than those usually included:

> Development should not be limited to the satisfaction of basic needs. There are other needs, other goals, and other values. Development includes freedom of expression and impression, the right to give and to receive ideas and stimulus. There is a deep social need to participate in shaping the basis of one's own existence, and to make some contribution to the fashioning of the world's future. Above all, development includes the right to work, by which we mean not simply having a job but finding self-realization in work, the right not to be alienated through production processes that use human beings simply as tools.
>
> (Galtung *et al.* 1980: 385–421)

Even if these explanations or qualifying considerations were to be set aside, there would still be enough evidence to show that the performance is clearly below what could have been achieved, were the Third World countries to meet the challenge of underdevelopment with the resolve it called for, to mobilize and intelligently use the human and material resources at their disposal, to seek political stability and administrative efficiency, and to promise only what they thought themselves capable of delivering: in brief, if they had attempted to provide sound answers to the type of questions we have been examining here. That the conditions just listed are very exacting for most of the politicians and other leaders that the Third World has had, and that external factors most connected with the colonial legacy have combined to militate against the Third World, is no doubt also partly responsible for the shortfall. But the internal responsibility for much of the shortfall cannot and should not be shirked. In brief, self-reliant development has not been seriously, energetically and realistically attempted, and if at all attempted, then not in a sustained fashion. The exceptions to this generalization – prominently China and India – are very special cases that do not invalidate the judgement.

To come more directly to the fourth question being discussed here, it is necessary first to consider, though most briefly, the kind of socio-economic system within which self-reliant development can possibly be sought and, hopefully, approached. This can be done through a process of elimination. Thus, it seems warranted to assert that self-reliant development cannot be the product of the conceptualization and the machinery of development as understood and designed within the framework of the philosophy of unfettered or unqualified free enterprise and the operation of market forces alone – in brief, as guided by the operation of the 'invisible hand' of classical economic thought. Nor can it be the product of the tenets and guidelines of the modernization paradigm as expounded in mainstream Western sociology, with its emphasis on a unilinear approach to development, and on the Western brand of development – with its concepts, values and specifications – advocated as the only (that is, universal) model to emulate. In either case, the basic concern is with the form and the agents of development within Western tradition, cut off from the historical roots of underdevelopment, and the cultural environment and particular objectives of the development sought. This concern disregards the normative dimension in development and the quality and content considered crucial for it to be meaningful and relevant. Furthermore, the framework for free enterprise, like that of modernization, is much more relevant to growth than to development, the differentiation between which I attempted to make earlier on.

Likewise, the development advocated cannot be sought through the avenue of orthodox Marxism, if its concept of development and the process through which it is to be brought about are to be maintained. The concept is too closely identified, for analytical comfort and relevance, with a Eurocentric propensity, and too closely associated with capitalism and colonialism, in their nineteenth-century role and behaviour as vehicles or as conduits, to be acceptable in the contemporary Third World. Indeed, Marx had serious reservations with regard to the ability of less developed countries, because of being 'primitive', to make the move to capitalism (as 'development') on their own, without colonialism. He had regrets about this, because of his awareness of the cruelty of colonialism, and must have viewed the latter as a necessary evil. Hence also the 'useful function' in the transition from feudalism to communism claimed for the European bourgeoisie in the *Communist Manifesto*. This work also assigns a lower status to 'old wants, satisfied by the production of the country', in the place of which, the authors assert, 'we find new wants, requiring for their satisfaction the products of distant lands and climes. In place of the old local and national seclusion and self-sufficiency, we have intercourse in every direction, universal interdependence of nations' (Marx and Engels 1888: 13, 14).

Furthermore, Marxism, at least as embodied in practice in socialist countries in the contemporary world, before Gorbachev's *perestroika* initiative in 1985, left hardly any room for private enterprise, thus foregoing the advantages of its dynamism and pre-empting a considerable part of society's economic endeavour. Aside from that, the socialist system in application, until very recently, violated a number of prerequisites for a healthy development worthy of the hopes and sacrifices of the masses. Human rights, and wide political participation making possible, among other things, free economic choice, are two of the prerequisites that have been largely missing until the last years of the 1980s.

Lenin had a clearer perception of development and a greater awareness of the obstruction which imperialism (particularly financial imperialism) builds in the face of development in what we now call Third World countries (Lenin 1948). He was also cognizant of the likelihood of collusion between foreign capital and the ruling elites in less developed countries against the masses. All this qualified him better to provide a guideline to development. However, his formulation is still less than satisfactory for present-day purposes. This is so because he had faith in the ability of political independence to make capitalism of necessity more progressive in its dealings with less developed countries. This view assumes away the lingering ties and forms of control of the former colonial powers with their former colonies.

Indeed, neo-Marxism seems today to be the most relevant strand of Marxist thought for an explanation of underdevelopment and dependence, and because of the understanding it reflects of the dynamics of development. At least it is free of the Marxist faith in the beneficial role of the capitalism of the advanced industrial country in bringing about development to the less developed country, through the former showing the latter 'an image of its own future'. This faith is echoed by subsequent writers adhering to orthodox Marxism. It is akin to the faith of those Western development thinkers who believe that the less developed countries will inevitably become in due course the mirror image of the advanced countries of today. To this extent, there is parallelism between the views of the two socio-economic systems, even if their overall philosophy and mechanics differ fundamentally. And both systems reflect a notable belief in determinism in the present context.

The process of elimination we have applied seems to leave us with two avenues that merit consideration. The first leads to socialism with a Third World 'flavour' as a socio-economic and political system capable of nurturing self-reliant development. The second leads to a nationalist system upon the satisfaction of three necessary conditions: (a) a large and dynamic public sector alongside private and co-operative sectors, where the first submits more effectively to criteria of efficiency in its operation, and the latter two submit more effectively to ones of social consideration and to an outer framework of public authority around their operations; (b) a strong government which has a sound understanding of its functions, and attempts to steer the administration efficiently in a manner compatible with these functions, in the service of society's objectives; and (c) a progressive philosophy and orientation as well as a belief in the right of the people to basic rights and freedoms and to the exercise of political participation.

I have not expanded on the characterization of socialism as an appropriate social environment for self-reliant development, for two reasons. The first is that the principles and tenets on which socialism is founded, and its structure and dynamics, together make it capable of providing a suitable climate for self-reliant development, on condition that human rights and political participation constitute high-priority values in society and are properly respected and protected by the polity. The second reason is that I consider the ability of a nationalist system, with the three conditions stated, to uphold self-reliance as a strategy for development as still very much an open question worthy of exploration. It is my purpose to attempt this exploration in the last chapter of the book, with particular reference to the Arab region. As this is a large enough region, hopefully the analysis will prove both relevant and significant for much of the Third World in general.

Without anticipating the discussion to follow later, the dynamics and machinery of self-reliant development will now be identified, in the context of a progressive nationalist state (or a community of states) that embodies the socio-economic system which I will be considering all along in this study as a possible environment-to-be for self-reliant development. What, then, are the dynamics of self-reliant development – that is, what are the dynamics that can activate a society to pursue such development, and sustain the pursuit? In simple and direct terms, it seems to me warranted to expect the very components or elements which give self-reliant development its particular features and strength, and its special flavour, to provide the desired dynamics, once the components become internalized as an essential part of society's collective consciousness. The components in question are: concern for independence of the country's process of economic decision-making; the drive to satisfy basic human needs as a top priority; the pursuit of harmony with the environment and its sustainability; internal motivation; and emphasis on inner-directed developmental effort. While it is strongly arguable that these components will operate against the background of the pressure of poverty and maldistribution, it is also arguable that the pressure itself will provide the urgency of far-reaching economic and associated non-economic transformation in society.

Thus, the components of self-reliant development make it crucial that all social groups should have significant functions in the shouldering of the various developmental tasks, from conceptualization and determination of objectives, all the way to execution and review. This would be so because all would be involved both as active agents and as beneficiaries. But each of the social groups involved would have its specific role and function. It is essential to indicate here, in the light of the nature of the discussion conducted so far, that development where the public sector dominates the economy is not only for the 'professional developers' to undertake – that is, for the planning and executing agencies in government. The kind of development that these professionals are capable of bringing about will of necessity turn out to be heavily dictated, centralized and bureaucratized, and overly concerned with statistical indicators of performance, even while these can be grossly misleading and almost meaningless.

On the other hand, the kind of development that market forces inspire, motivate, activate and dominate, will of necessity be spearheaded and undertaken by the business community, and will therefore be mainly profit-orientated and overly led and steered by the locus, intensity and directions of purchasing power in society. Thus, again of necessity, it will be very patchy, having areas or pockets of over-development as well as ones of underdevelopment – areas of enormous riches and abundance alongside vast areas of abject poverty, joblessness and dispossession. However, neither of the two models just referred to rarely ever appears in pure form in the Third World. But the two almost everywhere appear in combination, the mix depending on the relative power of the determining group of actors in the private and the public sector in society. Such a two-sector economic system is necessary for the pursuit of self-reliant development, but only if the appropriate specifications of such development are sought by society.

China and India offer two very plausible examples of countries pursuing self-reliance. China (before the recent move towards 'economic liberalization') embodied the dynamics and suggested the machinery of self-reliant development in a socialist environment. India does this in what I have designated as a 'progressive–nationalist society, two-sector economy with socialistic features'. But the two countries can hardly be considered prototypes to be set as examples for Third World countries in general to emulate; they are a very special, unrepresentative sample: indeed, a minuscule sample although (and because) they are the two most populous countries in the world. Apart from them, there are barely a handful of Third World countries that can rightly claim a socialist system, or a progressive–nationalist, two-sector system actually in sustained operation.

Given all this, it is doubly crucial to explore the feasibility of self-reliance as a strategy for development in the vast majority of less developed countries, that is, everywhere except in those instances where the countries concerned have the size of population and the variety of resources that present a prima facie case for self-reliance. The question of size also invokes the need to consider, as an alternative to self-reliance in one country, collective self-reliance – that is, regional association and co-operation, and complementarity among a community of countries with a shared cultural heritage, close interests and a common outlook. The enquiry that will follow later in the book will centre around the possibility of self-reliance in the Arab region, considered as one entity or as a group of sub-regions. The system that will be assumed will be that of a progressive–nationalist society and a two-sector economy, possibly with socialistic features, or at least with broadly based ownership of the means of production.

If the dynamics of self-reliant development in such a society reside in the power or the driving force of its main components, and of their interaction, as stated earlier, against a background of pressing poverty and maldistribution, then its machinery has of necessity to consist essentially of those social groups and forces that are concerned with the substance and implications of these components and are eager to see them embodied in the development sought. If, and once, these groups and forces feel and express the conviction that need-orientated, self-generated and socially mobilizing development is crucial for society's well-being, and furthermore that it is the only desirable course which it is possible to take that is capable of leading to the objective sought, then this conviction will constitute the necessary dynamics of action. In its turn, the conviction can be diffused in society on a wide scale, and can be deepened as well, through properly orientated education, socially motivated intervention by the media, and development-directed public policies and institutions.

The social groupings which can, and will, have to shoulder the responsibilities and tasks involved are three: (a) leaderships in the significant areas of society's structure and life, that is, in politics, education, public opinion, labour, private business and professional activities; (b) socially concerned and committed intellectuals who occupy an important place in the esteem and recognition of Third World countries in general, and (c) above all, those segments of the public which are already politicized or amenable to being politicized and mobilized for participation, especially when problem-solving and a propensity to constructive action are incorporated into the process as a distinct value. These three groupings, in their action and interaction, can determine the course of self-reliance at the national, sub-national and local levels, as well as at the regional level (involving several national states). Likewise, their functions and impact will be seen in the public and private sectors and the performance of their respective tasks.

The identification and allocation of functions among the three groupings, the manner in which each grouping will perform its functions, the internal relations and interactions among the groupings, as well as the misgivings which obviously will have to be borne in mind with regard to the possible malfunctioning of one or more of them and the setbacks which the whole process will suffer as a result, are all matters that deserve the closest scrutiny. So will the likelihood of the appearance and operation of what one might call 'the counter-dynamics of development'. Counter-forces such as hesitation and awe in the face of the enormity of the tasks of development, impatience with the slow pace of development, and the coalescence of internal special interests and external forces hostile to self-reliant development may well abort the drive for development.

But all this is a matter for later chapters in the book to undertake. Only then can the question which the discussion in this chapter suggests be answered, namely: will the promise of development through the pursuit of self-reliance as a strategy for development not be betrayed, and will the frustrated pursuit of the post-war years be turned into distinct fulfilment?

2 The dependency paradigm: promise, limitations and qualifications

INTRODUCTION

This chapter sets out to sketch a major course which a number of economists and other social thinkers with concern for development have pursued since the early 1960s in the search for an explanation of underdevelopment. This is the dependency paradigm. Two reasons explain why the work of the dependency school of thought is singled out for special consideration and focus here. First, because it has claimed and earned considerable merit for providing a plausible explanation of underdevelopment in much of the Third World. And although the approach has come under questioning and attack since the late 1960s, it can still be said to contain a main body of jointly shared ideas which enjoy explanatory value worth preserving.

This is a defensible position to take along with the admission that the paradigm has come to face serious scepticism with regard to its claim for general applicability, and that the dependency school that evolved it has gone through several schisms, to the point where many think it can hardly be said still to have a unified and coherent message today. However, the central core of ideas relating to the historical connection between dependence and underdevelopment remains of crucial value in explaining a large part of the causes for underdevelopment. Consequently, a forward look in search of an appropriate strategy for development will in turn necessitate the search for an antidote to dependence. And here lies the second reason for an examination of the dependency paradigm. Self-reliance as a strategy for development possesses force and appeal as the antidote to be applied. Essentially, therefore, the present chapter paves the way for the discussion of self-reliance in the chapters that follow, rather than being an end in itself. The introduction of this book stressed this point earlier on.

The majority of Third World development economists and sociologists of underdevelopment in the immediate post-war years, who had been trained in Western neo-classical liberal economic and sociological thought relating to development and modernization respectively, on the whole sought an explanation for underdevelopment through the intellectual tradition with which they were familiar, the development model based on its socio-economic concepts and guidelines, and the experience of the advanced industrial countries which evolved it with the processes of growth and development. The search and pursuit within the confines of this tradition and experience provided 'intellectual comfort' for most Third World social scientists, owing, on the one hand, to familiarity and intellectual and political – even ideological – conditioning and affinity and, on the other, to their acceptance of the belief that there was one universal model to examine and emulate: the Western model (Eisenstadt 1983).

By the early 1960s, the course of intellectual search just referred to had come to a point where it failed to continue to provide comfort to many economists, sociologists and political scientists in some parts of the Third World. It had become the object of serious questioning as to its relevance, applicability and credibility. This was essentially because the neo-classical Western analytical framework and model had failed to provide a key to the understanding and explanation of underdevelopment, mainly owing to the obvious fact that the development expected as the outcome of the content and logic of that framework had not materialized as expected. Even allowing for the over-ambitiousness and non-realism of the expectations themselves, there was still a serious and gaping shortfall in developmental performance, both qualitatively and quantitatively, as the last chapter tried to show.

This judgement can be made with respect both to countries with a market economy, and to those which claimed to have accepted the tenets of socialism, followed a socialist path to development, and structured their economies as centrally planned systems.

Awareness of the failure of the conventional wisdom absorded from the Western capitalist industrial countries, or else (but more belatedly) from textbook Marxism and the actual experience of communist countries, to explain underdevelopment and to prescribe for development came at varying points of time in the four post-war decades. But it can probably be said that it was rather slow in coming in most Third World countries. Politicians concerned with political myths and with their image and durability in office, and development technicians and practitioners concerned with indicators of growth and its outward statistical manifestations, still show less awareness than social thinkers, even if they are not altogether unaware of the shortcomings of the development performance measured against the more quantitative targets of development plans and programmes. And, when it comes to private businessmen, the whole notion of macro-economic performance, or of the social dimensions of development, is of no concern to any but the odd idealist among them, so long as their profit innings are satisfactory.

If the Arab region is singled out, then it can be said that awareness of the failure of the 'imported' frameworks to provide an explanation of underdevelopment with a good fit is coming much more slowly than the awareness that the frameworks have, on the whole, failed to lead to meaningful, concrete and wide-embracing development. On the other hand, the clearest and earliest awareness in Third World regions came to a number of social thinkers in Latin America, and led to probing intellectual questioning, research and writing – and to certain policy reorientations of relevance. It may be useful at this point to elaborate somewhat on the questioning and the groups voicing it.

Three groups among the social thinkers who articulated their misgivings about the neo-classical economic and the sociological lines of thought contributed to the literature on underdevelopment and, by extension, development. First, there were the Marxists and neo-Marxists. The second group consisted of Western and Third World thinkers sensitized to structural factors in the genesis and persistence of underdevelopment, and beyond in the pursuit of development. But probably the most important group, the one of particular pertinence to this book, consisted of those Latin American social thinkers who were to become known as the 'dependency theorists' – the *dependentistas* – after developing the dependency school of thought. (The last group came to include neo-Marxists, structuralists and progressive Third World nationalists, who all – expect perhaps for the structuralists – emphasized the role of dependence forced on Third World countries by the colonial capitalist countries in the genesis and persistence of underdevelopment.) With the emergence of this school, it can be said that the intellectual comfort characterizing the preceding post-war years gave place to dissatisfaction with the conventional wisdom reigning supreme in development thinking, whether capitalist or orthodox Marxist. The era of 'intellectual restlessness' thus set in.

Only the main ideas and approaches of these groups that touch directly on the shaping of the dependency line of thought and its evolution and differentiation, and ultimately on its crisis, will be brought into light during the discussion of this chapter. But they will not be presented in their entirety and in an integrated manner that deals with their whole systems of thought: such a course would diffuse the focus of the chapter and, in any case, would necessitate the devotion of much space to permit adequate treatment.[1] Consequently, the chapter will essentially discuss – albeit briefly – the genesis and development of the dependency line of thought, and its main intellectual tributaries; attempt to identify its main content or theme, and the variations to this theme, as they brought with them qualifications, made certain limitations necessary, and roused misgivings which have, since the late 1970s, come cumulatively to beset the dependency paradigm and to cast doubt on its analytical and explanatory usefulness; and finally pose two central questions in the context of what can be called the 'paradigm crisis' (see Hirschman 1977).

The first question is: is dependence (as a state or condition) still a relevant and useful explanation of underdevelopment in our changing world, when almost all Third World countries have acquired at least the outward and formal trimmings of political independence and sovereignty, and the power of independent economic decision-making? And, if the answer is in the affirmative, even if heavily qualified, then the second question is: what lessons can be learnt from it, particularly with reference to the credibility and usefulness of self-reliance as a strategy for development essentially expected to halt and correct the state of dependence? In conducting the discussion and attempting to answer these questions, there will be more emphasis on present-day realities relating directly and closely to underdevelopment than on theoretical abstractions. However, the significance and implications of theory will be kept in mind as factors that explain and put order into the behaviour of the many variables in the operation of reality.

BY WAY OF BACKGROUND: CRITIQUE OF THE NEO-CLASSICAL, MODERNIZATION AND MARXIST PERSPECTIVES OF DEVELOPMENT

Dependency,[2] whether designated as notion, perspective, approach or line of thought, or yet as paradigm, did not descend on one or more theorists as a coherent, unified piece of inspiration. Rather, it evolved or developed initially in Latin America through the convergence of different intellectual tributaries. But it can probably be said that all these derived from the same main source: dissatisfaction. This dissatisfaction was motivated by different reasons and had several targets. The prime target was the neo-classical theory of development (or of growth looked at as identical or nearly so with development). A very close target was the modernization perspective or paradigm developed by mainstream Anglo-Saxon sociology, basically in the United States. This paradigm was used as a tool of analysis and explanation of underdevelopment by many Western economists, obviously in addition to sociologists. (Rostow (1952, 1960) and Hagen (1962) are leading examples of economists who delved deep into the kit of definitions and analytical tools of the sociologists.)

The central cause for discontent and the critique that followed was that both development and modernization within the Western capitalist tradition were thought of as universal, unlinear, unidirectional processes, and thus that both had their embodiment in one basic model, even if this allowed small marginal variations. And, because of this characterization, neither development nor modernization, as understood by mainstream economics and sociology, took into account the historical, objective background to underdevelopment in the Third World, with the political, economic and sociocultural dislocating and unbalancing impact that capitalist penetration had brought into play in Third World countries through their subjection to colonialist control – no matter what benefits happened to be brought in alongside. In other words, this very crucial differentiation made the experience of the advanced, capitalist industrial countries specific to their own history, culture, location and endowments, as well as to the timing of their experience, rather than a case of general applicability.[3]

It is important in this context to remember that the critics had the experience of Third World countries in general in the post-war years available, to be observed and learnt from, but essentially – and much more significantly – they had the large expanse of the Latin American continent to use as a testing ground for the extent to which the neo-classical prescription for development could actually bring about the promised results. Thus, they could draw both on their theoretical and analytical endeavours, and on the down-to-earth developmental experience all around them, to learn from in assessing past performance and suggesting avenues for future theorizing and action.

Parenthetically, it would be useful at this point to comment on the place of Keynes within the neo-classical tradition, though demonstrably Keynesian theory came in the mid-1930s as a protest against, and as a fresh corrective to, this tradition. While Third World economists by and large eventually welcomed Keynes's *General Theory of Employment, Interest and Money* as a new gospel carrying fresh ideas with regard to the activation of stagnant economies, the realization only gradually grew that Keynes was not essentially concerned with development (obviously a long-term process), as much as with (short-term) growth.[4] Furthermore, his message was basically directed at developed economies whose infrastructure, capital, technology, labour skills and markets were already well developed and at a high level of performance, the main deficiency being in effective demand (a monetary phenomenon arising from insufficiency in the volume of income). In this situation, the major problem that needed crucial attention was the fuller utilization of capital, know-how and labour resources, already in abundance and of good quality, by the creation of more effective demand through government intervention and the use of monetary and fiscal instruments. This brief summing up of the special features of the Keynesian thesis is enough to show that Keynes addressed a situation vastly different from that of underdevelopment in Third World societies.

On the other hand, a quarter of a century later W. W. Rostow seemed to be more relevant, and appealed to large numbers of Third World economists and sociologists reared on the Western intellectual tradition and deeply conditioned by it. Rowstow's best-known work, *The Stages of Economic Growth*,[5] which he claimed to be 'A non-Communist Manifesto', initially enjoyed vast intellectual and operational appeal because it dealt directly with development, suggested a phased process of growth and development, and identified what he saw as the crucial factor in this process, namely capital investment. He went so far as to suggest a minimum specific proportion of national income to be directed to investment, which would make possible graduation into the take-off stage in development. In spite of its credentials, Rostow's book was soon severely criticized very tellingly by a number of Western scholars of repute like Simon Kuznets, Alexander Gerschenkron, H. J. Habbakuk, Phyllis Deane and others (see Rostow 1963). The criticism was concerned with concepts and analysis, specific facts, the sequence and dating of stages, and methodology, rather than with the kind of issues that neo-Marxists and dependency theorists found absent in his system of thought, such as the role of the colonial connection in the underdevelopment of a large part of the world, and the need for a large measure of self-reliance to enable Third World countries to free themselves effectively from dependence on their erstwhile colonizers.

But the main and central objection to Rostow's system was its rather automatic evolutionism, and its contention that the underdevelopment countries formed some sort of caravan, the members of which were at different points or stages on the road to development (and mass consumption), but that the road was unique, and all members were destined to arrive at their target sooner or later, once they satisfied the conditions for the take-off. Furthermore, the sociological notions contained in the system were derived from the conventional sociological wisdom of the post-war years, according to which the socio-cultural traits of nations were paired in pattern variables, one part of which fitted the developed, the other the underdeveloped.

The modernization perspective or paradigm was criticized by dependency theorists essentially because it had certain basic tenets similar to those of the neo-classical development theory, and because the latter used certain inputs in its logic and structure taken over from the sociological thought of modernization theorists. Broadly speaking, the critique of the modernization paradigm, viewed as the other side of the coin of the development process in the neo-classical tradition, focused on three central points.

These were, first, that modernization was viewed by its theorists as an evolutionary, transitional process which moved with unilinearity, thus transforming societies from traditionalism to modernity in stages.

Second, it was claimed that modernization meant the adoption essentially of one model that had universal value and applicability; in this sense the paradigm – with ethnocentric overtones – did not allow for differentiation except marginally, implying absolutism for the Western traits or variables of modernity. Hence the traits and features associated with traditionalism (and underdevelopment) were to be shed off if Third World countries were to aspire to have the image and substance of the advanced Western industrial countries and to acquire modernity. In this connection, heavy (though not total) emphasis was placed on the internal cultural and structural causes of traditionalism, and glaringly little on external causes associated, for instance, with the burden of the colonial legacy under which most Third World countries laboured. Therefore, quite sweepingly, modernity was associated with development, as traditionalism was with underdevelopment.

Third, a number of pattern variables like the traits or features of modernity versus traditionalism (or development versus underdevelopment) were identified and assigned a central function in causing underdevelopment (if the 'bad' part of the pattern variables were adhered to), or in being instrumental in leading to development (if the 'good' part were adopted instead of the 'bad'). Talcott Parsons (1951) developed the pattern variables that were to become well known in the literature and widely used both in connection with the unfolding of the process of modernization, and also in connection with the unfolding of the process of development.[6] The literature on theory and area studies dealing with modernization within the general context of the present discussion is voluminous, and quite a few works deal specifically with the Arab world (under the designation of the Middle East or the Near East).[7]

It is useful to characterize some of the leading works in order to point to certain objections that I have, in addition to the three areas expressed by the critique of modernization by dependency theorists. Thus, in twenty-five essays edited by Myron Weiner (1966) only passing references are made to the strains and agonies, the disruptions and even unsavoury connotations of modernization. Other authors who moved in the Parsonian tradition or borrowed from him in their writings on modernization and Westernization[8] (including Hoselitz, Smelser, Apter, Moore, McClelland), and political scientists dealing with the political aspects and the politics of modernization, are open to one basic criticism. This is that

> even when they show awareness of the conflict between the old and the new, or the traditional and the modern, or of the cultural, social, and psychological costs of modernization, they fail to suggest what safeguards can be established in order for modernization to have built-in concern for the masses and protection for the poor and the weak (be they individuals, groups, or nation-states) versus the rich and the strong.
>
> (Sayigh 1978b: 41)

This failure can tell us a great deal about the kind of development that the modernization advocated might bring about.

Not only neo-classical development theory and the modernization paradigm were targeted for criticism, but also Marxist thought. This was because Marxism, too, saw the historical process unfolding in one-directional fashion. Thus, although countries stood at different points on the scale of development (depending on their mode of production at the time), they were expected, according to the logic of the Marxist analysis and framework, to achieve capitalist development in the end. This phase they were expected to reach through the development of their bourgeoisie, and therefore of industrialization and an industrial proletariat in due course, which would co-operate with the bourgeoisie for a time. It is only in the second phase that a proletariat-led revolution could unseat both the bourgeoisie and capitalism, and replace the latter by socialism, according to a two-stage strategy.

Thus, the two schools of thought and systems – the neo-classical and the Marxist – through their different analysis and their widely differing reading of history (and their expectations for the future), ended up having a rather deterministic attitude to the matter of development of the underdeveloped countries – an attitude according to which the advanced industrial country showed the retarded one how it would be in the future, sooner or later. In other words, the process was unilinear and one-directional, and it led to yet another embodiment of a universal model of development. All this notwithstanding, the most telling critique of orthodox Marxism in the present context came from neo-Marxists who addressed specific points relating to underdevelopment and development. But it would be more advisable to identify and discuss these points in the following section of the chapter.

THE DEPENDENCY SCHOOL: ITS SHAPING AND CENTRAL THEMES[9]

The strands of dissatisfaction with the neo-classical, modernization and orthodox Marxist perspectives of development emanated essentially from Latin America, but with contributions from the Caribbean region, India and, to a certain extent, some parts of Africa. Latin America merits the greatest credit not only for the originality and breadth of the debate led by a number of its social scientists, and the sharpness of their sustained critique of conventional development theory, but also for their probing speculation and research on the roots of underdevelopment, and, indeed, for the fact that the dependency perspective which they developed came to point directly to the necessity and urgency of the pursuit of self-reliant development. In other words, they also deserve credit for promoting the evolution of a relevant development perspective and strategy, one which would be rooted in the soil of Third World countries and address their particular conditions, and would therefore be less ethnocentric than the conventional perspective which was almost solely the product of Western thought, history and experience (see Wiarda 1984). For all these reasons, the discussion will be concentrated on the Latin American contribution.

It is fair to say that the Third World began, with the dependency school, to contribute to development theory and to have its voice heard internationally, rather than to continue to depend on received orthodoxy in silence. In the process of freeing itself of the straitjacket of conventional development theory, the dependency school contradicted the claim of universality for this theory, and established the imperativeness of the acknowledgement of the multiplicity of avenues to and models of development – in other words, the imperativeness of the recognition that theory and action had to spring from the history, culture, endowments, experience and dynamics of each country concerned. If there were still concepts, mechanisms or approaches of relevance to development for which universality could be claimed, such as capital–output ratios, multiplier and accelerator effects, the marginal propensity to consume and to save, or national accounting – to list a few examples at random – then these related basically to certain technical, operational or methodological tools in the analysis of development, not to the philosophy, rationale and orientation of development.

Latin American social scientists ought also to get credit for the critique they directed at Marxian development thought. (And, in addition to criticism, they offered alternative avenues of thought and action with respect to what they criticized.) The emergence of a neo-Marxist body of thought is a matter of special significance with respect to Marxism, as we will have occasion to see later. In addition, neo-Marxist social thinkers had the courage to direct a forceful attack at the circumscribed manner in which communists in Latin America read the history and political reality of their countries, and the degree to which they merely echoed the policies and positions relating to socio-economic and political processes and developments, as conceived, elaborated and declared in the Soviet Union, and issued as guidelines for action by communist parties abroad.

The dependency perspective and its basic components or fundamentals evolved even as the flow of criticism against it thickened, mainly by Marxists, neo-classical economists, and by the very developers of the perspective itself. In other words, it would be very difficult, if not impossible, to trace the genesis of the perspective and the shaping of its content in isolation from reference to the criticism, from without but basically from within the dependency school. However, what will be attempted in the present section is a survey of the main contours of the background of the perspective, and of its fundamentals, with only an occasional reference to controversy relating to specific points in the content.

In 1948, the United Nations Economic Commission for Latin America (ECLA) was set up in Santiago, Chile, and soon attracted a number of talented Latin American economists and sociologists who were in subsequent years to initiate and maintain a widening debate on the causes of underdevelopment and the sound approach to development.[10] At the head of the ECLA, and certainly the noted economist who left the deepest mark on the debate, in its genesis and deepening, was the Argentinian Raul Prebisch. He and the ECLA economists came, as the years went by, to constitute what can rightly be called the 'ECLA tradition', and thus to influence not only thinking on underdevelopment and development issues in academic and other intellectual circles, but also official policies as well in a number of Latin American countries. This tradition shaped the ECLA neo-Marxist and emphatically structuralist strands in the genesis of the dependency school of thought.

Although the development debate generated by ECLA economists centred around a number of issues, foreign trade theory stood at the heart of their concerns and questioning. According to classical, and also neo-classical, theory, foreign trade was without question beneficial to both parties engaged in it as importer and exporter, as the logic of 'comparative costs' and 'comparative advantages' determined. The international division of labour, which optimized the pattern of allocation of goods in the streams of production and external exchange, was considered benign and rational. This was so because the theory assumed the automatic correction or adjustment of any deviations from the pattern determined by the operation of the principles of demand and supply, and of comparative costs and advantages. Free trade was thus the mechanism *par excellence* for this optimization, to the good of both trading partners.

In addition, foreign trade was considered in classical and neo-classical thought to be 'an engine of growth', as can be seen from the writings of Gottfried von Haberler, Jacob Viner and others.[11] The ECLA economists (and, like them, the larger group of neo-Marxists in and out of the ECLA) disagreed with this analysis on more grounds than one, though in all of them the strong influence of structuralism could be discerned.

First, they objected to the static nature of the analysis, which subsumed what can rightly be called a 'natural' international division of labour, according to which the advanced Western countries would continue to buy primary products from the Third World countries, and export manufactured goods in payment. The ECLA economists refused to consider this pattern of production and exchange as given once and for all, and were set on finding ways of breaking through its containing wall. Their position derived from the conviction that the pattern was forced on their countries in the unequal relationship (military, political, economic, financial and technological) between the advanced industrial countries and the underdevelopment countries – especially under the influence of colonialism. In their view, this pattern must and could be broken through. The various factors shaping the external sector were not to be considered unchangeable and unchanging: technology, financial resources, labour skills, market openings and certainly policies should and could all undergo substantial changes that would alter the pattern fundamentally. And that would turn the situation into a dynamic one.

In the second place, the ECLA economists disagreed with the empirical underpinning claimed for a dominant pattern of foreign trade. Neo-classical economists claimed that the terms of trade were necessarily shifting, even if slowly, in favour of primary producing and exporting countries, against advanced industrial countries, which made their products less and less costly to produce – other things being equal – while savings in the cost of production of primary products, if any, were smaller and slower to materialize. Therefore, the argument went, the underdeveloped countries were the beneficiaries of the drop in the cost of the manufactures imported by them. This, it was also claimed, would provide them with more financial resources to invest domestically in infrastructure, education or housing, or yet to import more goods for the same volume of exports. Prebisch, and other ECLA economists, challenged this analysis; their research showed that the underdeveloped countries were not benefiting from technological advances and the drop in the cost of manufactures, and that the structure of the supplying markets, and the power imbalance in favour of the suppliers, enabled the latter to retain the fruit of technological gains and the savings achieved in the cost of manufacturing.

The third cause for dissatisfaction with the classical/neo-classical analysis of foreign trade was that the logic of this analysis strongly suggested that, in effect, the underdeveloped would remain underdeveloped or at best, develop very slowly, while the developed would develop much faster and become much richer. This was contrary to the contention of the neo-classical analysis that there was a direct causal link between foreign trade and economic growth. Thus, according to the critics, the underdeveloped countries wanted to seek industrialization as the process capable of making a breakthrough in underdevelopment. But, to achieve this, these countries ought to halt (or at least drastically revise) the operation of the prevailing pattern of external exchange. This would call for a set of policies that would enable the underdeveloped countries to industrialize so that, at a certain future point when a solid enough industrial base had been established, they could join the world pattern of foreign trade more fully – but then it would be a new pattern in which they would have a new role and from which they would reap a larger benefit, not only in financial terms, but also in terms of economic diversification and real development.

Even before we move on to identify and examine the imputs made by neo-Marxists, both from within the ECLA and outside, to the dependency analysis, we can discern certain distinctive notions and positions that have come to characterize the dependency school. Foremost among these was one which related to what Prebisch recognized as the structure of the world economy and the pattern of relations between the two main groupings of countries. The structure, according to him, was one in which the units in the international political set-up belonged either to a very small grouping of advanced Western industrial countries which were at the centre or core of the world system, or to a much larger group of underdeveloped countries which were at the periphery. This structure was the product of centuries of capitalist development on a world scale, buttressed and solidified by colonial penetration by the strong advanced countries in the weak underdeveloped ones. The process through which the structure was shaped drew the lines of the relationship between the two groupings, and set this relationship in deep grooves.

Flowing from this first point was a second one which spelt out the content of the relationship, as one of domination and exploitation by the few centre countries, and of helpless acquiescence and dependence by the many peripheral countries. This dependence came gradually to be seen not merely as one involving the pattern and composition of foreign trade where the centre countries exported a wide range of manufactured goods to the periphery against imports of a narrow range of primary products, but one that went much beyond. Thus it involved terms of trade which deteriorated against the underdeveloped countries, and political, cultural, technological and financial dependence.

It is to be noted that the ECLA social scientists indicated their awareness of the changing political realities of the post-war world, with special regard to the independence of many Third World countries, and what all this implied for the relationship between centre and peripheral countries. Consequently, the social scientists in question acknowledged the growing difficulty for centre countries to overtly impose dependence on the peripheral countries, with which they had a long dominating/dominated relationship, through the use of force, direct appropriation of the economic surplus, and like methods.

However, the governments of the centre countries had recourse to two new mechanisms whereby they were able to maintain their economic domination. These were the transfer of a large part of their power to their private transnational corporations (TNCs) and the skilful disguise wrapped around their own power and influence. This diguise took many forms, such as 'foreign aid' which was heavily self-serving to the donors; action through multinational organizations like the World Bank and the International Monetary Fund; technological and financial 'transfers' on terms which were onerously unfavourable to peripheral countries, and stiff resistance to drastic change in international relations and in the structure of power allocation in the international economic order.

The third notion and position to emerge was twofold. The first aspect of it was that, contrary to the neo-classical analysis, development in the advanced capitalist countries did not automatically mean development for the underdeveloped countries associated with them (dependent on them), owing to the observable fact of economic exploitation made possible by the many strands of dependence, and the inhibiting control exercised by centre countries over the prospects of industrialization and development in the peripheral countries.

The second aspect of the point being discussed must be obvious by now: that, because of the various restrictive policies and measures adopted by the industrial countries, development in these countries necessarily led to underdevelopment in dependent countries – or at least to the slowing down of the development of the latter. Indeed, any development that slipped through the fine mesh of the net of restrictive policies would turn out to be no more than dependent, distorted and patchy. This meant that it would be heavily conditioned by and conditional on the will of the advanced capitalist countries on which the less developed country or countries concerned were structurally dependent. Furthermore, the extent and context of this development would be determined – at least largely influenced – by the interests of the advanced countries and the limits they were capable of setting to such development. In effect, all this meant that the development of the centre capitalist industrial countries spelled out the underdevelopment of the peripheral countries: it implied a negation of the thesis that underdevelopment was an 'original sin' or original state; instead it meant that underdevelopment was a state brought about by the dynamics of capitalist development in the advanced industrial countries.

A fourth notion or position can also be discerned in the process whereby the dependency analysis evolved. This is that although dependence as a state was caused by what one might call 'the external imperative' – that is, the logic and impact of the nature of the relationship between centre and peripheral countries, or the impact of external factors – yet these factors, though predominant, were not all alone in operation. There were internal factors to operate inside the peripheral country, and provide dependence with a stronger grip on the economy, the society and the polity. These internal factors were basically structural in nature: they related to class structure and relations, vested interest groupings, institutions designed to serve the powerful, the rich and the influential, and so on.

The four notions and positions identified as central to the dependency school of thought and its analysis enjoyed the agreement of non-Marxist and neo-Marxist *dependentistas* alike. In fact, they were also on the whole acceptable to the structuralists who, however, placed major responsibility for the state or condition of dependence on internal rather than external factors. In this connection, it is appropriate to usher the structuralists into the heart of the discussion here, since they provided a major strand of the dependency analysis. But this point calls for some elaboration. Thus, if we take the core of the position of structuralists, such as Raul Prebisch, Hans Singer, Gunnar Myrdal, Dudley Seers, Paul Streeten and Hollis Chenery,[12] we find that they were highly sensitive to the unhealthy manner in which internal structural and institutional factors confirmed and deepened dependence, or lengthened the unbalanced centre–periphery connection to the disadvantage of the latter. But the tone of the structuralists was always rather mild: they stopped short of indicting colonialist capitalism explicitly and harshly, not only for being the source of the external factors that had brought about the genesis of dependence, but also for nurturing the internal forces and structures that gave dependence its longevity.

One outstanding illustration of the point relating to tone or style can be found in an interview given by Raul Prebisch to the editor of the *Third World Quarterly* in 1978.[13] Prebisch emphasized the imperativeness and urgency of transformation of the social system in peripheral countries, along with the implementation of a sound redistribution policy, if development was to reach the poorer segments of Third World populations. (In the course of the interview he indicated that he had reached this position rather later in life.) Yet he continued to insist on the recourse to the democratic process to achieve this transformation, while admitting that the communist countries could reach this objective more speedily through appropriating the means of production (rather than merely appropriating the economic surplus). He explained the paradox by saying that the communist approach to the problem could achieve its purpose only at the expense of certain political desiderata. Hence his shunning of the communist option.

The analysis of the structuralists could be considered reformist neo-classical – somewhere between the neo-classical and the neo-Marxist analysis. Its main virtue was perhaps that its leading proponents were Western social thinkers. Thus it was a sort of 'palace revolt' from within neo-classical thought. The structuralists were intensive users of the term 'dependency'; they must be acknowledged not only as contributors to the analysis, but also as forerunners of it. Further, even if their emphasis on internal factors in the genesis of dependence was excessive, and their indictment of external factors was mild, yet the emphasis was not misplaced if one took into account the persistence of dependence under the umbrella of independence and sovereignty in Third World countries.

Finally, it is worth noting in the present context that it can rightly be said that all *dependentistas*, whether non-Marxist or neo-Marxist, were structuralists to a certain extent, since they all attached importance to the role of systems, social structure and relations, and institutional factors, in the operation of external but also of internal factors, and in the interplay of the two groups. But the structuralists were on the whole not neo-Marxists but non-Marxists: they stood out as the advocates of reform of the capitalist system, though the degree of the radicalism of the reform they advocated varied from one writer to another. (It is quite possible that their anlysis could have become more radicalized if a larger measure of political participation and democratization, and the enjoyment of human rights, could have been successfully woven into the political system of socialist countries and could have been genuinely and meaningfully enjoyed.)

The promotion and programming of industrialization which the ECLA advocated, and which met gradually but increasingly with official approval and application in most ECLA member countries, led to notable growth in Latin America in the 1950s. But, by the 1960s, stagnation set in, the industrialization process became sluggish, balance of payments problems intensified in spite of the import substitution policies resorted to in the preceding decade, and development was seen to stall. Thus, the development gap between the industrialized and the newly industrializing countries seemed to be widening. Criticism of ECLA analysis and of the solutions it was proposing intensified and became more widespread, and more radicalized. The neo-Marxist influence became greater, both in criticism and in the advocacy of the new approach to the understanding of underdevelopment and the pursuit of development. In this, the neo-Marxists were helped by younger and more radical ECLA economists.

Needless to say, the orthodox Marxists were not slow in capitalizing on the theoretical and operational difficulties in which the ECLA found itself. It was in this phase of the later 1960s (and beyond into the mid-1970s) that the dependency school of thought received most of the contributions that were to enrich it and make it more sophisticated – but also to pull it more strongly in different directions. It is this phase that will occupy the rest of the present section in the chapter, but essentially with regard to the contributions made to the analysis rather than the fragmentation of the school.

Neo-Marxism, whose contributions constituted the third major strand in the dependency analysis, along with those of the structuralists and the non-Marxist *dependentistas* in the ECLA, was urged into being and growth as a critical reaction not so much to neo-classical thought as to orthodox Marxism, as understood, practised and translated into political reality by Latin American communist parties. The central criticism was that the textual Marx was not relevant to the capitalism of the twentieth century which had witnessed many changes in class power relations and orientation since the appearance of Marx's major writings in the latter part of the nineteenth century. Indeed, the neo-Marxists probably saw Mao Zedong as much more appropriate and relevant to the objective conditions and mood of the second half of the twentieth century, especially because of the nationalistic strain in his Marxism.

If Raul Prebisch was the undisputed leader and catalyst of the non-Marxist wing of the ECLA school and tradition, Paul Baran, with his book *The Political Economy of Growth*,[14] was the leader of neo-Marxism, and the catalyst in the upsurge of the radical wave designated as the New Left. Hence, the deflation of hopes with respect to the unfolding of development based on the prescription of programmed industrialization formulated by the ECLA, ECLA's (possibly excessive) caution in raising socio-political issues closely connected with the development being advocated in order to avoid official disapproval and sanction, and the insufficiency of the ECLA's focus by itself on the fallacious faith of the neo-classicists in foreign trade as an engine of development all combined to create or strengthen the new radical wave, both inside and outside the ranks of the ECLA. Baran's thought was the major intellectual influence in this wave. Under this influence, some scholars who had belonged more comfortably in the traditional school, changed convictions and came to belong in, or to have affinity with, the neo-Marxist school.

One leading example of these was Celso Furtado,[15] a Brazilian who initially followed the neo-classical line by investing great hope and faith in capital availability as a major factor in development. This position naturally led to great concern with the inflow of capital into underdeveloped countries, which as a general rule were short of this important input. But it also led to rosy expectations of foreign investment flowing in, and to dependence on the export of primary products – and, in brief, to a marked emphasis on the external sector and external factors. The speeding up of industrialization in the 1950s added to the rosiness of the expectation that import substitution would save valuable, and scarce, foreign exchange for Brazil and other countries in the continent. But Furtado was soon to see that the industrialization that had been materializing increased rather than decreased dependence on the advanced industrial countries, most notably the United States. So did the export of primary products and dependence on it, again instead of decreasing under the impetus of faster industrialization. Furthermore, foreign investors were seen to align themselves with rich and powerful interests in Brazil and elsewhere, at the expense of much of the population.

All these developments made Furtado better aware of the role of internal structural factors in underdevelopment, and the need to change these radically if meaningful and sustainable development was to be effectively sought. Thus, Furtado shifted from an economistic view of development to one with a much wider angle of vision and a fuller awareness of non-economic factors along with strictly economic ones, with special emphasis on internal socio-political structure. The natural next step in his thinking was to emphasize the need for underdeveloped countries to seek a larger measure of self-reliance in development, along with a restructuring of the economy and a strong public commitment to development.

Osvaldo Sunkel,[16] a Chilean economist who had worked with the ECLA, had even stronger views than Furtado with respect to the appropriateness and feasibility of a strategy of self-reliance in development, close attention to and reform of economic and social restructuring in Latin America, and greater concern with internal factors and forces supporting their external counterparts in maintaining underdevelopment. He also emphasized a nationalist commitment to self-determination with a strong developmental content, and widely based political participation with particular emphasis on the criticality and practicality of close co-operation and joint action between certain segments of the middle class, urban labour, and the rural population. Because he believed that self-reliance could be sought within a nationalist framework by various groups that otherwise belonged to different classes according to rigorous class analysis, it was evident that he did not consider the adoption of socialism as the only road open to underdeveloped countries. Thus, even more than Furtado, Sunkel's awareness of the burdensome legacy of dependence did not lead him to a strong Marxist position, though he did not reject Marxist theory altogether, and thus fitted into the left wing of the ECLA. Again, even more than Furtado, he emphasized the force of internal factors within a structuralist framework of analysis.

Sunkel is to be credited with the formulation of what he designated as 'global dualism', a concept within which be observed and discussed the emergence of TNCs which side-stepped national states and had disruptive effects on them. This process he summed up by the phrase 'transnational integration and national disintegration'. Within this understanding and formulation of such a global system, the process affected both developed and underdeveloped countries, with small parts of the former and large parts of the latter in effect belonging to the periphery in the world system, and large parts of the former and very small parts of the latter group of countries fitting into a characterization of the centre. This allocation of positions is based on the degree of dependence oι inability to develop from within, in a sustained manner, and on the basis of internal dynamics.

Before we turn to more decidedly neo-Marxist theorists, it is necessary to refer again to Paul Baran. Baran's contribution was essentially contained in his book *The Political Economy of Growth*, to which reference has already been made. As the title suggests, Baran underlined the non-economic factors in growth and development. This involved the recourse to a historical perspective and to the structure and content of relations between the capitalist industrial countries and the underdeveloped countries standing at the feudal stage or somewhere between feudalism and capitalism. A predominant feature of this relationship was the skimming by the colonial power of the economic surplus generated in the colonized country.

According to the wording of a careful work on development and dependence by Magnus Blomström and Bjorn Hettne, 'Baran abandoned the view of capitalism being spread from the "centre" to the "periphery"; instead, he introduced the idea that "underdevelopment" was an active process following the development in the centre' (Blomström and Hettne 1984: 35). Baran's view with respect to the stultification of development in the underdeveloped countries is quite different from Marx's, as the authors just referred to note. And although they also note that the position taken by Baran with regard to the causal connection between the development of the centre and the underdevelopment of the periphery 'was more or less hinted at, or implicit in Baran's analysis' and 'It was . . . brought to its logical conclusion in the works of André Gunder Frank, in which the idea of "the development of underdevelopment" was brought forward' (Blomström and Hettne 1984: 35), this position embodies the central message of dependency, irrespective of the way in which the school subsequently branched off.

Theotonio Dos Santos (1970, 1973), a Brazilian who reflected neo-Marxist influence more than Furtado or Sunkel, saw the relationship of dependence within a global context, rather like the 'world system' context elaborated notably by Samir Amin, André Gunder Frank and Immanuel Wallerstein. In his view the global context accounted for the external factors influencing the state of underdevelopment through the process of the internationalization of capitalism. However, dependence reflected the impact of the internationalization (that is, the external factor) *within* the Third World countries. The contribution specific to Dos Santos is his introduction of the concept of 'new dependence' in Latin America, to describe the shift of United States investors from investment in the production and export of primary products to investment in industry. Although this shift was very visible in Latin America, it was also a world-wide phenomenon. Dos Santos hastened to indicate his concern in this respect, for, in spite of the faith developmentalists usually have in industrialization as a sure path to development, the process of Latin American industrialization unfolded under such conditions that it did not contain independent dynamics, owing to its unfolding within a context of dependence.

The shift was seen by Dos Santos as being in line with his characterization of dependence as falling into three phases, with their distinctive particularities and emphasis. These were: colonial dependence, financial–industrial dependence and technological–industrial dependence. It can be asserted without danger of serious challenge that the more underdeveloped a country, especially if its colonial connection has not been severed for very long, the closer would its dependence fit into the first phase or category, and the more advanced an underdeveloped country, the nearer it would fit into the last category.

It is arguable that the 'Four Little Tigers' – South Korea, Hong Kong, Taiwan and Singapore (to whose experience we will refer again later on in this chapter) – whose capitalist development has been highly publicized as evidence of the fallacy of the dependency perspective, and of the possibility of development under the influence of world capitalism and within the context of dependence, instead provide an illustration of dependence of the third type, considering the web of relations that they have had and still have with transnational corporations that are leaders in technology and manufacturing industry.[17]

Such an interpretation would most probably not violate the conviction derivable from Dos Santos's writings, since the only options he could see for Third World countries seeking development, given the handicaps in their path (like small markets, low purchasing power, the drain of economic surplus, and insufficiency of capital for industrialization), were Fascist military regimes, or socialism. His system did not allow for a third option worthy of exploration like a progressive nationalist society, with an important public sector, and wide participatory political rights and freedoms. However, as we shall see later on, the socio-political and economic systems prevailing in the four countries listed, and their development policies, are not typical of Third World countries and are therefore largely responsible for their untypical development.

André Gunder Frank,[18] who is the last of the neo-Marxists to be discussed very briefly at this point, has made a considerable contribution to the dependency school, especially as far as the English-speaking readership is concerned. In the process of thinking out and shaping his understanding of dependency, he directed strong criticism at the conventional neo-classical theory of development. The reference to Baran and to Frank quoted a few paragraphs earlier, with respect to their reading of the causal relationship between the development of the centre and the underdevelopment of the periphery, made it inevitable for his view on one process to lead on to the other process. This is because, according to Frank, incorporation of countries into the world capitalist system made some developed and many more underdeveloped. The relationship between the few and the many is one of a metropolis and its satellites (Frank's terminology for centre and periphery).

However, to satisfy the claims of reality, Frank allowed for a more complex hierarchy, whereby a country within the world system which was a satellite to another higher up in the hierarchy of development and power, may well act as a metropolis (mini-metropolis perhaps?) *vis-à-vis* some other country or countries further down the hierarchy. The main determinant in development/underdevelopment was the access to and the size of the economic surplus. This hierarchical structure is world-wide, but it is not fixed for eternity: it can witness changes under the pressure of crises or wars. However, the reader is left undecided whether such a shift in position in the scale or hierarchy can be so radical that a country which is much more satellite than metropolis can turn into one which is much more metropolis than satellite. One could only surmise that such shifts would remain only marginal, so that the essence of the relationship would remain as it was under world capitalism, until the global system itself was basically transformed.

Two writers who also contributed richly to dependency analysis belong to another category, as they came from a Marxist background – neither neo-Marxist nor non-Marxist ECLA. They were Fernando Henrique Cardoso, a Brazilian sociologist, and Enzo Faletto, a Chilean historian, who jointly wrote a book in 1969 which appeared in English translation in 1979 (with expansion) under the title *Dependency and Development in Latin America*.[19] This book has since become a basic work on dependency.

The distinguishing ideas and position of the two authors were a strong emphasis on the socio-political aspects of dependence; emphasis on the need for historical and empirical research into cases of dependence, rather than satisfaction with aprioristic judgements; a belief that the intensity of dependence could change over time, owing to change in class combinations because of change in class interests lying behind the combinations, and furthermore, that the extent of dependence varied with the dependent country's response to that relationship and its implications; and insistence on the complexity of the relationship and interaction between external and internal factors and forces. Though influenced by Marxist thinking, they did not believe that the process of development was linear, or that it was characterized by stages that could be identified or labelled in advance. Finally, the two authors did not consider dependency an independent theory – it lacked the basic specifications of a theory. Instead, they considered it a part of the Marxist theory of imperialism. However, unlike leftist dependency theorists, Cardoso envisaged the possibility of development under dependence: the two were not logically irreconcilable.

The preceding survey is, understandably, partial and restricted to Latin American theorists (except for Baran). But it is meant to highlight the main points of contribution to dependency analysis by the leading theorists. The main components of this analysis and the perspective it has produced have emerged from the brief identification made of the main points in the work of the leading writers on dependence. Together with the four points I had identified as central to the dependency analysis earlier on in this section, they are sufficient for present purpose.[20]

THE DEPENDENCY SCHOOL UNDER CRITICISM: DOES IT STILL CARRY A RELEVANT AND USEFUL MESSAGE?

For about a decade, from the mid-1960s to the mid-1970s, the dependency analysis enjoyed the widest spread and acceptance in its rather brief active history, and was capable of providing many Third World and some Western social scientists with leftist leanings with a credible explanation for underdevelopment, and, by extension, with a pointer to what meaningful and real development ought to be and how it ought to be sought. Yet at no time, not even during the decade of its vigour, was the analysis free of attack. It is noteworthy that this attack came from foe and friend alike – from neo-classical as well as Marxist theorists, both groups of which were basically hostile to the perspective and challenged virtually all of the components of its intellectual and empirical underpinnings, and therefore its tenets and conclusions. It also came from *dependentistas* within the school itself who criticized and sometimes flayed each other in disagreement.

The issues which were the subject of dispute varied in weightiness and centrality in the analysis. Thus, at times the debate sounded highly polemical, overly concerned with marginal issues, and unworthy of the talent and time of the contestants. At least this is definitely how parts of the debate appear to me now in the early 1990s, when concern should be focused on those central issues that still enjoy broad agreement and together constitute the heart of the dependency perspective. The determining consideration should rather be whether this perspective could conceivably be seen still to have explanatory value and analytical power worth preserving and using, even after the introduction of a number of adjustments, elaborations and qualifications.

But before we move on to a discussion of the main issues which were the subject matter of debate, it would be worth noting that the structuralists, who were the one group which was the earliest to be instrumental in the genesis of the dependency analysis and its evolution, made their contribution with less assertiveness than the non-Marxists from within and outside the ECLA, and were equally moderate and soft-spoken in their critique. In fact, perusal of a substantial part of the relevant literature seems to suggest that when structuralists entered the debate and addressed certain issues on which they were in disagreement with one or another *dependentista*, they did so more as neo-Marxists or as nationalists than as structuralists. In other words, they were in such instances drawn into controversy more by their neo-Marxist or nationalist stance, than their structuralist analysis.

A surprisingly small number of neo-classical economists seem to have found the dependency analysis worth criticizing. It is difficult to assign the reason for this disregard, but if one were to venture a guess it would be that most Western (or Westernized) neo-classical economists considered dependency a transitory diversion of Third World economists, guided more by ideological predilection and/or based on questionable research, in the face of well-established, widely accepted, neo-classical theory. But, whatever the reason, the very few who took the trouble to examine the dependency literature critically, whatever course they took in their examination and whether they emphasized dissatisfaction with the methodology of *dependentistas* or with the content of their analysis, concluded that the dependency analysis proved unable to prove its basic thesis scientifically and unable to show that dependence and development were incompatible. The views of three leading economists will now be considered.

The first is P. T. Bauer, whose various writings since the early 1970s have presented a strong case for capitalism and the development that it brings into being. Indeed, according to him it is the only socio-economic system capable of nurturing development. He makes this point especially strongly in his two recent books, *Equality, the Third World and Economic Delusion* (1981) and *Reality and Rhetoric: Studies in the Economics of Development* (1984). He pursues his argument both deductively and on the basis of empirical facts. And, not surprisingly, he draws attention to the widely quoted four success stories designated 'The Four Little Tigers' or, alternatively, the 'Gang of Four' in the Far East (South Korea, Hong Kong, Taiwan and Singapore), all of which were underdeveloped countries right after the Second World War and considered dependent by dependency theorists.

The central point he makes is that if these countries could achieve a notable measure of development, in terms of industrialization, land reform, technological progress and a tangible rise in national and per capita income, then that should lead to one forceful conclusion: that what these four have achieved, others too could achieve, if they followed the course of capitalist development and formulated and implemented the appropriate policies, basically *because* of a relationship considered 'dependent' with the advanced Western industrial countries, rather than *in spite* of it. However, the long-term significance of the role of TNCs in the development of the four, and the implications of the penetration of these TNCs, as well as the political promotive factors centring around alignment with the industrial West, and what this implies for the society and polity of the four countries, does not receive the attention and consideration it legitimately deserves in Bauer's examination.

Nevertheless, it ought to be admitted that the experience of the four countries in question, despite the fact that they are not typical of underdeveloped countries in general, has shaken the conviction of a number of Third World countries in the soundness and assertiveness of dependency analysis, and led to serious questioning of its tenets, and of the absolutism of some of its advocates who maintain that development and dependence are incompatible. The four cases cannot be dismissed by mere debating skill or recourse to ideology-loaded statements detracting from their successful performance simply by associating it with close alignment and co-operation with Western advanced capitalist countries. This would be begging the question.

I believe that the development of the 'Four Tigers' could well be considered the result of a serious effort at self-reliance, reflected in their development policies and behaviour, rather than of their dependent status. The case can be made that these countries are freeing themselves of the shackles of dependence by purposeful self-reliance pursued cautiously, intelligently and consistently.

The central issue that has to be addressed is this: what are the long-term economic, social and political implications of such alignment and co-operation with the advanced West for development, independent decision-making and social justice in the four countries? It would be highly speculative and inconclusive to argue that they would have been better off in the very long run, again in terms of the criteria just listed, had they refused to take the course of action they have taken in the last few decades and, instead, insisted resolutely on following a course of 'delinkage' and self-reliance in development with all that it means in political, social and economic terms. The question is important enough to receive yet more examination further down.

The critique of the second economist to consider here is perhaps more telling, because it is methodologically more rigorous. The economist in question is Sanjaya Lall, who framed two criteria or conditions to determine the soundness and relevance of the dependency perspective in an article that has had strong analytical impact (S. Lall 1975):

1 It must lay down certain characteristics of dependent economies which are not found in non-dependent ones.
2 These characteristics must be shown to affect adversely the course and pattern of development of the dependent countries.

Upon the application of the first criterion, Lall established that certain characteristics of dependence considered significant by dependency theorists could be found in many advanced, non-dependent countries (financial penetration, technology imports, and so on). From this he concluded that such characteristics, though discernible in underdeveloped countries, were not sufficient reason for the classification of countries into dependent and non-dependent. It seems to the present writer that while the observation is correct, the conclusion does not necessarily follow, since what matters is the relative size and significance of the dependent sector or pocket in an advanced industrial country, not the mere presence of a small such sector or pocket. The question is therefore warranted: would the conclusion be as firm and final if Lall had recognized dependence only in cases where it predominated in a very substantial part of the economy under examination? If not, then his identification of dependence pockets in countries like Canada or Belgium would by definition be discounted as evidence of overall dependence.

The application of the second criterion led Lall to conclude that the characteristics of dependence referred to in the Latin American context were static and showed no causal connection with underdevelopment. Here again, the nature of the conclusion centres around the designation of the characteristics as 'static'. It would seem quite puzzling to consider the socio-political and economic aspects of dependence as static; a strong case can be made for their designation as dynamic and active, though their dynamism and action are 'downward-pulling' in their effect on the development performance of the society and economy.

The characteristics in question are not listed in the dependency literature as traits or events, or yet as socio-political or economic ailments that describe a state or a condition, and which show no action or movement over time, and no dynamics, singly and in interaction. The opposite is true, even if one thinks of the colonial or imperial connection in historical terms, or of the appropriation of the economic surplus in the context of dependence, whether this occurs 'freely' in the market place or in 'unequal exchange'. In both instances, the connection and the appropriation exert undeniable sustained influence (even if the intensity of this influence changes over time and under changing circumstances), and have a 'debilitating dynamics'.

But, having said all this, it remains true that Lall's two criteria are valuable, not in declaring the fallacy of dependency or announcing its demise, but rather in pointing to the need for a flexible and relativist understanding and interpretation of dependence, and in recognizing that it ought to be looked at in a dynamic framework and frame of mind, with a view to providing it with the qualifications that new analysis and research bring to light and necessitate. In other words, dependency analysis must not be absolutist and dogmatic, nor should it cut itself off from the specific realities of time and place, within and for which it is researched, identified or tested. The implications of Lall's analysis, as I identified in the last sentences above, endow dependency with greater relevance to present-day realities, but also qualify the anlysis as an appropriate prelude to the pursuit of a strategy of self-reliance in development.

The third neo-classical economist whose critique of dependency theorizing I will now consider briefly is I. M. D. Little. His fullest examination of dependence can be found in his book *Economic Development–Theory, Politics and International Relations* (Little 1982: Ch. 12). In my view it is the most comprehensive and serious critique undertaken by neo-classical economists that I know of. Little sets out, patiently and in detail, to examine the grounds and conclusions of dependency theorists from the main angles which they identify as manifesting the dependence of peripheral countries on centre countries. The angles chosen are:

- trade dependence;
- dependence on external financial transfers;
- industrial dependence;
- technological dependence;
- TNCs and dependence.

After assessing the degree of truth in the claims of dependency theorists in each of the areas enumerated, Little moves on to examine the credibility of the contention that the elites in Third World countries get contaminated through contact with their counterpart in centre countries, essentially because of trade relations and association with the TNCs. He then examines the meaning of underdevelopment and its real causes, in the light of his preceding analysis, and ends his long chapter with final thoughts on dependence and capitalism.

Although the general tone in Little's treatment is critical, and the analysis distinctly disapproving of anything associated with or drawing on Marxist or neo-Marxist thought, it still reflects a large degree of fairness. The central line in Little's critique is the denial of the possibility of dependence between peripheral and centre countries in the era of political independence, so long as there is competitiveness among centre countries or TNCs in the supply of goods and services through external trade, in financial transfers, in the outflow of investment capital, or in technological transfers from centre to peripheral countries. While he admits a certain degree of influence over the latter group of countries in the course of the conduct of bilateral relations between them and strong industrial countries, he sees this as unavoidable in international relations. Likewise, he rejects the notion of 'unequal exchange' as used by neo-Marxist *dependentistas*. Finally, he comes to the conclusion that many of the complaints by dependency theorists are unsupported by reality and untenable, but to the extent that they have some substance, it is the governments and societies of Third World countries that should bear responsibility. Capitalism should therefore not only be exonerated, but should indeed get credit for promoting development in Third World countries.

A fourth writer, whose attachment to the capitalist system seems to go beyond what sober analysis calls for or justifies to reach into ideological faith, is Deepak Lal. In his book *The Poverty of 'Development Economics'* (1984), he makes more of a crusade than just a critique of the whole arsenal of 'development economics', on the basis of the proposition that there is no such discipline: there is just orthodox (Western) economics, and it is absurd to contend that there is a special branch of economics to deal with development issues whose content and rules differ from the classical, conventional discipline developed by writers of the capitalist world. Lal devotes the two pages of his book in which he discusses dependency theories (1984: 43–5) to an assault on these theories, but squeezes into this small space two long quotations for a concentrated attack on one well-known dependency theorist, Samir Amin. What is worth mentioning here is that the quotations come from a Marxist whose attack is essentially because Amin is believed to have strayed away from the Marxist path. It is certainly ironical that a confirmed neo-classical economist should base the bulk of his critique on the views of a Marxist attacking a neo-Marxist for being a deviationist!

Finally, in addition to the serious critique of a number of points in dependency analysis by neo-classical theorists Bauer, Lall and Little, there is one other point which has drawn criticism. This is the inclusion by a number of dependency theorists, especially Samir Amin,[21] André Gunder Frank[22] and Immanuel Wallerstein,[23] of the theory of 'unequal exchange' in their analysis. This theory draws attention to the exploitative aspects of exchange when two goods being traded have two different prices even though they have the same value (the latter determined by the *numéraire* used, such as working hours). The difference in prices will then be occasioned by difference between the two wage levels, and it provides scope for the exploitation by the high-wage country of its low-wage trading partner. Without going into the details of the controversy, it is sufficient for present purposes to mention that both neo-classical and Marxist economists take the neo-Marxists to task for the way they use the notion of unequal exchange, the former because they believe that this notion is a factor of disturbance in foreign trade theory. Furthermore, while this notion provided the neo-Marxist critics of trade theory with yet another weapon of attack, the neo-classicists considered the weapon theoretically blunt, because fallacious.

The Marxists, who shared with the neo-classicists their dissatisfaction with the use of the notion of unequal exchange as one of the arguments of dependency, had other issues as well on which to attack this school. One of these they also shared with neo-classical theorists. This is that, contrary to the position of *dependentistas*, development and underdevelopment are *not* two sides of the same coin – that development in the advanced capitalist (colonial, neo-colonial or imperialist) centre countries leads to underdevelopment of the peripheral countries, by the logic of history and the nature of the situation. In other words, both schools, the Marxist and the neo-classical, envisaged development as possible with dependence, within the orbit of a world capitalist system. Indeed, it is ironical that they both believed that the process of development could unfold (outside the socialist system) only through capitalist transformation. We do not have to go any further in elaborating on this point as we have already had occasion to sketch the outline of the Marxist theory of development in the context to which we are now referring.

In general, the Marxist critique of dependency, and particularly of neo-Marxist *dependentistas*, was essentially motivated and shaped by the belief that the latter were errant Marxists, and all that was called for was their return to the correct path of (orthodox) Marxism. The reader of the relevant literature, especially as it relates to A. G. Frank, S. Amin and I. Wallerstein, gets this impression. This is basically because while the critique is often harsh, it always leaves a route of escape open to the prodigal sons of Marxism, a route which if taken, will lead the neo-Marxists back into favour.[24] But it would be unfair to the Marxists to claim that their critique merely reflected disappointment or pique: it did go into basic issues of disagreement. One of these was the neo-Marxist advocacy of one-stage revolution, with heavy involvement by the politicized rural masses, in contradistinction with the two-stage strategy advocated in Marxism – to which we referred earlier. The disagreement here was both historical and analytical. And Frank was the main target.

Another issue where Frank again was targeted more than any other neo-Marxist, related to the implications of his notion of 'sphere of exchange' within which the centre (the metropolis) skimmed off the economic surplus of the periphery (the satellite). The Marxists, on the other hand, insisted that it was the difference in the modes of production and the class relations within them that made the appropriation of the surplus possible. Hence, the neo-Marxists' casual reference to class relations was a serious point of disappointment, particularly that they accused labour in centre countries of taking part in the process of exploitation. In other words, capital and labour in the centre exploited capital and labour in the periphery, although labour was in its turn subjected to exploitation by capital within the centre as within the periphery.

The wide disparity in the weight of emphasis laid on external factors by the dependency theorists, and on internal factors by Marxist theorists, was another area of disagreement. It was entangled with other issues, such as the Marxist belief in the beneficial role of the capitalist penetration in bringing about development, while the neo-Marxists attributed underdevelopment to this penetration. In this connection, the Marxists accused the dependency theorists of over-simplification in attributing underdevelopment solely to the system predominating in (or enveloping) centre countries. Once again, the Marxists reminded the *dependentistas* that it was imperative to identify the deeper causes – namely, internal factors in the peripheral countries. Finally, the two schools disagreed on the definition of the geo-political entity appropriate for a consideration of dependence. Hence, while neo-Marxists generally identified dependence within the context of the world capitalist system as a whole, Marxists considered national states as the appropriate context for the identification of underdevelopment.

While these were not the only issues around which disagreement and debate raged, they may suggest sufficiently the wide divide between the two groups of theorists. But notwithstanding the number and intensity of issues in dispute, there are Marxists who continue to believe that the neo-Marxists will again join ranks with them, after the parting of roads of one or two decades. Indeed, the internal debate and disputes within the dependency school; the increasing emphasis laid by some of its leading theorists on internal factors rather than on external disruptive influences emanating from the centre; the signs of some rethinking by Marxists of certain issues on which the two sides did not see eye to eye before; and finally the very telling impact and implications of development achieved by a number of dependent countries in spite of the insistence by 'textbook dependency' that development and dependence are incompatible – all these developments give Marxists hope that some readjustment in the neo-Marxist thought will most probably take place and end in steering it towards the orthodox fold.

It is appropriate at this point, before moving on to the last category of critique and dispute, to present a Marxist whose writing defined a special position that irritated *dependentistas* considerably, and even a number of Marxists – the latter considering these views as socially and politically embarrassing, coming as they did from another Marxist. The writer in question was the late Bill Warren whose book *Imperialism: Pioneer of Capitalism*[25] contained a complex of rather heretical arguments and took a number of provocative positions relating to development in Third World countries (Warren 1985). Thus he argued that colonialism was a strong promotive influence for social change in underdeveloped countries, one which had been instrumental in removing old social systems and replacing them with capitalism. He maintained that this had improved the scope for capitalist development in a number of Third World countries – indeed, it had led to concrete development that could be seen in such countries as Brazil, Argentina and Mexico, but strikingly in the Far East in the four countries (the Four Little Tigers) referred to earlier on in this chapter. This process could also be expected to spread into other underdeveloped countries.

The implications of the position just defined are far-reaching. They first suggest a beneficial role for imperialism/colonialism, but also suggest that as imperialism recedes capitalism advances. In such a situation, the internal impediments to capitalist development emerge visibly and as increasingly significant – more so than imperialism. Finally, Warren's argument and assumptions led him to consider the anti-imperialist stance of nationalists and consequent self-reliant (or autarkic, in his view) tendencies of nationalist political systems to be erroneous and counter-productive, in so far as the drive for development was concerned. Furthermore, he considered the mobilization of the proletariat in Third World countries, through nationalist slogans and appeals, to be ill-directed, harmful to the long-term interests of the proletariat and, again, counter-produtive for capitalist development. Though his was a minority view, Warren has provoked a great deal of discussion. The message of this book can be said to contain some truth, but it should not be generalized, especially since it overlooks or underplays a number of harsh and painful aspects of imperialist history. We will have occasion to touch on this message later on in the chapter, when we assess the extent of the relevance and usefulness of dependency analysis.

The debate among dependency theorists themselves, to which we now turn, did not have the degree of harshness that the critique by neo-classical or Marxist theorists displayed. This was understandable, inasmuch as the main objective of this debate was not to destroy the dependency analysis but to refine or improve it, and make it more compelling, or else to remove some excesses that had crept into it in the early years of its enthusiastic genesis and led to rather dogmatic, over-assertive generalizations. But, though well-meaning on the whole, the debate no doubt contributed to the fragmentation of the school.

However, the school can still be said to share a central core of ideas relating to the historical and causal connection between colonialism and capitalist penetration by centre countries on the one hand, and dependence and underdevelopment of peripheral countries on the other, and thus can still be said to emphasize external factors. It can also be said to contain a global view of capitalist development within which there is a small number of centre countries in a position of dominance, and a very large number of peripheral countries whose development is essentially severely restricted (if not altogether blocked) by acts of omission or of commission by centre countries and their TNCs. Against this area of broad agreement, there is another area where the views of dependency theorists diverge. There is no reason to list here these points and the theorists who uphold them, since the survey conducted in the preceding section of the chapter identified many of the points and their supporters. It will be sufficient now to point out the major issues of internal debate.

One of these relates to the apportioning of responsibility for underdevelopment between external factors associated with the global capitalist system and its exploitative dynamics on the one hand, and on the other hand, internal factors associated with the internal system and structure, and its political, social, cultural and economic components. Furtado and Sunkel, and also Cardoso, stand out for the tangible emphasis they placed on the latter group of factors. However, no dependency theorists placed all, or even most of the blame on internal factors: to do so would be to deny the very foundation and *raison d'être* of dependency analysis. But the various theorists differed among themselves in the extent to which each went in blaming internal as against external factors. Behind this issue was a basic dispute with respect to the choice of reference social formation, or geo-political area of reference: is it the national state, or alternatively the whole capitalist system? Amin, Frank and Wallerstein stand out as the principal upholders of the latter view. The more firmly the latter view is held, the greater the emphasis on external factors, and vice versa.

Also related to the point of dispute just referred to is the question of whether capitalist development is at all likely at the periphery, and, if it is viable, if it proves at all possible. In turn, this question is tied to another one: is it possible for a Third World bourgeoisie to emerge as a promotive force for development and to co-operate with labour in the drive for development and, to that end, to abstain from exploiting labour or at least to minimize the exploitation? Phrased differently, the question would be: can development at the periphery be approached and achieved outside of the framework of socialism? And are there other alternatives besides the extremes of socialism or fascism? Cardoso stands out as a theorist who answered in the affirmative to all these questions. And he is not alone in taking less dogmatic, less absolutist positions than those that characterized views and attitudes in the early years of the rise of the dependency paradigm.

In the present context, it would seem to the present writer that the most notable change in views and attitudes, among theorists who basically accept the dependency analysis, currently centres around three themes:

1 That socialism is not the only framework for the true and meaningful development of Third World countries, and that there is another desirable and realistic option, which is a progressive nationalist mixed (private and public) system. This contradicts the early polarization: either socialism or fascism.
2 That although dependence by peripheral countries on centre countries was made to come about by the capitalist/colonialist and later imperialist policies of the latter group, and that there is still strong evidence of the persistence of multifaceted dependence today, though enforced by newer instruments, it is nevertheless possible to find escape routes, even if narrow and partial, in the era of national independence and sovereignty. And, furthermore, along with the independence of Third World countries there is the 'wider spread of the centre', namely the inclusion in the centre of a large number of advanced countries – both capitalist and socialist – that have marked economic and technological capabilities to which underdeveloped countries can have access, and thanks to which they can enjoy a stronger bargaining position.

3 That, therefore, it is crucial today to focus more on internal structural handicaps to development (while keeping a watchful eye on external handicaps). It is also crucial to direct action against underdevelopment in a way which expresses the understanding of the new political realities in the world, the interaction between external and internal factors, and the possibility of the management of the problem in a number of Third World countries or, more feasibly, within groups of countries sharing policies and acting collectively. In other words, these countries do not face an impasse even without taking the socialist option.

The immediate availability of the socialist option itself is now being questioned by a few theorists who, not many years ago, saw it as the only true and credible option. A leading such Arab theorist, Samir Amin, has very recently started a new line of thinking and writing which deserves to be reported on at some length in the present context. Amin has recently published four essays in which he has set his assessment of the relevance and appropriateness of the socialist option for the pursuit of self-reliant development as a way out of dependence. The writings under reference, which began with a seminar paper given in April 1986, are so far all in Arabic to the best of my knowledge.[26] This justifies the space devoted here to the presentation of Amin's central thesis.

To begin with, Amin notes that the changing political, economic, socio-cultural and structural situation and conditions with respect to the world capitalist system, and likewise to the socialist system as it has been put into application in the European communist countries, have not been matched by changes in theoretical perceptions and frameworks. (This is obviously because theoretical analysis lags behind the realities which it is supposed to explain.) Thus, the marked ability of capitalism to adjust to crisis situations, as it has done in the decades after the Second World War which came at the end of the Great Depression, on the one hand, and the failure of socialism, as it is concretely visible in the communist countries, to constitute a credible and appealing option for most non-socialist countries, on the other, have combined to necessitate the rethinking of the conventional wisdom of the critics of capitalist development, especially dependency theorists.

This does not mean a discarding of the dependency paradigm altogether, but instead the willingness of its advocates to make the necessary conceptual and analytical adjustments, with a view to enabling theory to catch up with reality. Nor does this mean the discarding of the world capitalist system framework and analysis by its advocates, since it still basically embodies a true characterization of reality, especially with respect to the persistence of the structure which it describes with centre–periphery relations and their implications.

The significance of the current developments, in Amin's view, is that they necessitate the search for new systemic frameworks of action capable of effecting a breakthrough in the impasse of underdevelopment. At this point of his argument, Amin takes a long look at socialism as we see it in operation today. Without going into the details of his discussion in this context, we can discern two main lines of thought. First, that socialism has been unable to provide scope for broad-based, free political participation by the masses, and has not permitted the enjoyment of human rights outside the purely socio-economic areas of work opportunities, income distribution, education and health services, and the like. In other words, the record with regard to freedom of expression and association, and political choice, still leaves a great deal to be desired. Second, that socialism as a system has not yet been able fully to embody the principles of social ownership of the means of production, to function efficiently in the economic sphere, or satisfactorily to solve problems of scarcity in certain critical areas of production essential for a marked improvement in the level of living of the masses.

This process of observation and thinking leads Amin to consider that a meaningful and all-encompassing socialist transformation is still a matter on the agenda of the very distant future, so distant as to require many more generations of radical change and adjustment within the political, social, cultural and economic spheres of life. But what of the foreseeable future? What is the system that can provide an effective option for self-reliant development capable of enabling peripheral countries to break out, even if gradually, of the state of dependence and of underdevelopment? In other words, what is the viable post-capitalist option, if not socialism?

Amin's answer, in his own words, is *dawlanah*, the Arabic word (in my view) for the French word *étatisme*. The essence of *dawlanah*, as he sees it, is closest to what I have designated in the first two chapters as a progressive nationalist structure (a national state or, in the Arab context, a community of nation states constituting the Arab region and acting collectively), where the public sector occupies a central place in the economy, and where basic human rights and freedoms are assured within the scope of broad-based political participation.[27]

Such an interpretation of *dawlanah* goes beyond *étatisme* which, narrowly defined and carefully observed in, for instance, *étatiste*

Turkey, reveals a very scanty socio-political content with respect to participation and political freedoms. It would not be far-fetched to describe the system or structure advocated as capitalist/socialistic. The word 'socialistic' means no more here than having a socialist flavour or socialist tendencies – something beyond the currently applied form and content of state capitalism, though not deserving the unqualified designation 'socialist' in its proper meaning.

I admit that the formulation suggested could be viewed by critics as no more than verbal acrobatics. Or perhaps no more than an escape from the constricting belief that the world capitalist system in its global behaviour cannot permit the underdeveloped countries to liberate themselves from dependence, but that the only option left for them – socialism – is not one many of them wish to take (nor is it promising in Amin's view). Yet, the experience of a few Arab countries in the post-war period (especially between the mid-1950s and mid-1970s) suggests that the option of *dawlanah* adopted in practice proved promising and fruitful, even if it was ultimately beset by serious reverses brought about by a combination of external forces and factors (including war) and internal forces and factors (including the failure to institutionalize the socio-economic transformation and to permit broad-based participation and basic freedoms).

I hope I have not done Amin an injustice while summarizing the core thesis in his most recent writings which have appeared in Arabic. As would be expected, the argument is long and complex, covering as it does four long essays, as already indicated. But the summary presented here is at the centre, surrounded by many elaborations called for by the need to develop the argument for the thesis. We need say no more in the present context, except that a good deal of debate must now be expected, once Amin's readers become aware of the substance of his recent writings. The internal discussion among dependency theorists will ramify, and perhaps there will also be further fragmentation in the school. On the other hand, greater flexibility in analysis may as well ensue. One leading Arab economist at least, Ismail Sabri Abdalla, is bound to take issue with Amin's dilution of the monopoly of the socialist option of the answer to dependence. Although he sees socialism as the only course open for self-reliant development, Abdalla admits that there is today no pure theory of socialism with which he can have theoretical affinity.[28]

At this point it becomes legitimate to ask: is the dependency school coming to the end of its life span? Have we already witnessed the demise of the dependency school, and are we therefore invited to explore 'new trends in development theory', as two authors we have already referred to tell us (Blomström and Hettne 1984: ch. 8)? And, if the school is not yet dead, but ailing and in need of treatment to be able to give to development theory what in a healthier state it could give, what should it undergo by way of rethinking and qualifications? To the examination of these questions we now turn in the next (and final) section of this chapter.

MATURING PERCEPTIONS, CHANGING REALITIES AND THE NEED FOR QUALIFICATIONS

The answer to the question of whether the dependency paradigm is in crisis, and thus whether the time has come for a drastic paradigm change, cannot be a straightforward 'Yes' or 'No'. In my view, the paradigm (or the main body of ideas in it) is in crisis, judging by all the debate around its components, the many inroads that have been made into its content, and the notable discrepancies between its assertions and the real world around it currently. Consequently, there is need for rethinking and elaborations, urged on by the recognition of limitations to the relevance, usefulness and generality of the paradigm, and therefore the need for qualifications. But the answer would be 'No' if it is claimed that the crisis is fatal, and that the paradigm is dead or dying. In this latter case, the argument can be made that dependency still has a useful explanatory function, particularly if what is expected of it is realistic, and it is not viewed as a rigorous theory with interpretive value for past experience and predictive value for future expectations, for all underdeveloped countries.[29]

Indeed, the very fact that the paradigm is considered in need of elaboration and qualification is in itself an indication that, far from being dead, it is still useful, worth revising, and continues to have promise as an analytical tool, once it is used with the necessary caution and flexibility. All this suggests that there is a desire for the paradigm to be more nuanced and sophisticated than it had been in the early years of its development, and a need for it to be used with more prudence: with less assertiveness, dogmatism or absolutism, and with an avoidance of excessive generalization.[30]

The foregoing statements are made in spite of the critique from fundamentalists – whether liberal, neo-classical economists, modernization theorists or Marxists – and in spite of the attempts by all these to contain dependency analysis or incorporate it in their own. In this latter context, the rejection of dependency is probably not as widespread today as it used to be a decade ago. There is greater recognition that it has at least some historical justification for many countries, especially those with a colonial legacy – and at least some theoretical strength – but in both cases it is still considered by most fundamentalists as having exaggerated its historical and theoretical underpinnings.

Furthermore, there is now wider acceptance of some of the dependency theses, like the existence of a global capitalist system, with a structure the contours and components of which continue in broad outline to exist and to be operative, although capitalism undergoes changes itself. Likewise, the (external) influence of the global system on the (internal) situation in individual peripheral countries is recognized, and the interaction or dialectic of both sets of forces and factors is acknowledged. Furthermore, the shift from internationalization to transnationalization is admitted, with all that it implies in polarization (centre/periphery or metropolis/satellite) within countries as between countries. Finally, there is general acceptance of the notion of system articulation or the coexistence of different modes of production.

On the other hand, the *dependentistas* themselves have accepted the principle of some accommodation and adjustment warranted by maturing perceptions and changing circumstances. These adjustments include recognition of the transnationalization of capital and its flow from core or centre countries into the periphery for investment in different sectors, including manufacturing industry. In consequence, there is wider admission of the occurrence of some tangible transformation in the pattern of international division of labour, and the feasibility of the acquisition of appropriate and effective technological capability by underdeveloped countries – even if patchily, slowly, and at a high cost – through the dual process of the establishment of a science and technology base at home, and the formulation of reasonable and firm but realistic policies for the import of capital goods and technical skills from abroad.

But the most notable adjustment (even if still mainly implicit) is awareness of the possibility of development in the periphery even outside a socialist framework (though it would still be called 'dependent or distorted development', possibly as a face-saving nomenclature), particularly under the aegis of development-orientated governments and with the instrumentality of appropriate policies. The emergence of this possibility has occurred thanks also to the multiplicity of centres and the greater manoeuvrability which this factor now permits. We refer here to the existence of a socialist community of countries that acts as a 'source of countervailing power' to help peripheral countries in their drive for development, as well as to the readiness of several politically acceptable advanced industrial countries in the Western world which have the technological capability to help in the promotion of development in Third World countries. Finally, there are also several international bodies with a similar capability and readiness.

All this is being mentioned in order to indicate that changing conditions, and changes in analysis, diagnosis and the assessment of experience and reality, have been taking place within both sides to the debate: the dependency theorists and their adversaries. This is proof that the dependency analysis is not dead, but instead is alive and readjusting, thanks to the influence of praxis.

Related to the point discussed in the preceding few paragraphs is the fact that the attitude to the modernization paradigm has also undergone some change. Thus, while the core of the paradigm is still refused and refuted by dependency theorists – namely its insistence on a universal model of Westernization to emulate, and that the model is characterized by certain traits or pattern variables – there are certain components of the paradigm that are acknowledged as relevant. These relate to several aspects of traditionalism which are considered hostile to development and social transformation.

But the admission is not a blanket acceptance that all aspects of traditionalism are to be shunned and fought; it is rather that careful study and history-related research should be undertaken to determine what aspects constitute a blockage to the transformation desired, and what aspects do not.[31] The change in attitude with respect to modernization does not go as far as to accept the notion of the oneness of the avenue to modernity – in other words, the ethnocentrism of the modernization paradigm – nor the notion of 'stages of growth' with a large sociological content taken from the modernization paradigm.

Yet, even with the achievement of some mutual recognition by dependency theorists and their adversaries, there is still need to emphasize that the former ought to recognize that their analysis will always have its limitations – like all analyses that tend to find one central and general explanation for all historical phenomena. To begin with, by the same token that *dependentistas* strongly criticize the concept of a universal model of or path to development, as neoclassical (including modernization) and Marxist theories all claim, each in its system and framework, the *dependentistas* should not themselves claim universalism for their analysis either. Dependency falls into a contradiction in this respect: while it insists on the recourse to historical experience in defining the colonial connection between centre and periphery, and the resultant influences which have produced underdevelopment in the latter, it ought not to claim general applicability of its theses.

To realize the need for differentiation, one needs no more than a careful look at the past experience and present situation of Latin America, which has been the soil in which the dependency school has grown, as against the Arab region, which likewise has been subjected to far-reaching capitalist/colonial/imperialist penetration. While it is true that the former region is much richer in natural resources (hydrocarbons apart), the latter has relatively considerable financial resources, a rich cultural heritage in science and the arts, a wide experience in international trade stretching long before the Ottoman incursion into the Arab lands began in 1516, and a not inconsiderable market. Yet, today, it is obvious that several Latin American countries have acquired considerable technological capability compared with the Arab countries, and a more creditable economic performance, particularly in the area of manufacturing. To find the reason for the discrepancy one would have to explore very thoroughly and profoundly the many elements that govern each of the two situations.

The exploration will have to comprise political, socio-cultural and economic components over time, in their national and international context, and will have to include the place of each region in the world capitalist system in the relevant past and in the present, and consider the change in the place of resources in economic life and in the composition of world trade, as well as the change of trade routes regionally and internationally. Surely all these considerations have a relevance to the unfolding of the course of development, or alternatively to its blockage. The need to include so many questions and variables in any exploration suggests that greater modesty is called for when claims are made in sweeping terms with respect to the general applicability of dependency analysis.

This is all the more necessary when it is recalled that dependency is not a general theory with proven power to interpret the past and predict the future for a whole category of countries – in the present instance that of former colonies. Indeed, dependency cannot become a general theory unless such exploration and research has been undertaken and has revealed uniform results that can all be interpreted by the theory. And in our state of knowledge we are distant from that, to say nothing about the improbability of finding enough common features attributable to underdeveloped countries in their various historical perspectives to justify including them all in one meaningful category.

Another limitation that calls for appropriate analytical qualification, which it is necessary to recognize, relates to the impact of changing circumstances with the passage of time and change of context. Thus, it is warranted to emphasize that the kind of judgements passed with respect to the conditions of dependent countries that have acquired independence only recently, cannot be the same as for ones that have been independent for many years, and have exercised their sovereignty and power of independent politico-economic decision-making for a long enough time to make them self-assured and eager to protect this power, and able to do so. This point has serious implications for some central theses of dependency. One of these is the incompatibility of development and dependence; phrased differently, it is the incompatibility of independent decision-making with conditions of dependence. Here the question arises: can this incompatibility continue to be upheld with the same tenacity for the large and/or well-endowed countries with a long experience of political independence and the exercise of decision-making, as for those smaller and/or poorer countries which have just acquired their political independence, and are still of necessity heavily forced into dependence on the advanced capitalist countries? And should there not be recognition that there can be a tangible difference in the degree of independent decision-making enjoyed by developing countries?

The danger of generalization in the present context can be seen if attention is turned to another direction, that of the impact on Third World countries of penetration versus isolation. The relevant thesis here is that penetration blocks capitalist development. But this cannot be reconciled with the fact that some capitalist development is frequently encountered in countries which had experienced especially deep and widespread colonial/capitalist penetration, while certain countries that had been sealed off against such direct penetration have failed to achieve anything like the same degree of development experienced by the former group.

In the Arab region, for instance, by the end of the Second World War the only two countries that had not come under direct foreign domination or experienced notable economic and cultural penetration were Saudi Arabia and North Yemen. Yet these two countries were distinctly far less developed than the rest in the region, notably less than the Maghreb countries (Morocco, Algeria and Tunisia), and the Mashreq countries in general, but Egypt and Lebanon in particular. This judgement is true whether it is related to levels of education and sophistication, the development of journalism and literature, the establishment of physical infrastructure, manufacturing industry or technological capability. Such examples can be multiplied from other regions in the world. In contrast, however, there is Japan where isolation (though by no means the only strategy) led to phenomenal development and technological excellence.

The value of establishing such contradictory realities is not merely to indicate the limits of the generality of dependency theses, and the consequent need to present them as broad tendencies with some modesty and appropriate tentativeness. Probably the greater value lies in the implications of the facts in question for the notion of delinkage from the world capitalist system which some dependency theorists (like Samir Amin, Frank and Wallerstein) and, less vigorously, Galal Amin, have advocated for peripheral countries, if they wish to seek development.[32] Here again too much of a good thing can prove bad. Thus, a certain degree of isolation coupled with the marshalling of society's internal will and resources for development, and very great attention to its own market and ability to satisfy its demand, are not only essential but crucial. But realism and the wide experience of the Third World which is there to be seen and learnt from, together suggest where the critical line lies between isolation that can be useful, and isolation that will be counter-productive. The position of this line will naturally differ as between one country and another.

The advocacy of moderation here is by no means dissociated from awareness of the dangers which accompany dependence and excessively close linkage. The thesis which is suggested here is that the dangers which the unavoidable links carry with them can be more effectively reduced or better controlled, the more clear-sighted the dependent society is, and the more determined it is seriously to seek self-reliance as a consistent strategy for development and national regeneration. Furthermore, these dangers must be measured against the extreme sluggishness in the process of development, or even its blockage, if delinkage is taken to extreme limits, particularly in view of the heavy requirements in capital investment and technological capability, both of which generally entail the need to seek foreign aid and co-operation. Undoubtedly a society ought to mobilize the maximum it can of its own resources and capabilities before turning to foreign aid, and thus to balance between the two extremes in attitude. But the balancing cannot be undertaken without attention to two significant considerations.

The first is the need for underdeveloped countries to seek capitalist development, whether or not they intend to end up attempting to undergo a socialist transformation. I am aware of the neo-Marxist thesis that this transformation can be 'jumped' – brought about in one stage from a base of underdevelopment instead of the two-stage strategy stipulated by orthodox Marxism. Yet, what seems to be appealing in theory does not necessarily have the realism or feasibility to match it, judging by Third World experience. Furthermore, an argument can be made for precedence to be accorded in the context of underdevelopment to the promotion of productive capability, rather than to distributive justice and the speedy narrowing of the income gap between socio-economic classes. This is not to deny the causal link between the level of wages and social services of the lower-income strata and economic performance; but the translation of the causality into wage and income policies can be so exaggerated as to make these policies counter-productive.

The second consideration is that the socialist countries which can be seen in the real world suffer from several economic and socio-political shortcomings. Indeed, now in the early 1990s, the leading socialist countries, the USSR, some other European socialist countries, and China, are 'liberalizing' their economy (and society) in what can only be called a receptive response to the challenge of capitalism, as concretized in the socio-economic systems of Western Europe and North America. On the other hand, it is also a manifest fact that the Western capitalist countries are a long distance away from fully-fledged *laissez-faire* and a submissive faith in the workings of the 'invisible hand'.

It would be rather anachronistic and unrealistic for dependency analysts today to preach extreme delinkage from the capitalist world, at a time when the socialist world itself is deeply rethinking its own system and is initiating drastic and profound changes in the application of this system – and also at a time when capitalism is actually applying certain *dirigiste* or interventionist policies (even if these are not at the macro-economic level but partial or sub-sectoral). What delinkage is advocated, and there is a strong case for a measure of delinkage, should be sought within the framework of a broad strategy of self-reliance, to the examination of which we will turn in the next chapter. But the appropriate measure will have to be associated with a number of political, social and cultural, along with economic and technological, prerequisites. In the final analysis, what is essential is more to control and calibrate, rather than drastically to cut the linkage.

The qualifications which, I submit, are called for in the dependency paradigm do not form a clean break with some of its elements or components, but the adjustment of the dosage, better to account for political and economic reality. One area in need of such well-calibrated qualification is that of the perception of the respective roles of the structures and policies deriving from the world capitalist system, as against those of the society concerned itself, and the dialectic of the relationship and interaction between them. Thus, in addition to the observation made earlier that there is today a greater awareness of the force of internal factors and forces, paralleled with the acquisition by virtually all underdeveloped countries of political independence, and their initiation of development efforts, there is a need for a dual process. One aspect of this process is the continued attention to the external set of forces and factors, and planning and action to reduce their influence on dependent societies. Needless to say, the attention must embrace not only the economic but also the political, cultural and information areas of dependence.

The second aspect is the need for much greater attention to the new modalities through which the external forces and factors exert their influence in the dependent countries. Two such modalities require careful monitoring and action. The first is the internal groupings of interests (usually a combination of financial/economic and political) whose basic alignment is with counterpart interest groupings in the core or centre countries (the alignment is outward-directed in its objectives and outlook). Relevant action to face this alignment cannot but involve reorientation in political, cultural and economic awareness. What is called for is no modest task, but to deal with the second modality under reference would probably be an even more daunting task.

This second modality is the TNC, whose penetration in underdeveloped countries is deep and many-sided, and whose influence on the societies of these countries is not only economic and technological, but has serious political, cultural and information aspects. Thus, the TNC has taken over many of the powers and much of the role of the capitalist/colonial country, and is today by far the most powerful instrument of imperialism. (Perhaps one could speak of the takeover as a case of 'transmigration of soul and role' between the Western industrial countries and their TNCs.)

But to say all this is not to deny the possibility for the operation of the TNCs to have a promotive effect in the fields of manufacturing industry, agriculture, finance and technology. I hasten to add that such a promotive effect will invariably be linked with adverse effects. Foremost among these are the control of a large proportion of capital investment in underdeveloped countries under various formulas of penetration and association; the shaping of the development and of the choice of technology in a manner that primarily and essentially serves TNC interests; the dangerously large outflow of capital from underdeveloped countries in the form of factor payments and the repatriation of capital associated with TNC inflows; directing consumption (and therefore production) patterns to suit TNC interests; and drawing large financial/economic interests within the underdeveloped countries into close association with the TNCs even when this is at the expense of the economies and societies concerned.

All this notwithstanding, the possible benefits of the operation of TNCs cannot be totally denied. The question becomes therefore: how can the benefits be made clearly to outweigh the damage? And, following on from this: do the underdeveloped countries enjoy some degrees of freedom which enable them to formulate policies and take action that can gradually – but tangibly – contain and reduce the damage, and give them the power to expand their control of the directions of the penetration, with a view to expanding the area of benefit? The contention here is that the answer is in the affirmative for many, if not all, Third World countries.

This is all the more tenable with the (slowly) growing cumulative power of Third World countries in the world political system, particularly within the United Nations which have taken several measures for the control of TNC work and the reduction of its adverse effects. Furthermore, the existence today of large numbers of TNCs from all over the advanced industrial world (and a few from such Third World countries as Brazil and India) provides greater room for manoeuvrability to underdeveloped countries. And, finally, the access which underdeveloped countries have to the expertise of the socialist countries weakens the stranglehold which TNCs from the capitalist world could otherwise have.

It must be clear by now that I attach a great deal of importance to the internal corrective power from within the underdeveloped country, and even more so from within the underdeveloped region comprising several countries that share cultural, political and economic interests and expectations. In other words, I consider it warranted to invest substantial trust in the ability of a self-reliant strategy, if designed and pursued in an enlightened and determined manner, to face the various aspects of dependence, and, even if slowly and gradually, to halt the growth of dependence and blunt the operation of its instruments. It is in this context that the experience of the 'Four Little Tigers' can be better understood.

This is so because the remarkable growth these countries have achieved since the early 1960s, and the acquisition by their manpower of a notable technological capability, must not be understood merely within the dogmatic context that they have sought to be sucked even deeper into dependence, and have become hostage to the TNCs. It will not bring their experience into the light to ignore the significant steps taken by these countries (especially by Taiwan) in the direction of land reform and other institutional correctives, the formulation of intelligent export and price policies, the propagation of a committed work ethic, the promotion of rigorous training, the support of energetic industrialization, and the evolving of especially efficient construction and contracting capabilities.[33] The relevant question here is: have these countries become, on balance, more or less dependent in the long term, as a result of the capitalist development that they have achieved? And do the policies adopted not in themselves reflect a large measure of self-reliance?

The least that can be said in reply is that they have generated internal forces that would potentially be capable of curbing dependence. Thus, even if dependence were intensified initially (in the short and perhaps the medium term, as the critics rightly maintain), in all probability the forces and capabilities generated and evolved should in the long run result in the reduction of dependence. In any case, the question posed in the last paragraph can well be faced by another: would a policy of stiff delinkage and isolation have resulted, on balance, in greater benefit to economy and society? It would seem warranted to suggest that the determination and success generated and achieved will be capable of turning what now looks like short or medium-term strength into long-term strength and confident self-reliance. However, it is also warranted to point to the fact that not all newly industrialized countries (NICs) are success stories in terms of social and political development alongside economic development. The experiences of Latin American and Arab NICs, for instance, have been marked by serious reverses in the economic sphere, and more so in the political sphere. (China and India are a special category by themselves, as I pointed out in the last chapter.)

It is appropriate now to end this chapter with some conclusions. These, and the discussion which preceded them in this last section, have a pragmatic orientation and approach. The reason why the basic question that the preceding and present sections set out to address – namely whether dependence still has a relevant and useful message and enough credibility to make it applicable to a large category of underdeveloped countries searching for an appropriate avenue to development – has been addressed in the way it has been, rather than through theorizing, is simply this: that the genesis and evolution of the school has witnessed a great deal of theorizing and considerable broad generalizing. In consequence, I consider it appropriate to put a number of dependency theses to the test of empirical fact and analytical consistency.

Hence the repeated reference to the contemporary political, economic and system realities, in the capitalist and socialist 'worlds'. A theoretical framework for social theses will have to be continuously measured for good fit against the realities which it sets out to interpret, if it is not only to provide a fitting, coherent and credible interpretation, but also to point to future developments within the same context. If alert reassessment and adjustment are not undertaken, the theses, or the paradigm, will fall into serious crisis. Such a crisis has befallen dependency with respect to many of its components, but it seems to me tenable to say that the heart of the paradigm is still sound, given a number of revisions, alterations and qualifications made in the light of experience, like those I have submitted for consideration in the latter part of this chapter. The exercise undertaken seems to justify the following six conclusions which are drawn from the preceding discussion:

1 The core of the dependency paradigm, namely that penetration and domination of the vast majority of Third World countries by the advanced capitalist countries, over the past generations or centuries, and the precedence which the latter countries gave to their own development and interests, is sound and has considerable explanatory value. This generalization seems strongly tenable today, in spite of the three qualifications I have introduced into the discussion of the point presently under reference. These are: (a) that certain countries still suffer severe underdevelopment even though they remain closed to capitalist penetration and domination; (b) that certain other countries have achieved a tangible measure of development although they had been subjected to deep penetration and domination for long periods; and (c) that the external influence of world capitalism has almost always interacted with internal factors which have complemented and bolstered it. Furthermore, the internal factors have become stronger with the passage of time, political independence, and the increasing exercise of national decision-making. Notwithstanding these qualifications, the dependency thesis remains useful for the explanation of underdevelopment in a large number of cases, and hence as a pointer to the appropriate route to development, namely as large a measure of self-reliance as feasible and useful – particularly collective self-reliance.
2 To safeguard the core of the dependency thesis, the theorists need

to exercise greater control over their theorizing and generalizations, with a view to achieving closer contact with contemporary political, social and economic reality, and to reflect greater flexibility and sensitivity to the fact that the ground on which the theorizing is based changes, even if slowly. The other side of this conclusion is the need to avoid dogmatic absolutism, or assertiveness, as though the dependency theses were iron laws of nature that cannot be bent by struggle and the resolve of people, as well as under profoundly changing circumstances. In this context, nationalism can be seen to be a strong determining force, particularly when it is enlightened and determined rather than blinkered and submissive where the society's interests and the flow of new social processes are concerned.

3 The Third World countries that are set on freeing themselves as far as possible of dependence, and which therefore marshall their material and human resources and their determination and capabilities to that end, find themselves less and less alone in their struggle. There are the socialist countries to provide moral and material support, neighbouring countries to join in the effort to achieve collective self-reliance, the United Nations to provide a forum for exchange of ideas and, if necessary, heated arguments that generate some light along with the heat, and a greater awareness among progressive elements in the capitalist world itself, as well as a few Western governments with progressive orientation, of the reality of dependence and the blockage it constitutes to development.

4 Delinkage from the capitalist system, which is necessary but should not be attempted in extreme form if it is not to prove counterproductive, should be undertaken as a smaller strategy within the broader strategy of self-reliance, with attention to the requirements of economic performance and acquisition of technological capability. In addition, it should be understood as a prerequisite for true interdependence. This may sound paradoxical. But it can be explained by the argument that, only if a country (or a collectivity of countries) succeeds in isolating itself in certain respects, in order to escape the adverse effects of the predominant pattern of international division of labour which essentially serves the interests of the advanced and the strong, and only if such a country initiates a determined and sound drive to development under the prudently designed protective umbrella of delinkage, can it subsequently be able to become a true partner in interdependence. Only thus will interdependence not be a polite euphemism for dependence, or a mere verbal subterfuge.

5 A carefully measured policy of delinkage should also be advocated

in view of the fact that, contrary to the general tendency for greater self-assurance in many Third World countries, a number of these have actually sunk into deeper dependence, instead of surfacing nearer to the level of self-reliance. Being surer of my judgement in the Arab context, I cite here the incontrovertible fact that most of the Arab countries (and not just the oil-producing and exporting countries) today show many significant and telling signs of heavier dependence on the capitalist world. Paradoxically, this accentuated dependence materialized during the 1970s, when the Arab region took into its own hands the control of the hydrocarbon sector, and as a result received immensely larger oil revenues than ever before. However, many major faulty policies were formulated and implemented, not only in the area of economics but also in the political, cultural, technological and information areas.[34]

External forces and influences have undoubtedly been instrumental in the generation of heavier dependence, but I put *at least* as much blame on current internal forces and factors. Predominant among these are the uncritical alignment – to a tangible extent voluntary – with the policies and interests of the leading capitalist countries, particularly the United States; the formulation of development, trade and education and training policies that have unavoidably confirmed dependence rather than led to its retreat; and the repression of freedom and human rights, and the severe curtailment of political participation, which have blocked protest against repression and the struggle for liberation, as well as against faulty economic policies and patterns of behaviour, and have severely curtailed the accountability of political leaders to the people.

6 Finally, the focusing on dependence as an explanation of underdevelopment, for which credit must go to the dependency school, has been timely and useful. But it can perhaps be said that such focusing ended by becoming an obsession with a number of leading dependency theorists. As an obsession, it has diverted attention and effort from the urgent and crucial search for a breakthrough in the blockage which dependence constitutes. But having said this, I feel justified in adding that the dependency paradigm is useful beyond its instrumentality in explaining underdevelopment. This is because it points to the necessity of the adoption of self-reliance as a strategy for development and a corrective for dependence. Such adoption is feasible not only for those countries that take the socialist option, but also for those that for one reason or another do not wish to take that option, but are at the same time determined to face the

challenge of underdevelopment and external dependence. It is contended here that this aspect of usefulness justifies the space allotted in this book to the chapter on the dependency paradigm – a chapter which has necessarily been rather long. Indeed, it provides an essential and appropriate transition from Chapter 1, which focused on the crisis which besets development in the Third World, on to an examination (in Chapter 3) of self-reliance as a strategy for development capable of making a breakthrough in the blockage formed by dependence.

3 What is self-reliant development?

INTRODUCTION

A word on terminology is called for, before we turn to a discussion of the substance of self-reliance in the three following sections of this chapter. There are economists, mainly Arab, who use the term 'independent development' instead of 'self-reliant development'. One noted Arab economist has argued in an elaborate and nuanced discussion in a recent essay that independent development can be nothing but self-reliant development, or that independence in essence is self-reliance (see Abdalla in *CAUS 1987*). I personally find the connotation of the term 'independent development' not quite satisfactory and suggestive of the core of self-reliance. Indeed, as I shall argue later, the pursuit of truly independent economic decision-making is only one strand or aspect of self-reliance as a strategy for development. The concept of self-reliance carries with it significant additional attributes and suggests fundamental implications, beyond the independence of decision-making, in economic as in other areas of society's life. Therefore we will be referring to self-reliance as a strategy for development, or to self-reliant development, more or less interchangeably.

This chapter is designed to identify and elaborate on the meaning of self-reliance, since, as we shall see, on the one hand there is no one meaning adopted uniformly by different writers, and, on the other, the meaning has several aspects that are emphasized variously in the relevant literature. These aspects on the whole have general applicability and relevance to every country, developed and underdeveloped, rich and poor, but specifically have greater urgency for the underdeveloped, and enjoy particular applicability to the Arab region and to the potential pursuit of collective self-reliance in it. This region will accupy the central area of our concern in this and the next two chapters. The present chapter will also identify the conditions that have to be satisfied if Third World countries are to pursue self-reliance as a strategy for the development targeted in this book, and the difficulties which the pursuit will be bound to encounter and will have to overcome if dependence is to be largely escaped.

All along, whether this is explicitly stated or not, self-reliant development as referred to in this book is meant to meet the specifications set out in the first chapter. In other words, development is taken to be a normative objective, which is not value-neutral. It has clear and strong social components, since it is meant to possess the quality and content which embody, first, the precedence of the pressing needs of the masses of Third World populations and their right to a dignified life, decent and rewarding job opportunities, proper food and shelter, and all the other basic human needs; and, second, the determination to meet these needs. As these specifications have already received sufficient attention for the purposes of this book, we need not elaborate on them any further.

However, the examination of the aspects of, and the necessary conditions for, self-reliant development necessitates the exploration of the proposition submitted in this chapter, namely that the exercise by the populations of Third World countries of widely based political participation and their enjoyment of their human rights, and the guarantee of a wide measure of social justice, are two critical components of a meaningful and largely self-reliant development anywhere in the Third World. I submit further that a large measure of complementary and collective action among the Arab countries has to be added as a third component in the context of the Arab region, for reasons which will become clear in due course.

Finally, the present chapter, along with the remaining two chapters of the book, will contain an examination of the feasibility and credibility of self-reliant development within the framework of a national state (or a group of states acting collectively), whose socio-economic and political system stands somewhere between socialism and capitalism. The examination will start by being deductive in approach, then become inductive and empirical as far as possible, without burdening the book with a mass of quantitative information. In other words, the social formation, the feasibility of whose pursuit of self-reliance will be examined, is assumed to be nationalist and progressive in orientation, and in political and socio-economic values and structure, attitudes, objectives and behaviour. It is also assumed to have a mixed economy with an important public sector alongside a substantial and energetic private sector. As an abbreviation, we will refer to the system of this kind of social formation as national-progressive, or as a two-sector national-progressive system.

It was indicated earlier that this system was chosen deliberately as the one within which to explore the feasibility of self-reliant development. This choice was made rather than socialism at one extreme or, at the other, a fully-fledged market economy which attaches minimal importance to moral considerations in the functioning of the economy, and in which development is pursued without tangible concern for the kind of values to which reference was made in the first chapter. The reason for this course of action, again as indicated earlier, is a dual presumption. First, that socialism has a prima facie case as a system capable to a notable extent of escaping heavy dependence on the world capitalist system and of satisfying a large measure of the economic, social and political desiderata comprised within the content and quality of development as targeted in this book. However, we also indicated that many Third World countries, and many of the Arab countries specifically, would not want to take a truly socialist option for various reasons. Furthermore, a number of socialists are currently questioning some of the merits of the system, and/or its internal political behaviour as applied in the Soviet Union and similarly orientated countries, as well as its economic efficiency.

The second presumption behind the option of system taken here is that the market economy of the type referred to above by definition will not concern itself with the quality and content of development advocated. Furthermore, the philosophy, values and orientation of a market economy would not be conducive to a disapproval of dependence by society and reflect a pressing desire for this society to extricate itself from the constraining grip of heavy dependence on the advanced capitalist countries, economically, politically and culturally. This process of elimination, apart from the intrinsic merits (as here presumed) of the nationalist-progressive system, leaves the latter as the system selected as a framework within which to examine, in what remains of the book, the meaning, and later the feasibility, and finally the dynamics and machinery of self-reliant development. All through the examination, but especially in Chapters 4 and 5, the analysis will move within the context of the Arab region, on the assumption – justifiable I believe – that this region is large and important enough within the Third World to permit the conclusions drawn or tendencies discerned to be applicable and relevant, with appropriate qualifications, to many other Third World regions.

SELF-RELIANCE BY WHOM?

There is nothing new or necessarily location-specific in self-reliance as a principle. Virtually all countries seek a certain measure of self-reliance, understood or defined narrowly as self-sufficiency, either in food, manufactures, technology, education, finance or security. This can be said to be a natural tendency of states. To this extent, therefore, the pursuit of self-sufficiency as an indication of the propensity to be self-reliant is an inherent attribute of statehood, and therefore goes as far back in history as the coalescence of nation states and other communities as clearly-defined political entities. Even more relevant is the fact that self-sufficiency has been sought through history at the local village or small community level – in secluded areas within countries.

But surely this is not the self-reliance which is being examined here? Indeed, self-sufficiency, understood and sought by a country as blinkered autarky motivated by extreme nationalism and isolationism, is distant from the meaning of self-reliance as here discussed. However, if the appeal of self-sufficiency is motivated by the desire by a nation state to isolate itself from the international economic system and its division of labour, in order to re-enter the system after its features have altered in a direction more in its interest, or at least less hostile to its interest, then self-sufficiency (in this context and for the limited and specific purpose indicated) would be a tactical step within the strategy of self-reliance.

The differentiation just made, as part of a phasing process, takes us back to the notion of 'interdependence' to which reference was made earlier on, where the fear (if not the conviction) had been stated that interdependence is often a mere euphemism for heavy dependence, or, as a nomenclature, is a bit of sugar coating around the bitter pill of dependence. Yet there is nothing abhorrent or objectionable in interdependence in the absolute. Indeed, it would be a welcome state provided it is not the euphemism it often is in the terminology of the powerful, when they try to reassure the underdeveloped countries that their dependence is a mere expression of exchange between two parties, and therefore that each party depends on the other within a framework in which neither party must feel underprivileged or imposed upon. Thus, the unfolding of self-reliant development, if achieved to a notable extent within an economy and a society (that is, in a manner encompassing economic, political and cultural aspects), would entitle the self-reliant economy/society to seek and enter into interdependence without the danger of thereby swallowing a bitter but cleverly sugar-coated pill.

Self-reliance, as qualified in these introductory remarks by what it is not, is a strategy for development characterized by, and likewise influencing, both those economic and non-economic areas of decision and action which together express the determination of a society to seek regeneration, and for that purpose to depend on itself, to the maximum extent possible. This purpose would be to achieve the sort of development which it believes serves and embodies the cultural, social, psychological and political principles, values and interests it holds high, and serves the objective of economic and technological capability and performance, which would provide the non-economic objectives with a solid base. Such a strategy, even if only in part, can now in retrospect be identified in the experience of a number of countries, before it became noticeable and the object of large-scale comment in the world after its adoption by mainland China at the beginning of the 1950s. Indeed, Mao Zedong summed it up effectively by saying it involved 'regeneration through our own efforts' (quoted in Galtung 1980: 19). North Vietnam, under the guidance of Ho Chi Minh, also practised it in its economic, social, political and military struggle first against the French and subsequently against the Americans. And Mohandas Gandhi preached it and influenced many millions of Indians to live by its guidelines, even though there was no political structure around him to give substance to the strategy as ambitiously as Gandhi wanted it to be.

To give a much older example, this time from the Arab region, we can say that Mohammad Ali's view of development and the policies and approaches he formulated and followed to achieve it, during his reign in the first half of the nineteenth century (see Abdalla in *CAUS 1987*), can be described as embodying a strategy of self-reliance as he understood it. Without idealizing him in retrospect, Mohammed Ali's understanding or characterization of development, and his choice of strategy and policies, went well beyond the economic sphere, to include political, technological and educational components. His failure to achieve a large part of his objective was probably as much the result of Ottoman and Great Power machination and blockage (including military intervention), as of the fact that he bit off larger objectives than he could chew and digest, given his resources and the state of the arts then at his disposal, and the society and economy which were the field of movement for his strategy.

It is opportune in this connection to say that a valuable and enlightening academic and analytical exercise would be for some researchers to survey the past two centuries and identify other experiments in self-reliant development, even if fragmentary – apart from research into the course of dependence. Such a survey would probably reveal partial and brief successes and glaring failures, but it would shed light on the internal factors leading to the shortfall, and more so on the intervention of powerful external factors to abort the efforts. While considerable such research has been undertaken for some regions (notably Latin America), it remains largely to be undertaken for the Arab region. But it is not my purpose to go any further into the lessons which Arab economic and political history can reveal.[1] Instead, the period within which the developmental experience of the Arab region is considered is that stretching from the end of the Second World War to the present. And the exploration of the meaning of self-reliance and its feasibility is action-orientated, therefore concerned with the future.

But the immediate task is to answer the question: self-reliance by whom? The answer to this question is to a far extent influenced by the understanding of the individual writer of the principle and concept of self-reliance, and of its practice, since no large enough body of literature has emerged and led to the coalescence of a more or less unified meaning of the concept. In fact, most of the writings around self-reliance – and these are very small in number compared with those on dependence – deal with self-reliance in the context or within the frame of one sector of one economy, or even a sub-sector, or within a village or small community, or yet deal with self-reliance by individuals, whether in rich countries (see Wemegah 1980), or in poor countries. The list of references at the end of the book substantiates this generalization.[2] So do the contents of the most comprehensive work on self-reliance that I have perused and referred to several times, namely *Self-reliance: A Strategy for Development*, edited by Johan Galtung, Peter O'Brien and Roy Preiswerk.[3]

This is not to say that national, or even regional-collective self-reliance does not have a place in the literature that has appeared in English in general, and in particular in the work edited by Galtung *et al.* But that is not where the emphasis lies. On the other hand, virtually all writings on self-reliance in Arabic (referred to generally as 'independent development', as already indicated) have the nation state as their area of consideration, or the whole Arab region in but a few cases.[4] However, these writings are not numerous and are all, to the best of my knowledge, essays or conference papers.

The importance of the book edited by Galtung *et al.* justifies further comment. In fairness, it ought to be pointed out that Part III of the book includes three case studies, one each for a country (Paraguay), a region (the South Pacific) and a continent (Africa). And Part I, which deals with concepts and ideologies, does indeed draw on country experiences in presenting various aspects of self-reliance, or various senses in which it is understood, or in suggesting central principles which justify it and around which it revolves. Yet all of the essays here – even the first essay on concepts, practice and rationale by Johan Galtung, which is the least location-specific or sector-specific – seem to place most emphasis on self-reliance by the individual, the village or the local community.

Indeed, in one or two cases the reader gets the distinct impression that the writers believe that to carry self-reliance to the scale of nation states is a violation of the principle which is basically individual-orientated, or at most village-, commune-, or community-orientated (see Galtung *et al.* 1980: 11, 12, 19–26). An underlying fear is that self-reliance at the whole country level would amount to autarky and would help capitalism get entrenched more deeply, thus reducing the chances of a socialist transformation. Even when Rousseau is referred to as an early advocate of self-reliance, and Gandhi's teachings are invoked in the same context, it is mainly individual (or at most individual community) self-reliance which is invoked (see Sachs 1980 and Tickner 1980). On the other hand, China's experience under Mao Zedong and North Vietnam's under Ho Chi Minh remain inescapably experiences belonging to a whole society.

This concern with self-reliance at the individual or small-group level tends to lead to idealization. Naturally, one could, with a certain amount of utopianism and faith in human nature, expect idealistic individual human beings to practise self-reliance in a much purer form than whole societies, mainly because individuals are more influenceable than whole populations or political systems, or the decision-makers in any economy at large. These aggregates are understandably more strongly pulled in different directions by the vested interests of groups, centres of power, or by political and security considerations, and so on, than are the individual members of the aggregates, some of whom will no doubt be idealistic. But idealization is dangerous, and this tendency in several of the essays of the book under discussion seems to me to be on the brink of danger, if the essays in question have not already gone beyond. There is also a collection of pertinent documents in the Annexes centring around self-reliance. Here there is an even larger dose of idealization and utopianism, possibly more than can be encountered even in the book entitled *Another Development: Approaches and Strategies* to which I referred in Chapter 1.

What I am examining in this book is self-reliance in the context of individual Arab nation states, where the feasibility of the application of the principle is assessed and then transferred to the larger context of the whole Arab region or community of Arab states for assessment. Prima facie, this sounds paradoxical. If self-reliance is difficult enough for individuals or small communities within countries, how much more difficult would it threaten to be at the level of whole countries individually, and yet more so collectively within the frame of a region? The transference no doubt engenders greater difficulty, in addition to the 'negative' effects of self-reliance, to use Galtung's term (1980), and the problems associated with the principle and practice of self-reliance as perceived by him. But to transfer the focus from the individual or small village or community to the level of a whole country or a grouping of countries that are held together by many historical, political, security, economic, social and cultural bonds and aspirations is not necessarily to ignore self-reliance in the small village or the community at the micro-level. Indeed, the two not only could be related to each other but ought to be related and made complementary and supportive to each other.

This, then, is where I take my position with regard to the question: self-reliance by whom? However, the substance of the self-reliance in question differs. At the nation-state or collective (that is, regional) level, self-reliance is viewed as a strategy for development. On the other hand, self-reliance at the micro-level is more of a principle of co-operation within villages and communities, first, for the purpose of self-help internally, and then for co-operation and exchange with other villages and neighbourhoods – that is, between these villages and neighbourhoods. Furthermore, at the micro-level, self-reliance involves the inculcation of those principles and values, and the establishment of those structures and avenues of action, that together promote the sense of identity and authenticity. These are: self-help in a socially-orientated sense (as against an isolationist sense); awareness of the power of self-reliance plus co-operation among self-reliant subgroups within a national context; drawing on own sources of vitality, ingenuity, resourcefulness and inventiveness; harmony with own cultural heritage and richness; concern for the ecology and creative and considerate interaction with it – in brief, the promotion of philosophies, attitudes, values, patterns of behaviour, and policies which all serve the pursuit of self-reliance at the national and beyond at the regional level.

Yet, in this book, I will concentrate specifically on self-reliance at the nation-state and the regional level, subsuming that the pursuit of self-reliance at this level is based on a foundation of self-reliance at the micro-level. It is a fact that self-reliance at neither level is currently being seriously and consistently pursued in the Arab region, and that the pusuit should proceed both at the micro- and the macro-level together. It can even be argued that without the foundation at the micro-level, the superstructure at macro-level cannot be built. This is true to a far extent; but the foundation will take a very long time to put in place, and the state – with appropriate broad-based leadership, orientation and institutions – can influence the speed and effectiveness of the establishment of the foundation. Furthermore, I do not feel able to cope with the subject matter both at the micro- and the macro-level within the limited confines of the present book. Hence my option for the macro-level alone, always bearing in mind, though not explicitly indicating this, that the foundation is a crucial necessity, and that the superstructure will never be solid and durable unless it is accompanied or preceded by work on the foundation. In saying this, I will not be waiting for a *deus ex machina* to descend and undertake the task of providing the foundation. Instead, I will be presenting my analysis on the basis of the reasoned belief that the dynamics of self-reliance, seriously and responsibly sought at the macro-level, will force attention and effort to the micro-level, and bring about those socio-cultural and political transformations whose logic necessitates the building of the foundation. (I recognize that the imagery of foundation and superstructure used argues against my proposition, since a superstructure is inconceivable without a foundation. But the reader is asked not to take these architectural terms too literally.)

THE MEANING OF SELF-RELIANCE

What, then, is the meaning of self-reliance as a strategy for development, or that of self-reliant development? Ismail Sabri Abdallah notes that the recent disenchantment with neo-classical development theory and policy – which has manifested itself in dualistic and externally-orientated development tied to the transnational world capitalist system and its most prominent instrument, the TNCs, and designed mainly to serve external interests – has led to the emergence of concern with inner-directed and motivated development. Likewise, the ostentation of the consumption of the rich in Third World countries in the midst of general poverty, and the marginality of the poor, has led to the concern with development as essentially a process making possible the satisfaction of basic human needs. And the irresponsible overuse and depletion of resources has led to concern with eco-development. So also has a bursting awareness of dependence and the underdevelopment (or, more correctly, the distorted and dependent development) it breeds, brought into focus self-reliant development, or, alternatively, development using self-reliance as a strategy (Abdalla in *CAUS 1987*: *36, 37*). I can add, in this latter context, that self-reliance/development has emerged conceptually as the other end of the axis whose first end is dependence/underdevelopment.

There is no specific or even general and broad agreement on the aspects and components of self-reliant development in the literature on the subject; and the literature itself is very meagre. In April 1986, a symposium was held in Amman, Jordan, by the Centre for Arab Unity Studies around self-reliant development in the Arab region (designated 'independent' development in the symposium documents). It was attended by leading Arab economists and other social scientists. Yet the fifteen papers submitted contained, or referred to, as many different definitions of self-reliance and self-reliant development, and the discussion which followed the papers added to the diversity of opinions, although there was general agreement that self-reliance is the antidote to dependence, and that the development based on self-reliance would be healthy while that materializing under dependence would be distorted and generally patchy and ill-directed (*CAUS 1987*). It would thus seem that the field is clear enough for theorists to elaborate their own understanding of self-reliance, especially if and when the strategy of self-reliance comes to be applied on a large scale in many Third World countries, with positive results, at which time the interaction of experience and conceptualization would lead to a more widely accepted definition, if not consensus.

Much of what we understand by self-reliant development today has appeared in such documents as the Arusha Declaration (1967), The Cocoyoc Declaration (1974), The Marrakesh Declaration (1977) (see Galtung *et al.* 1980: Annexes), and The Pugwash Symposium Report and Proceedings (1975, 1977) – though the treatment in all these is very general and expressed in rather utopian terms. The contribution of Johan Galtung to the elaboration of the concept (but also to the discussion of the practice and rationale) of self-reliance, around which his essay referred to earlier revolves, must be acknowledged for the enlightening analysis which the author has produced. The core of this contribution, as far as the principle and concept of self-reliance go, emphasizes that the content of self-reliance comprises the desire to rebel against dependence, get rid of submissiveness, and seek the regeneration of society, as well as the readiness to struggle for these ends. In this, he is no different from other writers, as the term 'self-reliance' itself invokes this type of emphasis. But the concept as it qualifies one type of development acquires an additional connotation:

it means a socially-orientated development of the type described in Chapter 1 of this book. Although it means this to most advocates of self-reliance, this connotation remains largely implicit, as though the mere use of the term 'self-reliant development' is enough to make the reader recognize the normative development which it is supposed to be.

But Galtung goes beyond the broad aspect of self-reliance to distinguish in detail what he sees as the theoretical rationale of self-reliance. This he does in stating thirteen points, the headings of which indicate their content, and we need not therefore recapitulate his explanation of the points, whose openings are reproduced below:[5]

1 Through self-reliance (SR) priorities will change towards production for the basic needs of those most in need.
2 Through SR mass participation is ensured.
3 Through SR local factors are utilized much better.
4 Through SR creativity is stimulated.
5 Through SR there will be more compatibility with local conditions.
6 Through SR there will be more diversity of development.
7 Through SR there will be less alienation.
8 Through SR ecological balance will be more easily attained.
9 Through SR positive externalities are internalized or given to neighbours at the same level.
10 Through SR solidarity with others at the same level gets a more solid basis.
11 Through SR the ability to withstand manipulation because of trade dependency increases.
12 Through SR the military defence capability of the country increases.
13 Through SR as a basic approach today's centre and periphery are brought on a more equal footing.

As can be seen from the listing of the thirteen points, Galtung assumes a certain content for self-reliance which the term itself, strictly speaking and literally understood, does not necessarily suggest. But somehow – perhaps mostly thanks to the documents and declarations referred to earlier – this content has come to be taken for granted as part and parcel of the concept of self-reliance and self-reliant development.

We also note that Galtung moves between a micro-level and a macro-level understanding of self-reliance. The points themselves reflect, among other thing, the writer's concern for the liberation of society, or of communities within it, from the power and penetration of external (advanced capitalist) forces, whether the penetration is economic, cultural, political or military. As far as the dangers of cultural penetration are concerned, he is not as outspokenly emphatic as Ignacy Sachs in his essay in the same work (Sachs 1980). Sachs attributes to this penetration the largest responsibility for dependence, but sees the antidote to it as being self-reliance. However, Sachs, who admits the possibility of spectacular growth under conditions of technological and cultural penetration, as witnessed in post-war Japan, Brazil and Iran (Sachs 1980: 46–8) – and one could also add South Korea, Singapore and Taiwan – does not suggest what attitude to take that would be capable of explaining the paradoxical phenomenon. He goes further to say that cultural dependence, plus internal inequality in distribution and environmental degradation, can accompany growth or dependent development.

Without going any further into the discussion of the chapters in Part I of the book under reference, which is concerned with 'Concepts and Ideologies', we may note that most of the writers suggest, whether explicitly as Kanyana Mutombo (1980) does, or implicitly, as the others do, that one manifestation of self-reliance is not to take the model of development unfolding and evolving in any other community or country as one's own. Mutombo follows this point up by saying: 'As each nation can create its own ideology of authenticity in conformity with its cultural values and norms, it can also determine the specific content of its self-reliant development in conformity with its needs (Mutombo 1980: 113).

If I have dwelt at some length on *Self-reliance: A Strategy for Development* this is because in my view it is the most important book in existence on the subject that I know of. Yet, considering that it is a natural tendency for writers to emphasize one central point in their characterization of a concept, very much like the cartoonist who magnifies one feature of the face to bring out what he wants primarily to be seen in that face, each of the writers of the essays highlights one or another point as the heart and soul of self-reliance. In what follows, I will deviate from this practice in venturing to give my own understanding of what self-reliance and self-reliant development ought to mean, by suggesting what I consider the main several aspects of self-reliance, or the components of its meaning that matter for the drive for true development. This is an approach which, I hope, will not be viewed as mere eclecticism, but rather as one of integration of causally (organically) related aspects or components, which are all conceptually as well as operationally relevant to the pursuit of development. It is to be added that the discussion that follows has the Arab region as its focus, and the points made therefore include some that are specific to the needs of this region.

In my view, there are seven interrelated aspects through which self-reliance as a strategy for Arab social and economic development can be understood.[6]

The first aspect is a need for Third World societies to free themselves of the philosophy and content of the neo-classical economic and sociological model of development, which represents in the view of its many advocates the unique example worthy of emulation and capable of leading to development – namely the Western capitalist industrial example, with its principles, structures, guidelines and ultimate results. It presents Westernization as the environment (meaning philosophy, values, outlook, system, and instruments and structures) within which development can unfold only if sought seriously and energetically, in co-operation with the Western capitalist societies. This model stipulates the passage of development through stages, but in the context of the oneness of its course: in other words, development proceeds in stages which different societies reach and cross at different moments of time; but ultimately all are destined to arrive at the objective if they follow the rules of the game. Such a view of development is therefore essentially optimistic, economistic and deterministic, and can thus create a false sense of confidence (see Wiarda 1984). By its nature, as well as its implications, it is based on a universalistic conceptualization (Eisenstadt 1983), within the streamlined specifications, components and structures of which all countries ought to operate in their drive for development.

This first aspect of self-reliance is underlined by the conviction that development is a process of self-liberation which can be attempted only after political liberation. But this involves only one aspect of the studied and careful delinkage which ought to be made from the confines of the world capitalist system. The other aspects fall in the political, economic and cultural areas of life. The delinkage or dissociation does not mean insularity and blinkered isolation, as we shall emphasize later in another context. It is essentially a return to one's own sources of strength, resources, capabilities and interest, in the hope of achieving an inner-directed development, through the pursuit of the independence of decision-making, in a national economy which subordinates external relations to the needs of internal accumulation, production and interests.

However, to indicate the need for Third World countries to free themselves of the specifications of the 'universal' model, whether capitalist or Marxist, calls for some further elaboration and qualification. Thus, the rejection of the model is legitimate, while it is legitimate at the same time to say that certain perceptions and themes of development are suitable for all societies. In other words, there are a number of components of development that can be accepted generally as objectives worthy of seeking by all societies eager to achieve the liberation of the citizen and his (her) self-realization, in harmony with societal and environmental objectives.

Yet, alongside the acceptance of certain universal desiderata, there is also a certain pluralism that needs to be accepted. This involves the admission that there is need to take into account a number of different factors, which vary from one historical phase and from one society to another, deriving from the social, economic, political and structural realities of each time and place; which also vary with the various views, perceptions, outlooks and expectations of societies in general and of the forces determining them, and, finally, vary with the various problems and obstacles peculiar to each time and place in the path of development. Thus, self-reliant, independent development does not merely mean the rejection of imported universalistic models that are 'ready and packaged', but also means insistence on creativity and inventiveness by the societies concerned, based, first, on the particularity of their outlook, expectations, endowments, interests and needs; second, on the sufferings and anxieties of these societies turned into motive forces; and, third, on their capabilities and the cumulative wisdom gained from their experience.

Hence the need to emphasize the particularity of each society at each phase of its history, with what this implies for development with respect to conceptualizations and systems of thought, organization and the dynamics of action. Obviously these vary from one society to another, within the universality of certain central objectives of development. In other words, it is erroneous conceptually and methodologically to divide countries into developed and underdeveloped on the basis of the level of per capita income, that is, the point on the income scale each has reached. Indeed, it will be more correct to say that the vast majority among Third World countries have achieved varying measures of distorted or patchy development, in contrast with the advanced industrial countries of the centre. But even with such a correction of terminology, we would still face a certain serious misrepresentation because the developed countries themselves suffer from a number of socio-economic and structural problems, alienation, and certain heavy costs of the enormous growth achieved by them.[7] But this qualification is not a central concern of ours at this juncture.

The diversity of Third World countries is easy to observe and establish, even though a good many of them have one main common characteristic: that they had been under foreign domination, which resulted in their dependence on the centre countries to varying degrees in various spheres of life. The logical conclusion from all this is that there is not, and there cannot be, a general theory of development (although there could possibly be a theory of economic growth) applicable to all countries, capable of explaining past experience and possessing predictive power for the future. Individual countries seeking self-reliant development must therefore design their own model, with all that that implies in conceptualization, choice of objectives, formulation of strategies and policies, the drawing of plans and programmes, and the process of implementation and follow-up.

The second aspect of self-reliance to consider is specific to the Arab region: it is the necessity of bringing about a harmonious mix between the values of modernity and those of religious fundamentalism. This is imperative for the pursuit of development because of the close interconnection between this pursuit, on the one hand, and the motives, objectives, determinants and criteria of the development sought, on the other. In fact, much of what is still sought as 'development' in the Arab region is condemned by the Islamic fundamentalists as not only irrelevant, harmful or unnecessary, but also sinful. While one cannot but agree with much of this condemnation for a certain part of the content of modernity – namely, that part which represents a flagrant or an obnoxious violation of society's cultural heritage, values and sense of morality, or a violation of mere common sense in the use of resources – blanket condemnation often emanates from excessive dogmatism and scriptural literalism, or else from the refusal to take note of historical experience with respect to concepts, the principles of politics and government, institutions, social organization, and other basic matters in society's life and structure.

The harmonious mix necessary in the pursuit of self-reliant development involves the preservation – even if with certain adjustments made imperative by historical reality – of moral principles and basic values in the heritage of Arab society, which is overwhelmingly Islamic. But this ought to be combined with flexibility in the formulation and elaboration of ideas, concepts and institutions, and in the shaping of organizational patterns and the guidelines and instruments of social action, to be in tune with the accumulation and growth of Arab experience across past centuries. If such flexibility were allowed, the danger would be reduced that Arab Islamic history and heritage would become a 'cause for embarrassment',[8] in case fundamentalists rejected the necessity and the task of evolving systems of textual interpretation, and likewise of searching for solutions and answers to contemporary problems and issues within contemporary frameworks, as though the experience of long centuries past did not necessitate any change in the nature and the understanding of such problems and issues, and the solutions and answers called by them.

It is essential to emphasize that there is no contradiction between insistence that self-reliance ought to be sought in the drive for true, meaningful and especially self-generated development on the one hand, and, on the other, insistence on the application of the flexibility advocated in the last paragraph. This flexibility is necessary, even if the experience to be learnt from is that of other societies, on condition that independence is retained, and adaptation is applied, with Arab contributions to the study and interpretation of the 'borrowed' experience, to enable it to be in tune with Arab society and its basic values, needs, interests and endowments. This would involve a searching internal look into Arab capabilities and the mobilization of such qualities of enterprise, inventiveness and authenticity of which Arab society of today is potentially capable.

The third aspect of self-reliance lies in a sound and balanced awareness of dependence, and understanding of its meaning, its nature and origins, and its implications for the various areas of life. Of particular significance in the present context is awareness of the major instruments and ramifications of dependence, which, according to one noted Arab economist (Abdalla 1980) are:

a) Widespread use of the facilities and mechanisms of modern media and marketing, for the creation of new consumption patterns in Third World countries.
b) Direct investment [by the advanced industrial countries] in the production of primary products for export, or in the tourist industry or manufacturing industry, either for the satisfaction of internal demand or for export.
c) Encouragement of large-scale resort to foreign loans and aid for the modernization of infrastructure.
d) The use of international economic organizations (the World Bank, the International Monetary Fund, etc.) as an instrument for the direction and orientation of economic policies in underdeveloped countries.
e) The orientation of science and technology in such a way as to emphasize the position of predominance of TNCs, and to control

the markets of developing countries and determine the directions of their developmental efforts.

f) Capitalizing on the power to influence information and its sources for the purpose of consolidating the control of TNCs and ensuring the submission of developing countries to the orientations of the world capitalist markets.
g) Capitalizing on control over information and the use of leisure for the purpose of bringing about basic changes in values, orientations and cultures, and of the imposition of the Western capitalist consumer culture.
h) Large-scale use of aid in training and research, for evolving the systems of administration, planning and accounting, and for evolving and controlling information systems and those of national security.
i) Capitalizing on the need for armaments, arms purchases, military training and military assistance as an instrument of control and hegemony.

Awareness of the nature and role of dependence is a necessary condition for the assessment of the feasibility of movement to stop its spread, and then to force it to retreat on the various fronts where it is entrenched. The establishment of such feasibility will constitute a breakthrough in the obstruction, with which a relationship of dependence blocks sound and true development, and makes for the distortion of any development achieved. Hence the necessity of the assessment of the directions and degree of feasibility, for the sake of exploring the possibility of the development of Arab capability to launch self-reliant development, that alone can provide satisfactory answers to the four questions posed in the first chapter of this book.

If the exploration comes up with positive answers to the enquiry, then it would be possible to provide the necessary and sufficient conditions for the launching of an operation of liberation from dependence and movement towards self-reliant development – thanks to the combination of sound awareness, the availability/satisfaction of certain essential factors/conditions, and determined resolve and sustained effort. In this connection, the questioning with which the last section of the second chapter of the book ended – namely the one revolving around the viability, relevance and usefulness of the dependency paradigm for the understanding of contemporary underdevelopment and the design of action for development – becomes an input also in forging a connection between awareness of what dependence is, and the explanation of the meaning of self-reliance.

We need not recapitulate the relevant discussion already undertaken in the last chapter, except to underline the proposition that capitalist development is possible, under certain conditions, within a state of dependence, although this development would initially be, in some basic respects, dependent, patchy and distorted. However, as also indicated earlier, it is legitimate to ask whether even with such a characterization, the dynamics of development would not themselves lead, within a reasonable time and under the influence of a development-orientated national bourgeoisie, to self-reliance, thanks to certain liberating economic, technological, social and political forces that the dynamics and the pursuit of independence in decision-making will release. In my opinion, a voluntaristic not a deterministic attitude should be taken in the present context, in the sense that dependence is not what fate is to the fundamentalist of any of the monotheistic religions.

The fourth aspect of self-reliance is the need to evolve concepts, positions and courses of action appropriate to the conditions of the Arab region and the correction of its economic, social and political structures. While conceptualization is important, the crucial significance of action should be emphasized. For, while it is essential to have a theoretical construct within which to perceive how political, social and economic change can be engineered, such a construct would essentially serve to provide the guidelines for action. At the present, wrongly-directed action is the most serious bottleneck in the process of correction and therefore of development. This means that Arab society will be called upon, in consistency with self-reliance, not only to shun conventional conceptualizations that fit into the short horizon of growth economics, but also to formulate sound and appropriate answers to the four questions cited in Chapter 1, and therefore to map and pursue courses of action capable of translating the answers from the realm of perception to that of concrete reality. Thus, only answers that place the Arab masses, both urban and rural, in the very centre of concern for development, and that generally serve a largely independent and inner-directed, inner-motivated and internally-powered development can embody a sound mix of conceptualization and action.

The concrete end of the satisfaction of the conditions listed, and their ramifications, is the building/establishment of a strong socio-economic base in the Arab region, simultaneously with an intensifying process of careful and national delinkage from the centre countries and from heavy dependence on them. This base would ultimately be expected to be capable not only of promoting true, comprehensive development, but also of assuring Arab society and its territory and economy of reasonable security in the face of external threat, and of the capability to liberate those parts of the region that have already fallen victim to foreign usurpation.

The fifth aspect of self-reliance reaches beyond the imperativeness of elaborating a self-generated view of development, and of ensuring that this development is inner-directed and will cater to external markets only in so far as internal needs and interests have been catered to. Thus self-reliance is seen here to involve the placing of primary emphasis on Arab capabilities and resources – manpower, technology, natural resources, man-made capital and finance. And all the capabilities and resources involved will have to be understood and treated in a dynamic sense and manner. In other words, they ought to be assessed not only according to their actual abundance and availability at any one moment, but also according to their potential with respect to quantitative growth and qualitative improvement and diversification. This will call for the following tasks to be undertaken:

a) A careful and perceptive assessment of what society has available in terms of measurable or definable capabilities and resources, and what it has a potential to develop.
b) The mobilization to the fullest extent possible of the capabilities and resources.
c) The proper utilization of the capabilities and resources, with special attention to ecological soundness and prudence.
d) The redirection of manpower resources through cultural, educational and training channels, as well as through the extension and deepening of political awareness and commitment. Such redirection is essential in order to make the participation of manpower in the developmental effort more effective, and to enable labour to get a fairer portion of the national product. It is also essential in order to reduce waste, whether it is within the country or region, or brought about through the drain of manpower to the outside; and most importantly to raise the dignity of work by inculcating a work ethic appropriate to the requirements of self-reliant development. The point being discussed is probably the most central in self-reliance and the most relevant to its purposeful pursuit, for unless the value of self-reliance is inculcated, the developmental effort will fail to save the objective from distortion and underfulfilment.
e) The rationalization of the policies related to the utilization of physical and financial resources. Land, water and hydrocarbons

deserve special mention here (see Sayigh 1983). But beyond rational utilization, it is essential that Arab society activate the exploration of yet unexplored resources, and undertake the productive use of what is already explored and exploited in order to put an end to over-production (whether of oil, gas or other underground resources) at the expense of future generations, to stop the abusive utilization of land and the wasteful use of water, and generally to interact with the environment with concern for preservation, aesthetics and the proper definition of the end-user. Where financial resources are concerned, what is at issue is the need to mobilize much more effectively the resources available, whether through more prudence and less ostentation and wastefulness in the use of financial resources, or more determined and effective taxation of the higher-income strata of the population, or such social policies as would increase the incentives to the labour force in order to encourage it to make a larger contribution to the national product. Foreign borrowing and aid should be considered as the very last resort, not as the windfall which for much of the post-war years it has been wrongly thought to be.[9] Society should be sensitized to the moral, political, economic and social dangers and ills which dependence on foreign aid involves.

f) The establishment of a large and solid science and technology base (both at the single-country and the regional level), in order to develop an appropriate and effective scientific and technological capability within the region, and to sharply (though of necessity gradually) reduce dependence on external technological capability, for the supply of both capital goods and high-level technical services. This component of the aspect of self-reliance under consideration is closely tied to the reorientation and appropriate education and training of manpower and of human resources in general. The policies that need to be formulated for the two components ought to be co-ordinated and harmonized, both functionally and geographically (that is, at the national and the regional level).

The components of my understanding of self-reliance, contained in points (a) to (f) discussed above, commend self-reliance strongly and suggest that it should be attempted as far as possible. Yet this does not stand in contradiction with the advocacy made earlier of the imperativeness of openness to the experiences of other countries with respect specifically to science and technology. More than in any other area of knowledge, there is need for openness, considering the great advances made, the methods of research (both basic and applied) developed, and the criticality for the Arab region to gradually build the capability for it to be in line with those societies which are in the forefront. This is necessarily a two-way process, with give and take. If the contemporary Arabs are mostly (perhaps totally) mere takers today, this should not inhibit them from trying to become more resourceful in adaptation to begin with, then to move on to a stage where they can make scientific and technological contributions. This would make them recapture, though slowly and over a long period of time, a position of excellence not unlike the one they held in the golden age of the Islamic/Arab civilization and empire. Perhaps in no other area of action will the pursuit of self-reliance be as demanding of Arab society, in terms of effort, sacrifice and time.

Self-reliance in the sense which the present section of the chapter suggests has limits and implications that need to be considered carefully. The consideration has to proceed from seven angles of vision which involve issues that are of special relevance to the feasibility of self-reliant development. The relevance is highlighted by the suggestion of a large measure of introversion which self-reliance invokes. The angles are: (a) the size of the internal market; (b) the resource base available; (c) the composition and geographical pattern of foreign trade; (d) the extent of the availability internally of effective appropriate technology and manpower skills; (e) the availability of a reasonably sizeable reservoir of entrepreneurial drive and managerial capability; (f) the availability domestically of sizeable savings, for urgent investment in capital goods and the speeding up of capital accumulation, and of foreign exchange resources to finance essential capital and consumption goods imports, and, above all, (g) the availability of development-orientated leadership not only in the political sphere but also in the media, the educational system, the business community, the labour movement and the intellectual community.

The issues which the seven items listed comprise are serious bottlenecks for every Third World country. But they are not of equal tightness for all countries. The differentiation is not merely a question of quantitative availability. It is also a matter that relates to the effectiveness of the factors mentioned, the extent to which they are mobilized, the soundness of their use for development purposes, and the energy and inventiveness with which these factors as development resources are themselves developed.

Within the external sphere, the differentiation is a matter of the position and place of every country concerned in the international political and economic order. This in large measure determines the composition, size, and directions of foreign trade, the inflow of technology and finance, and the training and education afforded and undertaken. But, above all, it determines the ability of the leaderships to give concrete expression to any development orientation they have, in the face of the pressure of external economic and political forces in the advanced industrial countries, and the multilateral organizations which in the final analysis translate the policies of the latter group of countries.

Viewed in the context of the internal as well as the external sphere, the seven issues listed are the touchstones which determine the feasibility and operationality of concrete justifiable delinkage from the countries of the centre in the world capitalist system. Hence the need to examine the issues empirically as they relate to specific countries and historical stages – that is, not in abstract form and at a high level of generalization. In other words, the particular endowments and conditions of every country by itself, at a given time, should be taken into account when its candidacy for the pursuit of self-reliant strategies and policies is examined. In this context, the factors listed can be considered *criteria of adequacy* for self-reliance. As they constitute a central part of the test of the feasibility of self-reliance in practice, they will be examined at length in Chapter 4 below in the Arab context specifically. At that stage, the discussion will become less deductive and more empirical and inductive.

The sixth aspect of self-reliance is the need for the adoption of an Arab regional perspective in the conceptualization, design and pursuit of development. This perspective should be coupled with as large a measure as possible of independent decision-making within the region's individual countries, as against the submission to decisions formulated outside the region. But such decision-making within individual countries ought to be harmonized with its counterpart at the region's level. The latter is currently undertaken through the Arab heads of state in their summit meetings, the League of Arab States, the dozens of specialized ministerial councils and regional organizations and institutions in existence, and the hundreds of regional (joint) projects and companies – all within the framework of regional agreements and joint resolutions.

To insist on the independence of decision-making is not to deny that no single country or region in the world today, developed or underdeveloped, can claim absolute independence, whether in economic or political matters, and that the process of decision-making in major issues must invariably take into account the relevant politico/economic reality in the world at large. Thus, the independence cited must always be qualified as being sought within the maximum extent possible.

However, the adoption of a regional Arab perspective ought not to be understood as equivalent to ignoring national entities, with their diversity and those particularities which are enriching and often worth preserving. This adoption means that national perceptions, strategies and policies ought to be in harmony with their regional counterparts, while the drive for co-operation and complementarity continues. Through complementarity, compensation can be worked out for such national entities that might suffer as a result of the complementarity, or to make up for serious scarcities in resources here or there. The same principle applies here as that through which provinces or localities within the same country are helped to face hardship arising from national economic integration, or to obtain from other provinces the skills and resources which are short locally. But beyond the economic motivation for complementarity there is the integrative sentiment among the Arab peoples that populate the twenty-one countries – a sentiment that has its roots in a common history, religion, culture and economic background, and likewise in commonly-held aspirations and compelling common interests. This can be emphasized in spite of the presence of religious and ethnic minorities, or the different courses which the history of specific countries has taken during different periods in the past fifteen centuries of Islam in the Arab region.

If we go back to our central concern, we would see that the reason why a regional Arab perspective is a necessary condition for the pursuit of self-reliance is simply that a prima facie examination of the endowments and capabilities of the region's twenty-one states shows that none of them by itself has the basic prerequisites for self-reliant development. This is true whether we look at the components or aspects examined in this section of the chapter, or merely at the seven issues or 'criteria of adequacy' which were listed within the context of the fifth aspect above. On the other hand, also on prima facie examination, the twenty-one states would seem together to possess at least the minimum critical limit of the necessary endowments and capabilities, already in existence and potentially available, to permit a self-reliant approach to development. (We will try to prove the validity of this statement empirically in the next chapter.) But there is a further necessary condition that has to be added if the aggregate availability of the endowments and capabilities is also to amount to a sufficient condition. It is to this additional condition that we now turn.

The seventh and last aspect is the determination of society to seek self-reliant development with resolve and intelligence. This involves the willingness of Arab society to meet the challenge of underdevelopment and distorted development prevailing under conditions of dependence, plus the determination to do so resolutely and persistently, at the country level as well as at the regional level. The intelligent and well-calculated and graduated pursuit of self-reliance requires a well-calibrated mix of idealism with realism , of ambition with practicality. Such a mix will enable society to set its sights as high as it can reach by its own efforts internally, and externally with the co-operation, first, of other Third World regions that are likewise orientated towards self-reliance and, second, of such forces in the industrial world (both capitalist and socialist) as are sympathetic to self-reliance by Third World regions.

It is essential to emphasize that none of the six aspects discussed before, and not all of them together, can alone make the pursuit of self-reliance serious and promising. Only if the seventh aspect now being discussed can have its full impact, in addition to the other six, will the pursuit become meaningful and promise to help society pull gradually out of dependence. For, the question is not simply the economic availability of certain critical factors and resources, but further involves the maximization of the power of morale and the national and the regional resolve to challenge the forces, instruments, processes, and implications of dependence. Meeting the challenge is a function of the extra power which the community spirit and its dynamism can generate, through regional co-operation and a serious drive for economic and political complementarity, and ultimately some form of integration.

Finally, it remains to be added that the determination by the population at large, and by the leaderships at the various levels of authority in the different spheres of life, cannot emerge and be effective unless two critical conditions are satisfied (see *Sayigh 1982*). These are: first, wide participation by the people in the economic and political processes of deliberation and decision-making, in an atmosphere of respect for basic rights and freedoms, and second, the promotion of social justice. The latter must be achieved via the provision of social services, freely or at reduced cost, to the poorer strata of the population, the adoption of fiscal and monetary policies capable of narrowing the gap in income and wealth distribution, and the widening of opportunities for work, education and training for the underprivileged. But sight must not be lost of the compelling fact that an improved pattern of distribution can be meaningful only if there is more to distribute:

that is, if production expands in variety and volume, and improves in quality. As the two conditions just stated will be the object of analysis further on in the book, we will not elaborate on them any more, except to say that their satisfaction will raise the level of commitment to self-reliant development. While there is no or little meaningful political participation, and socio-economic and political opportunities are kept tightly restricted in the face of the underprivileged, little meaningful commitment can be expected.

THE TRANSITION TO SELF-RELIANCE

While it is rather easy to lay down the principles and identify the aspects of self-reliance, on an aprioristic basis, it is most difficult to seek it and put it into effect, and achieve a large measure of success in the process. Recapitulation of the seven aspects which I suggested in the latter part of the preceding section will reveal how hard it is to find *together* all the aspects, prerequisites and perceptions; to satisfy all the conditions stipulated, and to do all that has been indicated as essential to do, in order to carry the society and economy – anywhere in the Third World – to an effective state of self-reliance. This task would be especially hard if attempted in the Arab region, not only because of the heavy dependence on the advanced industrial countries currently prevailing, but also because the very few attempts made to move towards self-reliance in the post-war period have been aborted and indeed replaced by yet more dependence.

Yet this should not lead to despair. Rather than give up the endeavour altogether, on realizing how difficult it is to bring it to success, a society should, in its own self-interest, accept a measure of practicality in setting its targets and planning its gradual movement towards these targets, once its stocktaking of the endowments and capabilities it possesses seems to justify a promising outlook. Dependence did not develop overnight or even over one or two decades in any country's history. Generations were needed for dependence to take root and shoot out in different directions, that is, into the economy, the political and social structure, and the culture. Therefore the pursuit of self-reliance must be allowed many years before it may be justifiably subjected to the test of practicality and accountability.

Not only time will be needed, but phasing must also be built into the plans and expectations of society. For the sake of practicality and feasibility, the objective should be approached in stages, in the expectation that as each stage is reached, it will prepare for and make easier movement into the next stage. There are reasons to believe that it would be wise to set some very crucial objective as the first target, so that upon achieving it society can make movement onwards easier for itself. In this instance some central and critical aspect of self-reliance could be targeted to begin with, such as the shift of emphasis from the external to the domestic financing of the bulk of investment, or the take-over of ownership and control of foreign mining enterprises or of foreign-owned public utilities, or yet the undertaking of a fundamental overhaul of the perception, objective-selection, prioritization and policy formulation associated with the development plan of the country, to make this plan fit the normative, socially-orientated approach to development.

Yet most Third World countries will probably find such assignments very exacting for their capabilities and circumstances, particularly with respect to the exigencies of their external relations and commitments. Furthermore, the national leaderships might hesitate in front of colossal transition from dependence to self-reliance. The shock effect of a big push is something that can be justified, even urged, by theorists and advisers sitting at their desks. But decision-making to bring about a sudden and enormous transition will certainly not be equally appealing to the decision-makers, especially when that is seen to have serious external implications for the country's relations with very powerful Western advanced industrial countries, and likewise, to have deleterious effects on the vested interests of certain powerful political and economic leaderships internally.

No one formula can be composed that would be suitable for Third World countries in general. And no formula can be made by theorists or planners who do not have specific information and knowledge available to them about a specific country, to serve as input in the production of a formula. And the knowledge needed will have to derive from economic as well as political, social and cultural grounds, and likewise will have to relate to the country itself as well as to its place in the regional and international web of relations, in so far as the transition to self-reliance will impinge on these relations. Thus, a country seeking to make such a transition may well find it advisable to tackle first some crucial aspect of dependence which is less daunting than some more crucial aspects such as those cited earlier as a possible 'key' to an ambitious drive to self-reliance.

While the appeal of a big push is great, and the desire to speed the process of self-reliant development out of dependence is usually both pressing and attractive, realism is called for. The literature on the subject is over-full of superlatives in its description of 'another development', or 'alternative development', or yet of 'self-reliant development' and the utopia which each of these promises, to the point where politicians and social scientists, eager to move towards self-reliance as the promised land, may make the mistake of attempting too much in too short a time, with far too few endowments and capabilities, in the midst of too many handicaps, both internal and external. And it is usually much more dramatic for development advisers to counsel a big, ambitious, though unrealistic push, rather than judiciously rationed steps with a greater chance of being actually taken with safety.

These are observations of a general nature. But it remains true that each society must find and compose the formula appropriate to its own situation and circumstances: this by itself is one manifestation of self-reliance. It is probable that the formula that will actually be opted for in most countries will be a mix of objectives, some hard and some not so hard to attain. But in all instances, in its practice of self-reliance, every society must recall Galtung's dictum: self-reliance is a 'dynamic movement *from* the periphery . . . not something done *for* the periphery' (Galtung 1980: 23). And this includes the design of a formula with clear prioritization for the practice of self-reliance.

Galtung adds some more valuable advice. He warns that 'self-reliance cannot be at the expense of the self-reliance of others' (1980: 22). And, with regard to relations with other societies that are equally burdened with dependence, his warning is: 'The point is not to avoid interaction but to interact according to the criterion of self-reliance, also the self-reliance of others, *so that no new centre–periphery relationship emerges*' (1980: 23). But beyond these general statements, Galtung sets out what he considers the 'negative effect' of self-reliance. He lists five such effects (1980: 36–8):

1 Through SR inequities may decrease but inequalities will remain.
2 Through SR at the regional level, and also at the national level, local exploitation may solidify as long as the basis is unchanged.
3 Through SR organic ties between units may be reduced.
4 Through SR mobility between units may be reduced.
5 Through SR a new vertical distinction may be created between self-reliant and non self-reliant units.

These points invite some critical comments. Thus, with respect to the first, inequalities will remain only if self-reliant development is not already designed to have the value-laden and normative specifications which were discussed in Chapter 1 above, and if it does not satisfy the critical conditions cited in the last paragraph of the preceding section – namely, political participation, basic rights and freedoms, and social justice. If development is soundly designed, then the narrowing of inequalities will be one central specification to observe and attempt to achieve. The same kind of comment applies to the second point above for, in the view I have advocated in the preceding section of the chapter, 'changing the basis' is a prerequisite for the other changes sought to become possible. Points 3, 4 and 5 suggest that Galtung is using self-reliance to relate to local communities or villages within a nation-state, not to a nation state or a grouping of nation-states, which is the focus of my treatment.

Quite the reverse of what he fears is likely to happen if the focus is a nation-state, since the pursuit of self-reliance is likely to bring about more rather than less interaction among the units within the nation. This would be so, first, in order to make up for the reduced dependence on the external world, and second, because part of the ethic of self-reliance is co-operation among self-reliant units. The same argument would apply to a grouping of nation-states together seeking collective self-reliance.

Nevertheless, it must be admitted that, even in the context of a nation-state or a grouping of states, there is the danger that self-reliance itself may widen the distance between the entities considered – in the present case, between states. Furthermore, the vertical distinction mentioned in Galtung's fifth point may well occur between the more and the less self-reliant states (or the more and the less advanced), as between provinces or regions within the same state. This may well happen owing to the dynamics of the drive for self-reliant development promoting greater activity, and a more significant and positive response to the challenge, in some states rather than in others within the grouping seeking collective self-reliance (or in some provinces rather than in others within the same state). This would be a serious problem which the practice of self-reliance may encounter at the one-country or the regional level. Indeed, the widening difference in level of economic performance and capability which may occur may permit the more advanced to exploit the less advanced, and thus retard their development. In extreme cases, this possibility will amount to the extension of the centre–periphery relationship to the single country internally, or to the grouping of countries regionally.

Naturally, there will be references to and invocations for the strictest care to be taken in the formulation of the steps and stages of self-reliance, in order to protect the less advanced countries inside a regional grouping against such a contingency. But good intentions are one thing, economic and power realities another. Indeed, this is possibly the main handicap which stands in the way of a truly close economic complementarity among the Arab economies, though there is no shortage of sermons on its advantages, and invocations even for outright economic integration. If the long-term virtues of self-reliance retreat in the face of national selfishness and short-sightedness, then the outward, formalistic policies and structures of self-reliance will not in effect bring about the loosening of the grip of dependence. Furthermore, the expectation of long-term benefits will not be sufficient consolation to those provinces or sectors that might suffer because of the pursuit of self-reliance. What these will need will be some form of compensation, or practical advice which will guide them in an attempt to relocate their capital in sectors or industries, or yet provinces or countries, where the transition from dependence to self-reliance will be less painful or not painful at all.

Failure to bring about adjustment in case some province or sector, or yet some other country in a grouping of countries, suffers as a result of the pursuit of self-reliance, or failure to provide compensation from some fund set for the purpose, may tarnish the expectations built around self-reliant development. But this is not the only likely damage. The final outcome may well be deeper penetration by neo-colonialism (whether directly by advanced economies, or by proxy through their TNCs), not only in the less advanced countries within the grouping, but also within the relatively more advanced. Any serious crack in the effort to seek self-reliance will give the vested interests, which are hostile to self-reliance and aligned with external forces and interests in the desire for the state of dependence to continue, the opportunity to subvert the effort. Furthermore, the failure of the effort, even if partial, may shake society's confidence in the credibility and feasibility, and even in the usefulness, of self-reliant development, and bolster the forces and tendencies that favour the state of dependence to which the economy and society had been used, and in which some comfort must have been felt by influential segments of the population.

This is not the free play of hypothetical theorizing. It can be seen happening in the Arab region. Thus, most of the Arab countries, but especially the oil exporters among them, found themselves more deeply penetrated after the oil era of the 1970s than before, in spite of the relatively large oil revenues accumulated and the appearance of increased political power and influence in the international arena. And the penetration has not been merely economic and technological under the impact of vastly increased imports for consumption and for investment, and the need for capital goods and technical expertise from abroad. It has also been political, cultural (even if mainly touching on certain superficial aspects of culture), social (particularly with regard to consumption patterns and the adoption of new, ostentatiously expensive status symbols), and in terms of accelerated arms purchases which have added to defence arsenals but not equally to the will to struggle for liberation.

This deeper and more widespread penetration has led in many instances to further exploitation of the Arab region, as of the poor and weak by the rich and powerful *within* the region. To internal exploitation must be added oppression, which has been refined through the use of modern technology and what is euphemistically called 'systems of national security' – all imported also. The penetration has also led to a tighter collusion between some of the countries with the United States at government level in almost all spheres of life, parallel with collusion between Western arms exporters and Arab interests at both ends of the relationship.

There are four lessons at least which can be learnt even at this point before we come to the next two chapters. The first is that all the dangers referred to in the last few paragraphs lurk in the path of self-reliance, unless the principle becomes deeply embedded in the minds and hearts of the people, and unless the people are willing to struggle for the preservation of the principle and for its translation into action. This does not mean that the blockage of the pursuit of self-reliance simply arises from within the dependent society, since the external forces which have an interest in the persistence of dependence will try hard in various ways to abort the pursuit. It means essentially that the locus of the power to challenge dependence, and the dynamics of action in the struggle to free society from it, is basically within society itself. Furthermore, every success achieved in the struggle, no matter how small, will make the next move that much easier and likelier to succeed.

The second lesson is that self-reliance must not be viewed as a universal imperative which is equally urgent and pressing for all Third World countries, or as an objective which is both uniformly crucial *and* feasible, any more than dependence can be viewed as being equally deep-rooted and equally obstructive of development in all Third World countries. The understanding of both dependence and self-reliance must be attempted with flexibility and relativity, not with rigidity and absolutism, within the straitjacket of dogmatism. And in both cases the phenomenon/process must be searched for in different spheres of life, so that the extent of development in the various spheres may be differentiated, and likewise the escape from it through self-reliance may be differentiated, depending on the degree and the locus of obstructiveness.

Futhermore, inasmuch as the position of different Third World countries in the world capitalist system is not identical with respect to its generation of dependence, and as, in consequence, dependence does not befall all countries with the same degree of directness and with the same time sequence, self-reliance through delinkage from the world capitalist system must be sought within different degrees of directness and different time sequences.

The third lesson is that self-reliant development of the quality and content stipulated in this book, sought by a society with a nationalist–progressive system, does not represent an analytical and conceptual contradiction. Instead, this system could well be a third course to take between a socialism which it is still premature to adopt, as well as under questioning in the Arab context, and a capitalism which it is desirable to circumscribe and control, and also to qualify with certain socialistic principles and practices, and thus to outdistance in some concrete respects. The substance of this lesson will become clearer when we come to examine the dynamics and machinery of self-reliant development in the last chapter.

Finally, the fourth lesson is that the pursuit of self-reliance will demand all the intelligence, the foresight, the determination and the sense of community that the people can muster for the purpose. It will also demand the acceptance of tough sacrifices and an exacting work ethic. Even then, the pursuit will have to aim at that part of the ideal which reality can permit in any one phase of the struggle, even if 'reality' is to be understood in a dynamic sense where achievement extends the frontiers of the possible. Indeed, there is no easy formula for self-reliant development that we know of, though there are compelling reasons to believe that an appropriate formula can be found by a society which is determined to find one and to apply it.

4 The feasibility of Arab self-reliant development: a case study

INTRODUCTION

This chapter is basically designed to answer two questions in the process of assessing the possibility of self-reliance in the development of the Arab region. These are: can the Arabs shoulder the tasks and responsibilities of self-reliant development, that is, can they meet what I called in the last chapter the 'criteria of adequacy'? And, if the answer is in the affirmative, how will such development be made concrete: through what sectors, programmes and areas of action? The quality and content of the development targeted have already been characterized in the first chapter of the book. In contrast, it was shown that the development actually achieved in the Third World at large has been grossly distorted, patchy and dependent, and has failed to serve the interests of a large part of the populations of Third World countries.

As the multifaceted and far-reaching dependence of these countries was considered the main cause, directly and indirectly, of the distortion and patchiness, the second chapter was devoted to an examination of the dependency paradigm – its genesis, main ideas, evolution, impact on development thought, implications for development and relevance to present-day political and economic reality. This reality is distinguished by the fact that we now live in an era of national independence in which internal obstacles to development are prominent, but also in which transnational corporations enjoy a position of pre-eminence in the world capitalist system, and a communication revolution of global scale is in full force.

The second chapter ended with the conclusion that self-reliant development was the antidote to dependence. This led to the devotion of the third chapter to the concept and principles, and the practice, of self-reliance, which in turn led to the need to address the enquiry which the present chapter embodies, as to the feasibility of Arab self-reliant development. Though restricted to the Arab region, the enquiry is believed to be capable of serving as a test case of relevance to Third World regions in general, naturally with the necessary qualifications that will be called for in the application of the method of enquiry and of the findings to respond to the particularities of each region or sub-region.

The role assigned to the present chapter is determined by the contradiction between the present state of affairs with respect to the distortion and patchiness of development witnessed in the post-war period, even if the advances made in the forces of production are undeniable, on the one hand, and the relatively huge resources and energies devoted to capital investment and developmental efforts, on the other hand. What is conducive to even more anxiety and concern is that the current state of affairs threatens to persist and to worsen further. In addition, the upsurge in Arab oil production and in the inflow of revenue from oil export during the 1970s have not led to commensurate investment in the region at large. Instead, the relatively vast inflow of financial resources has, to a considerable extent, become an occasion for wasteful and misguided expenditure on ostentatious consumption, but likewise on the indiscriminate importation of over-priced capital goods and armaments. And it has also led to the build-up of enormous accounts in banks and investments in stocks and bonds in Western financial centres.[1] The recent awakening in the region to these realities is quite limited in scope, and has not been accompanied fully by the necessary corrective perception, policies and behaviour patterns in any of the basic relevant spheres of life. As these accusations are quite serious, they have received many references in this chapter and in the first as well.

Growing awareness of the contradictions just referred to, and of the identity and gravity of social and economic ills which are organically associated with them, has been restricted narrowly to a small circle of intellectuals – humanists, social scientists, journalists, educators – and a handful of persons in the higher rungs of authority. By and large, the vast majority of real decision-makers who hold the reins of power have either remained unaware that the region is going through a serious crisis in its economic, cultural and political life, or – what is worse – are aware but insufficiently concerned. Consequently, the groups which compose what I called earlier in the first chapter the 'development network' have not addressed the crisis with enough deep thought and seriousness to understand its nature and causes, and to suggest remedies. Hence the marginal and superficial concern with self-reliant comprehensive development, and the absence of consensus or near-consensus on the imperativeness of resistence to dependence.

The contradictions, and the failures in perception and in action accompanying and flowing from them, reflect a basic structural defect: the non-availability of social and political forces large and strong enough to visualize, engineer and generate radical change capable of bringing Arab society and economy to a satisfactory state of health. This realization carries us to the crux of the matter at hand: how can self-reliant development – understood as a broad and profound transformation in the cultural, social and political spheres of life, along with the economic – be initiated, intensified and sustained, given the present socio-political reality of Arab society? While consideration of this question will be the core of the last chapter of the book, it is also central to the enquiry of the present chapter. It will be recalled that the 'criteria of adequacy' formulated in the last chapter included the substance of the question just posed. Indeed, the satisfaction of the other criteria was stated as unfeasible without the determination of society to achieve self-reliance, and, for that purpose, to take the necessary measures in the fields of internal capital accumulation, acquisition of technological capability, sound and imaginative management of the economy, and the other criteria of adequacy.

The central and crucial function of this chapter is, therefore, to examine these criteria in order to determine in the end what chance self-reliant development has of materializing in the Arab region, and the course it will be likely to take in materializing. A later section will be devoted to the examination of these criteria. But first, the next section will briefly discuss the possible approaches to the enquiry with respect to the identity of the political entity or entities within which the criteria will be examined. This is essential in view of the fact that the Arab region contains twenty-one sovereign states,[2] whose size of population, area, resources, level of economic capability, basic social conditions, and political outlooks vary widely. These states can alternatively be divided into a number of groupings on grounds of certain common features, or, finally, they can be considered together as a region with one broadly defined economy.

THE REFERENCE POLITICAL ENTITY: ALTERNATIVE APPROACHES

As just indicated, there are three possible approaches, with room for combination as well. The papers submitted at the symposium held in Amman, Jordan, in April 1986 (*CAUS 1987*, referred to in Chapters 1 and 3) around the feasibility of independent (taken to mean self-reliant) development, followed two of the three approaches. To begin with, seven papers dealt with single countries,[3] each examining a single factor or criterion, or a very small number of factors or criteria, in the context of which the ability of the country concerned to seek self-reliant development was explored. The final paper, prepared by myself, had for reference political entity the region in its entirety. No papers dealt with the twenty-one states in their groupings according to some classificatory system, which is the third alternative approach. Although more than one paper referred to the groupings in one context or another, none tried to assess the feasibility of self-reliant development within them, individually or collectively.

There was one paper which did not fit into any of the three categories just referred to, although it overlapped in certain respects with the paper that dealt with the region as one entity. The former examined what in the region is called 'joint Arab economic action', within the 'joint Arab economic sector'.[4] I consider this paper to have moved closer to an assessment of the course of self-reliant development through the joint sector than any of the other country papers. This is essentially because it combined two important features: specificity, in so far as individual aspects of the joint sector were concerned and their impact on the course of self-reliance could be assessed, and comprehensiveness, inasmuch as the joint sector brought together in each of its aspects many or most (if not all) of the region's countries, and could thus provide a field for collective self-reliance.

Being small in size compared with the aggregate economy of the region, the joint sector is a good indicator of the very limited extent to which self-reliant development had been seriously sought on the regional level. This is because this sector was meant and designed to embody a regional approach to development. Its failure to have a considerable impact is therefore particularly telling about the meagre results in the region as a whole.

It seems to me fair, at this distance in time from the Amman symposium under consideration, and after careful rereading of the country papers, to state that on the whole they fell short of their objective, both with respect to methodology, and to reach of analysis, especially in view of the narrow focus on a very limited number of factors or criteria. Nevertheless, the conclusions reached indicate that in the majority of cases self-reliance had not been sought seriously, and in harmony with the definition of the concept of self-reliance adopted by the writers concerned; and, in those few cases where the pursuit of self-reliance during the past two or three decades had been well-intentioned and well-orientated, as in Egypt and Algeria, for instance, it had failed to be sustained and internally consistent. Above all, it had violated certain basic conditions without the satisfaction of which self-reliance would remain defective and at best transitory. (The conditions in question included democracy and human rights, and institution-building to reduce the extent of recourse to centralized and personalized leadership and decision-making, and to increase the recourse to the delegation of authority.)

Research that I have undertaken on the region's economies, over the past three decades, makes it possible to determine the strong and the weak points in each of the economies concerned, with respect to the relevance of these points to the pursuit of self-reliance. The findings of this cumulative research are presented in matrix form in Table 4 on p. 172. Understandably, my assessment of the satisfaction of each of the criteria, as recorded in the boxes of the matrix, must be considered somewhat tentative, since it is not justifiable to claim finality and precision where extensive qualitative judgement is unavoidable, and quantification seems to be a dubious approach (even where possible) in the absence of generally accepted data, coefficients, ratios or formulas for factor mixes. Above all, there is here the risk of 'misplaced concreteness'.

These difficulties notwithstanding, I hope the undertaking embodied in the matrix can be seen to hold some value for the enquiry of this chapter. According to the matrix, none of the twenty-one countries by itself meets the basic criteria of the feasibility of self-reliant development. This judgement will receive elaboration in the section to follow on the criteria of adequacy. The matrix shows many gaps which reveal how insufficiently the individual countries are equipped to meet the objective requirements of self-reliance. Although the analysis in the section on criteria does not follow the single-country approach, the matrix itself is an application of the demands of this approach.

The same matrix shows that the region considered as a whole has these requirements in sufficient availability to justify the expectation that it can pursue collective self-reliance effectively, even if the quality of the requirements is not always notably satisfactory. But two basic conditions must be satisfied for this positive assessment to have credibility: the setting up and earnest support of structures capable of giving expression to far-reaching complementarity and integration among the region's economies, and political determination to pursue the complementarity earnestly and intelligently, in a sustained manner, and on a larger scale, for the purpose of providing self-reliant development with the necessary *and* sufficient conditions which it will need in order to be launched. We need not go any further in this discussion, because we would otherwise be anticipating the detailed examination to come of the specific criteria of adequacy. But it has been essential to make the statements contained in this and the previous few paragraphs in order to indicate the justification for the choice of the regional approach as the main approach in our enquiry, along with basic information on individual countries provided as the need arises, sufficient for a profile of each country to emerge, with respect to the extent to which it meets or fails to meet the criteria of adequacy.

So far, little has been said about the third approach, namely the resort to the grouping of the twenty-one countries according to certain common characteristics, and the testing of the feasibility within each of the groupings. (The grouping under reference was used until 1987 in the preparation annually of the *Unified Arab Economic Report*, to which there will be repeated reference later.) I have resorted to this approach in the presentation of the matrix, by placing the countries which form the membership of each grouping together. Accordingly the extent to which the criteria are met within each grouping can be assessed. Although the gaps are fewer in the boxes of that part of the matrix relating to each grouping taken as one unit than for the individual countries, none of the groupings by itself, as the groupings are organized in the matrix, seems to give promise of self-reliant development.

Nevertheless, it can also be seen that the top four groupings – that is, all the countries except the six considered 'least developed countries' (LDCs), as they are currently referred to in the literature – can together seek self-reliant development without help from the fifth grouping of LDCs. In fact this statement could also be warranted for two or three of the well-endowed groupings alone, without all four being involved. However, the non-contiguity of some of the members of the groupings in question would certainly inhibit the integration – or at least the complementarity – which is essential for collective self-reliant development. In addition, the exclusion of the six LDCs which together comprise 20 per cent of the aggregate population of the twenty-one states[5] is not justifiable, particularly in view of the sense of community, the shared history and culture, and the broadly similar aspirations which tie the Arabs in the whole region together. Furthermore, the sense of collective responsibility for the development and well-being of the six LDCs is strongly felt by the remaining Arab countries.

The foregoing observations on groupings suggested to me the resort to a different system of grouping. This I have done, as can be seen in the next section. Even under this alternative system, no one grouping seems capable by itself of launching self-reliant development, if we are to rely on the degree to which the criteria of adequacy are satisfied. However, close co-operation between certain countries in three contiguous groupings is quite promising with respect to the feasibility of self-reliance.

This brief discussion of the alternative approaches to the testing of the extent to which the criteria of adequacy can be met suggests that the matrix to be presented later uses and conforms to all three approaches. However, apart from the matrix, the analysis in the next section dealing with the criteria will adopt the regional approach, although there will be references as the need arises to individual countries in the course of the analysis. The approach opted for emerged as clearly the most appropriate one, once the matrix was drawn in draft form in the preparation of the manuscript of the book.

But it also became clear that the decision needed more justification than the matrix could provide. I had to satisfy myself that I was not basing my decision to adopt a regional approach on ideological grounds connected with a strong commitment to Arab nationalism and the desirability of some form of Arab unity. Considerations were taken into account, connected with the conviction that collective self-reliant development, at the level of the whole region, was essential both for the social and economic well-being of the region, and as a solid economic base for National (that is regional) security, in the face of the existing loss of some Arab lands and possible dangers to some other lands. The decision had to be taken on the inherent merits of the case for self-reliant development, and how best this development could be sought – indeed, how at all it could be sought – important as the ideological and national security considerations were.

Consequently, the regional approach had to be justified on the grounds that there was actually an 'Arab economy' in existence, although its potential was vastly more impressive than its current reality. Furthermore, there was a substantial joint Arab economic sector, even though it could be much larger, show much more cohesiveness, and be better orientated to serve the purposes of self-reliant development more directly and effectively. The reasons why the actual falls well below the potential, with respect both to the Arab economy and the joint Arab economic sector, are both external and internal in interaction. The former category relates to the impact of long-standing dependence on the world capitalist system, particularly on the Western powers that had exercised hegemony over almost all of the region's countries, and/or enjoy vast economic and political influence today. This factor has acted in such a way that today individual Arab countries are more closely integrated with the capitalist system and its TNCs than with the rest of the Arab economy.

On the other hand, the internal factor is very powerful as well, in spite of the political independence already achieved, and the large measure of independent decision-making which has become possible. The components of the internal factor include political fragmentation within the Arab region; the state of estrangement between the peoples and the vast majority of the ruling elites; the severe limitations of broad-based political participation and human rights which mute the popular urge for radical political and economic change in the service of the masses; the social and political structures in dominance which permit the elites to corner power, affluence and privilege, and which are self-perpetuating; and the collusion between powerful vested interests in each of the countries and their counterparts in the dominant capitalist countries, within the fabric of the relationship of dependence.

All this notwithstanding, it can be argued that there is an Arab economy of limited reality in existence, and a substantial Arab economy that could emerge, given the satisfaction of certain conditions that are not beyond the reach of reason. Likewise, it can be argued that the joint Arab economic sector now in existence is not negligible. It is to these two arguments that I now turn.[6]

It is justified to question the legitimacy of treating the economies of twenty-one sovereign states as though they were one economy: indeed the correctness of such summation may be denied altogether. The critics may argue that there is no Arab economy in existence, and that the aggregation of data relating to twenty-one economies in as many states only produces the illusion of the existence of one Arab economy.

However, in defence of the claim of the reference to an Arab economy, it can be pointed out that the fragmentation of the Arab nation into many political entities, and their ultimate transformation into sovereign states, itself was an artificial dismemberment brought about by the use of force by Western colonialism. The fragmentation persists in spite of independence, because of the pressure of certain external interests, and the collusion of certain internal interest groups with them. This network of interests flourishes on political fragmentation, and also feeds it to give it longevity. Indeed, the strength of the existing international economic (and political) order benefits from the weakness of the economies at the periphery of the international order. The Arab region is one clear instance of the process of external influence operating on national leaderships to keep them away from the course of integration and unity. It can be argued that the absence of some meaningful form of Arab unity is a major debilitating factor which besets the process of development, if not the major factor.

Nevertheless, in spite of political fragmentation, the region enjoys the existence of a real regional economic circuit of life. This circuit runs through the national (individual) economies as well as through the joint Arab economic sector. This sector is the product of purposeful planning, design and action by the national leaderships concerned. Even when components of the joint sector are launched by the initiative of individual countries, the sector leaps across national frontiers and represents truly regional action. Admittedly, the joint sector still falls short of being an integrative determining force within the region, and is still far behind the integrative force of the Omayyad or Abbasid eras which covered hundreds of years of Arab history that were characterized by strong and far-reaching economic exchanges and interlocking relations. It even represents much less integrative reality than the long period of Ottoman domination which lasted till the end of the First World War. None the less, the significance of the joint sector cannot reasonably be denied or belittled in the context of present circumstances.

Many of the components of the institutional framework for Arab economic co-operation, complementarity and even integration have been in the process of formation since the early years of the independence of most Arab countries and the establishment of the League of Arab States in the 1940s and 1950s. The framework in question embraced official instruments – agreements, laws and machinery – to which some, many, or all the Arab governments were party. But, in addition, there have been since the 1960s certain private efforts by some business and professional communities, and these efforts have been embodied in intra-regional projects and associations. But the institutional framework experienced the most intensive expansion and diversification in the decade following the autumn/winter of 1973 when oil prices were adjusted, and the production and flow of oil to foreign markets expanded considerably. The price increases as well as the expansion in oil exports together brought into the Arab economies vast financial resources. Apart from the impact of this sudden financial abundance upon the economies of individual countries, the new resources permitted considerable financial flows from the major oil-exporting countries to the non-oil countries (and even to some oil-exporting ones with modest oil revenues). Several of the aid-receiving countries experienced a flow in the opposite direction: the movement of millions of workers from their native land to the oil-exporting economies to help in their development with the very wide range of skills at their command. Some specific indicators will now be selected to reveal the magnitude and reach of the joint economic sector.

At the policy and decision-making level, there is the formation of many ministerial councils in areas related to economic life (national economy, finance, foreign trade, planning, agriculture, industry, tourism, transport and communications) as well as to other areas of life. These councils serve co-ordinative, advisory, policy and operational purposes. Many more intra-regional bodies at lower levels (mostly designated 'specialized regional organizations') and literally hundreds of joint projects and companies have been established. Two regional funds were also established – the Arab Fund for Economic and Social Development and the Arab Monetary Fund – whose membership includes all the Arab countries. The former finances programmes and projects of development in needy countries, while the latter looks after monetary matters such as easing balance of payments crises. In addition, there are four national development funds which, though set up by individual countries, serve the development needs of the Arab region. Indeed, two of these country funds also advance aid to some very needy non-Arab countries.

Current official financial flows from the capital-surplus to the capital-short countries average $5.6 billion of aid annually, over the years 1976–87. A workforce estimated at 3–4 million strong have moved to the oil-rich countries to take part in the very extensive construction and development activity which the expanded oil revenues have permitted. This workforce is estimated to remit back home, or to save, an estimated $3–4 billion every year. The estimates quoted must have dropped since 1983 or 1984, as a result of the sharp decline in oil prices, production, revenues, and therefore economic activity. Finally, tens of thousands of students attend Arab universities outside their own countries. In all, the aggregate capital of the joint economic sector (including that of the various development funds, but excluding the capital of joint Arab commercial banks) exceeds $40 billion.[7] The significance of this sector goes beyond the size of its capital. It lies in the large degree of sharing of financial burdens arising from development effort, and of capabilities called for in the undertaking of the effort.

It must be admitted, however, that what is shared should and could be expanded considerably, if the joint sector is to become a major force in the process of strengthening complementarity and making it more meaningful – for the purpose both of promoting development and of enhancing security. The Summit of the Arab Heads of State, meeting in November 1980 in Amman, Jordan, endorsed the necessity of expanding the joint sector, and unanimously approved the documents of relevance prepared for it. The two most prominent among these were the 'Strategy for Joint Arab Economic Action' and the 'Charter of National [i.e. regional] Economic Action'. Subsequently, the two documents cited were translated into a plan and action programmes. Hopes were high at the time that, with financial and manpower resources available for the implementation of the plan and programmes, a robust and expanding Arab economy would be in the making, alongside and in harmony with the national economies. Although the Arab economy would still need a great deal of tending, its promise was seen to be considerable.

However, since the Arab Summit of 1980, the oil sector has fallen into crisis, with production, exports and prices, and therefore revenues, substantially reduced. The financial stringency felt since then (partly because of a real shortage of funds, partly because of injudicious large-scale expenditure during the 1970s) has led to the freezing of the plan and action programmes for the joint sector. While the promise just referred to is still considerable, it will need much more tending than the situation in the first years of the 1980s suggested.

The hydrocarbons sector is significant in the Arab economy as a whole, both directly for the oil-producing countries, and indirectly for the others through ripple effects reflected in financial and manpower flows, the setting up of joint projects and programmes, and the resultant reallocation of resources and capabilities. It is even more important for individual oil-exporting countries as the provider of funds for fixed capital formation and technical know-how, and for the importation of consumption goods and services. Yet this sector should not be referred to as *the* engine of growth, even though it constitutes a significant part of this engine. Consequently, the adoption of a regional approach to the assessment of the feasibility of self-reliant development must not stand or fall on the basis of the fortunes of the oil resource, whether it is exported crude, or subjected (as liquid or gas) to various manufacturing processes in the refining, fertilizer and petrochemical industries.

In other words, the Arab economy is not just oil. The latter has acquired significance as a result of the dramatic rise in the revenues accruing from its export, and the world-wide attention given to it at a certain conjuncture, when OPEC seemed to hold crucial power over the large oil-importing industrial economies. But, as events subsequently came to show, the industrial world has managed to absorb the price shock of the decade 1973–82 and to attract back a substantial part of the transfer of resources that seemed initially to take place. The backflow (or recycling) of funds went to the industrial countries to finance enormous purchases of goods and services from them, as well as excess savings seeking placement in Western bank deposits and in securities.

The critical question is, then, whether the Arab region can develop without the high dependence on oil exports which it came to experience in the 1970s. This is not the place to consider the question in detail. But my reasoned answer is in the affirmative, if the Arabs show determination, imagination, skill and discipline in the management of the economies of their countries and of their regional economy, within the framework of the pursuit of collective self-reliance based on the principle and practice of close and far-reaching complementarity. Indeed, the pursuit of self-reliant development acquires greater urgency with the shrinkage of oil revenues, since self-reliant development can serve as a corrective involving reliance on the other resources available – human, natural and manufactured.

THE CRITERIA OF ADEQUACY FOR ARAB SELF-RELIANT DEVELOPMENT

It is appropriate to move on at this point to an examination of the criteria as suggested in Chapter 3. This examination will be undertaken in the present section, with a sub-section for each criterion considered.

The size of the region's internal market

Since we have adopted as reference political entity the Arab region, we approach the enquiry by assessing the adequacy of each of the criteria as it is or can be met by the region as a whole. In other words, the shortcomings or stringencies of a criterion in one or more countries will not be an overall inhibiting factor, if the deficiency or insufficiency is more than made good in or by some other country or countries. This would reveal areas of complementarity, as we will see later at the end of the present section.

The size of the region's internal market consists of two components. These are exchanges of goods and services undertaken among the twenty-one Arab economies (which for the individual countries concerned constitute part of foreign trade), and exchanges undertaken with non-Arab countries. The region's international trade, or the sum of both components, is considerable, even though it has become smaller since the oil crisis became tangible in the early 1980s. Thus, total exports plus imports (of goods and services) stood at $235.1 billion for 1987, as against $379.6 billion for 1981, thereby revealing a drop of 38.1 per cent. Total foreign trade stood at 100.4 per cent of Gross Domestic Product for the region in 1981 (which was $371.1 billion), as against 61 per cent for 1987 (with a GDP of $385.5 billion).[8]

The drop in the ratio over the years is the result of a steep drop in the revenues from oil exports, and a much gentler drop in imports. (The value of oil exports from the Organization of Arab Petroleum Exporting Countries, OAPEC, members reached an all-time peak of $209.5 billion for 1980, but dropped to $195.4 billion for 1981, and then all the way to $74.5 billion for 1987.)[9] Nevertheless, even in 1987 the size of the external sector reflected an extremely high degree of dependence on the outside world, both for exports and imports, and showed that the region's economy produced largely for the external markets, and obtained a very high percentage of the goods and services it used from external sources. What is particularly indicative of this unhealthy dependence is that by 1987 the region's imports, though lower than those for 1980 or 1981, were substantially in excess of oil revenues ($129.2 versus $74.5 billion), and a large part of the shortfall had to be financed by drawing on Arab financial reserves held abroad, even though a substantial proportion of the imports were consumers' goods and services.

Foreign trade by head of population in the Arab region is considerable. In 1987, and in spite of the drop in exports as well as imports, it was still 15 per cent higher on the average than its counterpart for the world as a whole, or some $1,163 per head for the Arab region, as against $1,011 per head for the world.[10] Indeed, imports per head were the highest in the world for one or two countries during the peak years of the 'oil era'. While this is not a fact to be proud of, it must not be swept under the carpet. However, that part of foreign trade which constitutes intraregional trade is extremely small – 7.54 per cent of total exports and 6.77 per cent of total imports for 1987.[11] Thus, the significance of the size of the region's market must be gauged with both components in mind, trade among the Arab countries, and that between these and non-Arab countries.

To limit the measurement to intra-Arab trade only as it stands today would be misleading on two counts. It would involve an approach in static terms that does not take into account the possibility of considerable growth of the value of exchanges within the region; and it would not take into account the expectation that under the impetus of self-reliant development goods and services produced by the Arab economies could (and would) partly replace ones imported from outside the region, and the shift towards an inward-directed economy would make more of the production flow in trade among the region's countries. While trade with non-Arab countries may well increase during periods of energetic development work, owing to the necessary importation of technology, raw materials, spare parts and even food, appropriate policy and institutional and behavioural changes may and can themselves also promote intraregional exchanges.

As indicated earlier on in the last chapter, self-reliance is not taken here to mean autarky or blinkered isolation, even if a degree of isolation would be advisable within reasonable, well-considered limits. What is crucial in this context is the ability of a country or a community of countries seeking self-reliant development to determine, in the light of its interests, endowments and capabilities, the direction and the composition of its foreign trade, and to inculcate confidence and even pride in local products.

A dynamic approach will of necessity have to take into account growth expectations in the assessment of the size of the region's internal market. Aggregate Gross Domestic Product, GDP, per capita stood at a simple (unweighted) average of about $1,907 for 1987. It had risen considerably after the adjustment upwards of oil prices in 1973/4 and January 1980, and the expansion of production and export of oil. But it has dropped noticeably since the oil crisis started in the early 1980s.

However, the crude data on revenues, when aggregated for all the oil-exporting countries, fail to reveal that the pattern of distribution of wealth and income is grossly uneven, both within and between Arab countries, or that most of the rise in GDP is attributable to the rise in oil revenues between 1973/4 and 1980/1. The wide intraregional disparity in GDP can be seen dramatically in the fact that, at one extreme, GDP per capita was $16,179 for United Arab Emirates for 1987, but only $315 per capita for Somalia at the other extreme, according to Arab official sources.[12]

The disparity within countries is much wider still, with GDP for the many billionaires being no less than $100 million per capita (assuming only US $1 billion of wealth per billionaire with a net return of 10 per cent per annum), and, say $2,000 per capita for the lowest-income stratum in the oil-exporting countries. (This represents a ratio of 50,000 to 1.) While it is true that these sums cannot be found in official documents, they can easily be proved to be warranted from informed estimates and careful observation.

In spite of the scandalously wide wealth and income gap within countries and among them, it is still true that purchasing power has been generally rising, and the level of living has been improving during the post-war years, but particularly during the oil decade 1973–82, even for the lower-income groups. The official statistics show a sharp rise in consumption and capital formation, both in oil and non-oil countries, but particularly in the former. Even after the steep decline in oil revenues since 1983, the eleven oil countries members of OAPEC, plus Oman, financed investments totalling $85.8 billion in 1987, while the non-oil countries (including the six LDCs) together invested $7.3 billion. Thus total investment for the region of $93.1 billion, constituted about 24.2 per cent of an aggregate GDP of $385.5 billion.[13] And, in addition, there has been an outflow of substantial excess savings during the decade 1973–82 by the rich, and by governments, to the Western economies, after consumption and investment within the region were undertaken. Accordingly, Arab external holdings reached a cumulative total of an estimated $374 billion by the end of 1982.[14] To all this must be added a net population increase averaging 2.6–2.8 per cent annually, which has brought the total population by 1987 to 202.2 million.

Short of a further sharp drop in oil production, prices and exports in the decade or two to come – seemingly a remote possibility according to the broad consensus of experts in oil economics – the outlook is that the region's internal market is and will remain large with at least a moderate expansion in the years to come. But even if oil revenues remain at their current level, the outlook is not depressing, considering the size of the aggregate population of the region and the fact that its individual countries, according to World Bank data, enjoy an average gross national product (GNP) per capita which stands at about the middle of the scale for each reference GNP group of countries with which the individual country falls.

The same applies to the rates of growth of consumption (general government and private) and gross domestic investment.[15] However, in the context of consumption and investment, the Arab LDCs rank nearer the lower end of the scale. And with respect both to GNP and to consumption and investment data, the few Arab high-income oil exporters for which data are available stand as a class by themselves, with high GNP per capita but rather low rates of growth of consumption and investment compared with upper-middle income and many industrial market economies, again according to the World Bank's data already referred to. The low rates of growth are largely explainable by the high levels that had already been reached. Together, these facts and considerations permit the expectation of an internal market that is large enough to absorb a considerable proportion of the goods and services which the Arab economy can produce (except oil and gas), under the impetus of self-reliant development – given a sound appropriate pattern of investment, and a content of non-oil production that is essentially aimed at the internal needs of the region.

This rather favourable assessment will no doubt be tempered by the reality of the extreme modesty of intraregional trade at the present, as already indicated. A number of factors have shaped this situation, primarily the relatively small volume of production outside the sector of hydrocarbons, the narrowness of the range of products, the rather poor quality and therefore weak competitive position of these products in the face of similar goods and services imported, and insufficient purposefulness on the part of buyers to favour local production – even when the products are competitively attractive.

However, inhibiting as these factors are, they are not insurmountable if the pursuit of self-reliance is serious and intelligent, and the forces behind it are broad and determined enough to stand up to the forces that favour dependence or are permissive towards it, and that give preference to foreign products, even when these are not intrinsically superior. In this, as in the case of every other criterion of adequacy, the final determinant is the clarity and soundness of the national will, and the strength of the political and social forces pressing for self-reliance, as against those allied with foreign interests and pressure groups, and characterized essentially by an outlook on development which is outwardly directed. Hence the imperativeness of wide political participation, since it is the masses which have an interest in the satisfaction of their basic human needs, that care enough for an inner-directed, self-reliant development which serves them first, and are therefore expected to apply pressure to that end.

The directions and composition of Arab foreign trade

As indicated earlier, the region depends heavily on non-Arab countries, both as suppliers of imports and as markets for exports. This dependence – which began emerging in the early decades of the nineteenth century, when parts of the Arab region began to fall under

Western colonial rule, or within the sphere of influence of Western powers, if not direct rule – has been growing. The oil decade 1973–82 raised the dependence to a state of virtual integration with the economies of the capitalist world, essentially as a result of the pre-eminence of oil exports. Understandably, exports heading for Western industrial countries (including Japan) contained a very large component of crude oil.

The revenues derived became the main source of finance in the payment for vastly expanding imports, which also came mostly from the West. But the integration has been embodied in institutional arrangements, apart from its de facto aspect, through barter agreements which stipulate for the import of weapons, passenger airplanes or factory machinery against the export of oil (usually at a somewhat reduced price), and also through participation arrangements between the Arab oil countries and the TNCs of Western countries. It is estimated that the barter arrangements account for about 30 per cent of the oil exports of some producing countries, and that they may well reach 50 per cent by the end of the century at the prevailing rate of growth.[16] However, the heavy concentration of imports from Western sources of supply is more serious in the present context than that of the same Western markets as buyers of Arab exports, both because of the larger degree of dependence on the imports, and the composition of imports which include some very essential goods and services including capital goods, food items, technical know-how, chemicals and pharmaceuticals, and armaments.

The geographical distribution of Arab foreign trade is summarized in Table 1, which presents the relevant data for 1986, the last year for which they are available. As this table shows, the Arab region buys two-thirds of its commodity imports from the capitalist industrial countries, while a little over three-fifths of its commodity exports go to these countries. On the other hand, the share of the socialist community of countries is very modest, with respect to both imports and exports. A significant feature of the geographical distribution is the modest change over time in the share of the capitalist industrial countries as a group, both for imports and exports, with changes occurring within the group, mainly manifested in the drop of the share of the United States for imports as well as for exports, in favour of the European Economic Community and, less so, Japan. Thus, the feature of dependence on centre countries as a group has remained steady over the years of the oil era and beyond, even if the country 'shares' of this dependence have altered.

The degree of dependence on the industrial world for imports varies

Table 1 Geographical distribution of Arab foreign trade, 1986

Country grouping	*Exports (%)*	*Imports (%)*
Arab countries	7.54	6.77
Industrial countries	62.79	66.69
European Economic Community	(36.00)	(45.74)
United States of America	(8.22)	(10.98)
Japan	(18.57)	(9.97)
Socialist countries	2.44	3.78
Developing countries	19.18	15.74
Rest of the world	8.05	7.02
Total	100.00	100.00

Source: *Arab Unified Economic Report, 1988*, 'Statistical Appendices', Table 6/10

from one Arab country to another. Two generalizations can be made with respect to the pattern of the distribution in 1984 (the last year for which information is available). The first is that no one country received less than 40 per cent of its total imports from the capitalist industrial world except Syria (31.9 per cent). The second is more tentative: it is that the countries with the highest proportion of their imports coming from the industrial market economies (that is, above 70 per cent) included several of the major oil-exporting countries, but also one small oil exporter and one totally non-oil-producing country. This second category of countries consisted of Algeria, Tunisia, Saudi Arabia, Egypt, Qatar, Libya, Kuwait, Muritania, United Arab Emirates and Oman – in descending order – where the proportion ranged from a high 82.6 per cent to 70.4 per cent. On the other hand, Tunisia, Algeria, Saudi Arabia and Egypt had the smallest imports from the developing countries (including other Arab countries), with a proportion ranging from 17.8 per cent for Egypt, down to 13.6 per cent for Tunisia. Bahrain, Syria, South Yemen, Jordan, Sudan and Djibouti had the largest trade with the developing countries, with the proportion descending from 55.3 per cent (Bahrain) to 40.1 per cent (Djibouti).[17]

The pattern of the geographical distribution of exports in 1984 is less clear than that for imports, even though oil features importantly among the exports, and Western Europe and Japan are large buyers of Arab oil. Thus, the share of the Western industrial countries (including Japan) of Arab exports is highest for Mauritania (95.6 per cent), followed by Algeria (92.2 per cent), Qatar (79.7 per cent), Egypt (74.9 per cent), Tunisia (74.8 per cent) and Libya (73.6 per cent).

On the other hand, the share of the developing countries (including the Arab countries) in the region's exports is higher than that in its imports – 30.9 per cent as against 24.7 per cent. It is essentially oil exports that make up for this difference.

The geographical distribution of Arab foreign trade, and its relevance to an assessment of dependence and the feasibility of self-reliance, can be better appreciated if considered along with the composition of the imports and exports of the region.[18] In this connection, it would be warranted to expect the composition to have undergone considerable transformation, with respect both to exports and to imports, over the past three decades which have been characterized by energetic development efforts aimed, inter alia, at such transformation.

However, the results of the development pursued by individual countries, which has aimed at speedy industrialization, wider diversification in production, and reduction in the concentration on one or a few products for export – usually primary or partially-processed agricultural or mineral materials – have been very meagre. This is so particularly with the rise to distinct pre-eminence of oil among the exports, which has pushed back the results in relative terms of diversification efforts. Thus, by 1986, oil products constituted about 89 per cent of total commodity exports, while other minerals and raw materials accounted for some 2 per cent, industrial and petrochemical products for about 7.4 per cent, and food products for 1.8 per cent. It is to be noted that the efforts of the joint Arab economic sector have not resulted in any noticeable shift in the structure as created by the aggregate economic performance and exports of individual countries.

This assessment must not be understood to mean that the drive for industrialization has been a failure, even though Arab manufacturing industry still suffers from a number of defects, such as vacillation in policy, excess capacity, insufficiently efficient management, heavy bureaucracy and technological retardation. It means, rather, that there have been many stories of failure alongside some stories of success, and that several countries have suffered a relapse in their industrialization efforts for various reasons. These countries include Egypt, Iraq, Lebanon, Syria, Tunisia and Algeria, which represented the cases of the most notable industrial progress in the 1960s and a large part of the 1970s. The deeper reasons must be sought in two factors. The first is the insufficiency of the steps taken towards closer economic complementarity within the region, and therefore the non-realization of the potential of a notable widening in the regional market for Arab manufactures. The second reason can be found in the capitalist industrial countries which, at the point when Arab (and other Third World) industry began to expand and strike deep roots, and to acquire export-capability, started to impose a variety of restrictive measures on the entry of Third World manufactured goods.

Alongside protective and other restrictive policies by the developed world, the TNCs intensified their efforts to change the pattern of industrialization by energetically promoting the establishment of subsidiaries in Arab countries to produce final products under the TNCs' own trade marks, or intermediate products for use as inputs in their own production processes. In other words, the modest size of manufactured exports is in reality even more modest than it looks, once the production of the subsidiaries of the TNCs is segregated from that of truly national industry.

The picture is vastly different with respect to the composition of imports. Here we find for 1986 that the largest single group is that of machinery and equipment followed by manufactured goods (together accounting for 68.4 per cent), food products (15.3 per cent), petroleum products (8.2 per cent), chemical products (5.5 per cent) and raw materials (2.6 per cent). This pattern and the details behind it suggest some observations of relevance to the question of dependence and the prospects for self-reliance.

The first such observation is that the region still depends heavily on the advanced industrial countries for a wide variety of consumer goods as well as capital goods (apart from services, which are not included in the data being presented). The second is that, although the outlay on machinery and equipment imports, including means of transport and communication, is high, and has in fact risen over the past two or three decades, yet the region is still unjustifiably short of the productive capacity for a very wide range of products relating to manufacturing industry, transport, building, and public works and utilities. And this shortage exists alongside a very large potential regional market. Indeed, the outburst of building, public works, petrochemical, hotel, and other activities and industries since the early 1970s has in itself created a possible scope for industries to specialize in the production of capital goods for the very big new users just listed. Once again, the modesty of joint Arab economic action and of the complementarity achieved have limited the emergence of the necessary and feasible capital goods industries, which need a large market that individual countries could only rarely provide.

The third observation to make is that although the data as presented in aggregates do not distinguish between consumers' and capital goods sufficiently, the region receives substantial imports of the former category. These include luxury and near-luxury goods, and a wide range of gadgets not essential to everyday life or well-being. They are acquired at the expense of more essential and basic needs, or of capital goods to provide the region's countries with the capability for building a much larger productive capacity to produce consumers' goods that can provide greater utility to the general public.

Here again the expansion of the production base is inhibited through self-centred entrepreneurial and commercial impulses, and accommodating unduly permissive official policies. The most glaring instance of faulty policies in this respect is that of the importation of vast quantities of food products, estimated for 1987 to be $14 billion. (Earlier on in the 1980s, food imports had reached $23 billion.)

An imaginative and purposeful, regionally-orientated programme of agricultural development would remove the necessity for most of the imported food products in less than two decades, for an investment estimated to equal roughly two years' food imports. Even if these estimates proved over-accommodating to the argument, and the cost of the programme were distinctly larger, it would still be an eminently favourable and sound enterprise in terms of the long-term costs–returns calculus. Four countries out of a larger number with notable agricultural potential – namely, Morocco, Sudan, Syria and Iraq – can host a large part of the programme, and to a tangible extent reduce the degree of exposure of the region's food security.

It ought to be stated, however, that food production has achieved a clear rise in the 1980s, compared with the period 1965–79. Thus, according to the Food and Agricultural Organization's (FAO's) *Production Yearbook*, food production rose by more than population increase in all the fourteen countries which have an important cultivable land area, except South Yemen and Tunisia. Thus, with 1979–81 as base (= 100), the index for 1988 ranged between 120.7 for Algeria and 158.4 for Jordan; Saudi Arabia had an exceptional expansion, with its index for 1988 reaching 331.6. (However, World Bank statistics show a more modest increase in food production for the region as a whole.)[19] The drop in food imports between 1981 or 1982 and 1987 is attributable to two factors. These are the rise in food production over the years just indicated, and the drop in oil revenues. The latter forced the Arab countries to compress their food imports and restrict them to the more essential items.

There is no need to go any further into a description of the main features of the directions and composition of the region's foreign trade. But a number of observations can be made instead to conclude the sub-section. The first one is that the pattern of the directions and composition is fundamentally distorted, although on the surface both can be defended or at least explained. Thus, it seems understandable to have most of the exports go to the capitalist industrial countries, considering that they are large and intensive users of raw or partly processed materials and of crude oil. On the other hand, the logic of this pattern is itself a grave cause for concern, since the region should aim at speedier industrialization and the processing of raw or crude resources, and at the promotion of the marketability of its manufactured goods in general, and of petrochemical products in particular. Objections to the pattern relating to imports are at least equally serious. Here we need to go into some detail to specify the obnoxious aspects of this pattern.

One such aspect is the huge outlay on armaments, which have absorbed on average over $13 billion a year between 1972 and the end of 1987.[20] The importation of weapons systems is legitimate, in view of the region's need for the defence of its territory and the redress of grave injustices that have befallen Palestine and other parts. But there is warranted questioning about the seriousness of the justification given by Arab governments for the vast acquisition of arms. There is a wide discrepancy between the sophistication of the various arms systems, and the capability of the presumed users to understand, handle and maintain them. Furthermore, arms purchases are almost a bottomless drain, given the speed with which obsolescence sets in, and the persuasiveness of arms dealers and middlemen, and of arms manufacturers, who together prevail on the buyers to keep renewing their arsenals. The most serious objection is that the huge outlays involved are not justified in any concrete and substantial way in action in the field for which the arms were (presumably) bought in the first place. Thus, the means of defence are much more substantial than the will to defend Arab interests.

It should also be pointed out in connection with consumption goods that many of the markets of Arab countries are well-stocked with luxury and near-luxury goods, including many fancy gadgets, of varying styles and trademarks, which far outdistance the real needs of the consuming public. The addiction to consumerism, which began appearing in mild form in the 1950s and 1960s but intensified vastly during the oil boom, has been essentially promoted by widening contact with the West and Westerners, but more pointedly and deliberately by television programmes and marketing campaigns, and by other promotive efforts through various instrumentalities of the media.

This cultural conditioning is most serious in that it twists consumption habits, distorts the pattern of resource use, and leads to increased consumption in a region still in sharp need of larger savings and investments; and it strengthens the urge for emulation of consumption patterns characteristic of the upper-middle- and upper-income strata within the region, who in their turn emulate (and frequently outdistance) their counterparts in the industrial countries. Thus we witness the paradox of a wasteful pattern of conspicuous consumption in the region among the financially comfortable classes, superimposed on general income levels far below those in the industrial countries whose consumption pattern is being emulated.

To close this sub-section we need only draw attention to the fact that the production mix in the region is distorted, whether with respect to the production of goods and services in the agricultural or the manufacturing sector, in the hotel and resort industry or in housing, with the diversion of resources away from a number of the most essential to much less essential goods and services. In addition, many resources are left unutilized or very inadequately or irrationally utilized, particularly land and water. Others, like minerals and hydrocarbons, are exported in raw or crude state exccpt for a small proportion that is being processed to a point nearer to what the final user requires. Furthermore, the distortion of the production pattern is associated with the underutilization and underdevelopment of the real production potential of the region. All this enables us finally to say that the directions and composition of the region's foreign trade, as they stand today, are far from serving as an adequate and convincing criterion of the region's capability to pursue self-reliant development.

The resource and performance base[21]

This base is obviously of great significance and relevance for the growth and development of any economy.

> The natural resources available themselves promote or inhibit the diversification and productive performance of the economy – depending on their abundance, value, accessibility, and marketability. However, the resource base is not something fixed and final, or in itself independent. It is, instead, a function of the capital and technology available to the country, the studies and surveys undertaken to determine the quantity and quality of the resources, the markets accessible to them, the country's capability to process them, and the general management of the resources, and the seriousness in the efforts to develop them.

The region is only moderately endowed with natural underground resources of significant and direct value for large-scale development – apart from hydrocarbons which constitute a major resource by world standards, and phosphates further down in the scale of significance. Looked at individually,

> Arab countries vary widely with respect to their resource base. In some instances, as in Lebanon, this is mainly restricted to land, water, beautiful scenery, and a climate suitable to varied agricultural production and tourist activities. At the other extreme, as in Iraq, the resource base includes, in addition to abundant land and water and beautiful scenery in parts of the country, rich reserves of petroleum, gas, sulphur, and phosphates, as well as a few other minerals. Until petroleum was discovered and exploited commercially, the desert parts of the Arab world, particularly in the Arabian Peninsula and Libya, were considered very poorly endowed. Petroleum has revolutionized the endowment configuration. In general, it can be said that each of the Arab countries has some natural resource that is commercially exploitable, or otherwise usable for the production of some important marketable product. This is true of oil and gas where they abound, as of land or water [as in Morocco, Algeria, Tunisia, Sudan, Egypt, Lebanon, Syria or Iraq, or of the phosphates in Morocco, Tunisia, Jordan, Iraq and Syria, and the iron ore of Egypt and Mauritania] apart from the scenery and climate of several of the countries which enable them to market important tourist services.

However, even for the major oil-producing countries, the significance of the oil resources calls for a telling qualification.

> This is that until 1973 this resource formed a *financial* base for development – and even then a modest one – by providing the revenues capable of being translated into capital goods, education programmes, and other investment-related outlays. Only very recently did oil begin to become a 'leading sector' in the fuller sense of the term, activating other sectors and promoting industries and activities upstream and downstream through integration or the operation of backward and forward linkages. The non-oil resources, even the more important among them, have served neither function to a considerable extent; that is, they have neither provided a large volume of financial resources, nor provided the impetus for the accelerated development of the rest of the economy . . .
>
> [It must be borne in mind that] the impact of the resources on

growth and development is closely and causally tied to the quality and determination of the political management of the economy. Thus, even in the case of oil, it was only in the late sixties and early seventies that the Arab governments decided to insist on a more satisfactory return for their oil exports. It is true that the energy situation in the world then helped them in their decision, but their determination was a necessary condition for the improvement in their relative position *vis-à-vis* the oil companies and the large consumers.

Yet determination – though very relevant and important – is not enough by itself.

In addition, there is the factor of the organization of the industry concerned. Thus, such matters as the speed and efficiency of the exploitation of the natural resources available, their processing and marketing, and the bargaining capability of the agency in control – all these factors influence the extent to which the resources generate income for the country. In this respect, the Arab countries have registered some significant steps towards efficient and effective organization, administration, control, and operation. The bureaux or authorities that control the phosphates mines in Morocco, Tunisia, Jordon or Syria; the national oil ministries and/or companies in the oil-producing countries (but with varying degrees of success); the cotton boards of Egypt, Sudan, and Syria; the Suez Canal Authority in Egypt – all are manifestations of the realization of the role of the controlling agencies and the relevance of these agencies to the optimization of the exploitation of resources.

[It is to be noted, finally, that] the optimal exploitation (and by this we mean not just the mining or extraction of the resource, but also its processing, industrialization, marketing and distribution), to a certain extent depends on the performance base of the economy. This relates to the efficiency of manpower and of institutions, to their problem-solving capabilities, and in the final analysis to the level of national product per capita and the proportion of it used for investment purposes. The relationship between the resource base and the performance base is of great significance. A satisfactory performance base can go far in compensating for a feeble resource base.

The land and water resources, on the other hand, are still far from being a major, active factor in development. The deficitary foodstuff situation proves this amply, in spite of the rise in food production and the drop in the value of food imports between 1979 and 1987 – as already indicated. The agrarian reform measures undertaken in a number of Arab countries, like Egypt, Syria, Iraq, Algeria and Libya, have on the whole fallen far short of expectations and claims, for reasons related to insufficient institutional preparation, weak motivation, slowness in redistribution of expropriated land, excessively heavy bureaucracy, and other weaknesses in the whole concept and application of agrarian reform.

Land use data in the relevant issues of the *Production Yearbook* published by the United Nations Food and Agriculture Organization, FAO, and in official country statistics, show that cultivable land is no more than some 8 per cent of total land area in the region. Even allowing for methodological and definitional difficulties which confront a correct assessment of what is really 'cultivable', there is relatively very little land good for rewarding cultivation for the region's population (given capital and technology available), and what there is, is very unevenly distributed among countries. Furthermore, the total irrigated area hovers around 10–11 per cent of estimated cultivable land.[22] As a result of all this, both total agricultural production and food production have begun to catch up with net population increase only over the past decade, as indicated earlier, and even so not for all the countries of the region.

The smallness of the area under irrigation is, however,

> no true guide to the availability of water in the region. Rainfall on the whole is adequate only in small scattered parts of the region and is, furthermore, seasonal and undependable. Rivers are limited in number and concentrated mainly in Iraq, Sudan, Egypt, and Syria (with smaller rivers in Lebanon, Jordan, and Morocco). There is, moreover, a general inefficiency in the harnessing and use of water resources. Considerable waste is prevalent not only in the failure to catch the waters of torrential rains, or to utilize all river and wadi water, but also in the failure to make proper use of the water that is harnessed for irrigation and for industrial and household purposes.
>
> (Sayigh 1982: 20)

A well-known Arab authority stated in 1979: 'The volume of water used for irrigation purposes in ECWA countries [that is, Egypt and the Asian Arab countries] is estimated at 80–90 billion m^3' (Elgabaly n.d.). To all this we can add that 'the investments and efforts put into the expansion of irrigation dams and networks are to a considerable extent neutralized through the failure to provide parallel facilities for drainage. The imbalance has proved both costly and damaging in all cases' (Sayigh 1982: 20).

To conclude, the picture of the resource endowment of the Arab region with respect to underground minerals, including hydrocarbons, and to land and water, leads to a varied assessment with respect to the adequacy of this criterion for demonstrating the feasibility of Arab self-reliant development. It is probably warranted to say that the exploitation of underground resources has been more effective than that of land and water, but with one qualification. This is that the ores, minerals and oil and gas extracted are still on the whole exported in crude or partly processed form. But within this limitation, the current management of these resources is more creditable than that of land and water in all but a few exceptional cases (notably that of Egypt), even though such management with respect to land and water is more crucial for the very survival of the region's people.

> If we were to end with one sentence, we would say that the resources available constitute opportunities for development, which meet with serious constraints on the one side, and with efforts to overcome or loosen the constraints on the other side. The outcome determines how effective resources are as a factor in development.
> (Sayigh 1987b: 48)

The availability of appropriate technology and manpower skills

There is no doubt that the Arab region as a whole has acquired notable technological capability since the Second World War (expressed in the expanded availability of capital goods and equipment capable of use in improved productive performance; in manpower skills obtained through education, vocational and technical training; and in experience accumulated through participation in the growing economies). The advances made in education in all three cycles, and in the various fields of knowledge, are evident. Likewise, several countries – such as Egypt, Lebanon, Iraq, Jordan, Algeria, Tunisia – have moved to erect a science and technology base which is of promising value for a modernizing economy, and is capable of upgrading the forces of production. Coupled with these developments, one can observe greater and wider acceptance of technological change. The overall result of these factors has been improvement in the performance base of virtually all the region's economies, even if at widely different rates.

But the statements just made are tenable only when the achievements are measured against the situation at the start of the post-war period. When measured against the expectations of the early days of political independence, or against the vast outlays directed to the advancement of education, or yet against the achievements of such NICs as Brazil, Argentina, Mexico, South Korea, Taiwan or Singapore, they reveal a wide gap. This gap can be identified in quantitative as well as qualitative definiencies, in the adoption of insufficiently perceptive policies and outlooks, in excessive permissiveness towards technological dependence on the industrial world, and in the failure to mobilize and effectively utilize the resources available, whether in technological hardware or software.

More careful scrutiny shows that

> The Arab region faces a dual issue here: the failure to establish sufficient technological capability to meet its needs, and the adoption of the wrong policies in the attempt to correct this failure. The first aspect concerns not only the absolute shortage, but also the under-utilization of the region's capability. The second is associated with the drive for the 'transfer of technology', which has been thought by some to be the answer.
>
> (Sayigh 1982: 146)

Much has been written about the transfer of technology. In practice, this transfer has come to be largely understood in the region not as the acquisition and implantation of appropriate technological capability, but

> as the purchase of modern capital goods (machines, tools, equipment), and the 'purchase' of the services of foreign technicians and experts. Nothing could be further from a genuine implantation of technology than such a course. In fact, this course makes the 'transfer' harder to effect. What looks like a longer course of action, namely, the development of science, research, experimentation, and technical training, is in effect the *true* short-cut to technological capability. Furthermore, although such development may seem costly, in fact its cost represents fruitful investment. On the other hand, continued dependence on the importation of foreign machines and skills is a much costlier course, and one which does not promise independence. As far as cost is concerned, it has been estimated that the Arab region had been paying about $5 billion a year over the last few years of the 1970s and the onset of the 1980s, for the purchase of technological software alone, namely, skills, patents, managerial and training assistance, and design and consultancy services. In

addition, billions of dollars leak outside the region annually for the purchase of certain simple machines, tools, and equipment that could be produced by Arab industry right away or with minor preparation.

(Sayigh 1982: 165)[23]

This quotation is based on a study published in 1982, but is still relevant and fitting to present reality. What is yet more serious with regard to the assessment of the adequacy of the criterion under examination for the feasibility of Arab self-reliant development is that on the whole neither the perception and outlook, nor the policies for the acquisition of appropriate effective technological capability, have altered at the level of individual countries or of joint Arab action. Indeed, the developments that characterized the late 1980s suggest a relapse in the efforts to undertake corrective action both at the national and regional levels, in spite of some recent works that probe the nature of the problem penetratingly.[24] There is today definitely less enthusiasm than in the 1970s for joint action, smaller intraregional financial flows and movement of skilled manpower, and a manifest tendency to trim the activities of regional organizations and activities already in existence and institutionalized. This is all part of a growing 'country isolationism' (as against a sense of regional or pan-Arab identity), and of a willingness to accept a heavier dependence on the capitalist industrial countries and their TNCs, to which we have already referred.

A fair and realistic stock-taking of the situation with regard to the availability within the region of technological capability appropriate for the needs of development leads to a paradoxical conclusion. This is that the resource in question is relatively abundant, but that it is insufficiently and sub-optimally utilized, and therefore remains a potential yet to be put into proper use. Consequently, the criterion under consideration can become adequate at least for the present state of development, if not for a more determined drive, once the management of the resource becomes more rational and purposeful, and once this management at the regional and individual country's level is woven together with imagination and seriousness.

Obviously, this will call for a great deal of thinking and planning, since the different countries have disparate levels of technological capability and manpower skills, and do not seem sufficiently to realize the potential benefits to themselves from regional co-operation and management – judging by their narrow focus. Thus, a co-ordinated effort to raise the overall level will have to appeal also to the countries that are technologically ahead, so that they will not fear that co-operation and complementarity will mean freezing their progress while the handicapped countries try to catch up with them. On the other hand, the latter group of countries have to rid themselves of the suspicion that co-operation and complementarity will in effect make them susceptible to being exploited by those ahead of them, or at least will make them fear the freezing of the technology and skill gap, if not its widening through the dynamics of growth of the more advanced group.

What is essential in this kind of situation is for the region's countries to conceive of the appropriate path of technological progress which will enable them to build the capability that will match the needs and interests, as well as the resource endowments, of Arab society and economy, seen within a context of self-reliant development. This path can optimally consist of two lanes: individual country policies and action, and regional policies and action in intelligent co-ordination and purposefulness.

However, it must have become obvious from earlier comments in this sub-section that with few exceptions the leaderships in the region (economic, intellectual, syndical, but especially political) do not include the mapping of such a course of action within their pressing concerns. While there is greater (though still modest) concern with technological capability at the individual country's level, there is marked dilution of such concern by the leaderships of the individual countries in their deliberations and behaviour in a regional context, within regional summits, ministerial councils, organizations and institutions. Indeed, the strategy for Join Arab Economic Action, which was approved at the 11th Arab Summit, held in Jordan in 1980, allotted considerable attention to the imperativeness of joint Arab action to promote the region's technological capability. But eloquent statements and documents do not add up to plans of action, and plans of action without the will to act do not get translated into policies, concrete programmes, and implementation means and machinery. This trite wisdom has been manifestly proven fitting in the Arab experience since the early 1980s, and even in the 1970s, which were characterized both by a stronger sense of Arab community and brighter expectations for the region.

The availability of a sizeable entrepreneurial capability

The entrepreneur is given a place of honour as one of the factors of production in conventional economics. The textbook-entrepreneur, to whom Schumpeter gave pre-eminence in his classic work on development (1949: chs 2 and 4), belongs to the private sector. The entrepreneur and the manager, as a closely integrated team, have been singled out at one time as a most crucial factor for development during the post-Second World War period, when one factor or another, like technology, capital availability, or manpower were highlighted by economists writing on development. But there is less frequent mention of the entrepreneur now in writings emanating from Third World countries, probably because of the great emphasis on the role of the public sector in economic life and the expansion of this role within the scope of the drive for development, at the expense of that of the private sector.

We need not examine the 'entrepreneurial function' at any length, as it is a matter of common knowledge by now. But, in brief, this function

> is essentially understood to include innovation or adaptation, and the building of the appropriate organization capable of translating the innovation (or adaptation) into an operative, efficient economic unit. Basically, the entrepreneur perceives new opportunities, and in building establishments embodying these opportunities he expands the economy and introduces new products, techniques, or organizations, or discovers new markets. Once the societal setting in which he operates undergoes some important changes in technological, social (including demographic) and political institutions and ideas, and economic growth is registered, development is said to have been set afoot.
>
> (Sayigh 1978b: 68; also Schumpeter 1949: ch. 2)

If this is accepted as a generally agreed definition of the entrepreneurial function, then the public sector as an agent of development qualifies as an entrepreneur, or as discharging the entrepreneurial function.

Yet the differentiation must be realized between the leading motives of a private entrepreneur and his counterpart in the public sector. While both are sensitive to what David McClelland (1961: ch. 2) calls the 'need-for-achievement' motive, the private entrepreneur is more sensitive to the profit motive (in one of its variations) than the public entrepreneur who is normally more interested in physical targets of production, or in whatever criteria of success the authorities above him set for him to be guided by. But whatever the motive or motives that spur the entrepreneur to action (and there is usually a set or mix of motives in operation), he is a central part of the forces of production and the process of improvement in productive capacity, if he has the appropriate qualities of imagination, dynamism, motivation, and the propensity to bring about change in the economic profile. As an entrepreneur who has these qualities is likely to utilize all inputs necessary for achieving his goals, he will be favourably inclined towards research and the application of science, and therefore towards rationality, even though much of the literature highlights the flamboyant type who goes by his hunches and fits of inspiration! But whatever influences him most, he is certainly a crucial part of the motive force of the economic aspects of development.

It is appropriate at this point to address the questions: how well is the Arab region endowed with entrepreneurial resources? Where is the locus of entrepreneurial talent?

> A great deal has been said about the groups or communities that from time to time, and between one country and another, have shown or show particular entrepreneurial talent. Minority groups have often been said to be especially endowed with this talent; a qualification of this assertion has been that 'deviant' groups are so endowed. At the root of such assertions is the belief that such minority or deviant groups are usually not sensitive to the inhibiting cultural factors to which the majority is exposed.
>
> (Sayigh 1978b: 69)

While this may have been applicable to the early post-war period, it is much less so today, as the base of entrepreneurial talent has widened across the 'frontiers' of ethnic or social groups, and the threshold of the sensitivity to motivation and economic incentives has risen noticeably.

The situation in the Arab region with respect to the adequacy of the entrepreneurial resource varies considerably from one country to another. Until the civil war shook Lebanon in the mid-1970s, this was the country with the most dynamic and frontier-widening entrepreneurial talent in the region. Three other countries could point to their own impressive entrepreneurial resource: Egypt, Syria and, to a lesser extent, Jordan.

> While many [Moslem Arab] Egyptians displayed such activity, it is also true that in an important measure minority groups excelled in this field. . . . In Syria, the resource was mainly Syrian Arab, though some minority groups (originally immigrant) were active in the northern city of Aleppo and in the vast virgin plains of northeast Syria. In Jordan, the active resource was predominantly Palestinian,

and to a lesser extent Syrian. Nowhere else was entrepreneurial activity very substantial, or was the resource abundant, with the exception of the Maghreb countries. But then this resource was European – mainly French in Morocco, Algeria and Tunisia, and Italian in Libya.

(Sayigh 1978b: 70)

The picture as it can be seen today is substantially different in three aspects from the way it looked in the 1970s. The first is that the public entrepreneur has become much more evident and active than in the early post-war decades. Second, the minority groups, especially in Egypt and Syria, have become much less important as an entrepreneurial resource. Many feel inhibited or have opted for emigration. And third, in some of the countries which are not named in the preceding paragraph because of the modesty of the size of this resource (as in Saudi Arabia and Kuwait), national entrepreneurship has emerged and is playing a visible and active role which is of potential developmental significance. Yet it is necessary to add that some entrepreneurial inflows have enriched the national entrepreneurial endowments of the region's countries. Thus, in many instances, entrepreneurial drive has been activated or promoted through association with foreign enterprise, mostly TNCs setting up subsidiary business jointly with Arab nationals.

While the TNCs as a source of entrepreneurial promotion are not conducive to self-reliant development but rather to its opposite, another source is commendable because it is Arab. This is entrepreneurship moving into many Arab countries from other countries within the Arab region, through the avenue of the joint Arab economic sector, and the instrumentality of the establishment of the hundreds of joint projects and companies now in existence in the region.[25] This source is not national but regional, and is neither fully private nor fully public entrepreneurship within the strict definition of these two alternatives. It is some form of collective entrepreneurship nurtured and promoted through the regional controlling or planning agencies that have emerged since the establishment of the League of Arab States, but especially since the 1960s. And though the overall influence of this source of entrepreneurship on the course of development is very limited still, it has great potential and can play a significant function as an input in collective self-reliant development.

Finally, another category of entrepreneurship deserves mention because of its special features and its growing popularity. This is mixed public–private entrepreneurship, whose advocates claim for it special advantages. Thus it is believed to permit the public sector to be sensitive to the strong points of the private sector and able to avoid some of its weaknesses. Likewise, it is believed to make the private partner more concerned with considerations that motivate the public partner, and less ego-centred about its own motivation.

Our overall assessment of the adequacy of the criterion under consideration as a promoter of the feasibility of self-reliant development is that there is an acceptable degree of adequacy. However, there are four conditions that have to be additionally satisfied for this criterion to be satisfactorily met. The first is that public entrepreneurship should become more tangibly sensitized to notions of efficiency and the principles and guidelines of cost–return and market considerations, and freer to operate in line with these notions and considerations.

The second condition is that private entrepreneurship should show a larger measure of social awareness. This would be expressed in concern for the support of institutions and activites which render services to the public, like research foundations (whether in science, in medicine, or the arts), humanitarian causes which improve the quality of life and the climate of work and social relations, or syndical life which would promote the improvement of management–labour relations and thereby lead to smoother economic performance. But for all this to be reasonable to ask of the private entrepreneur, the public authority will have to allot a reasonable place for the private sector in economic life, in order to have a legitimate expectation of co-operation by private enterprise and a concrete contribution from it to development.

The third condition is that the fields or sectors of activity of the entrepreneur – whether private or public – must be directly developmental in orientation and impact. This would disqualify some lines of trade, the activities of non-essential middlemen, certain services associated with catering and entertainment – to name only a few. On the other hand, the condition being discussed would work in favour of agriculture, manufacturing industry, development finance, transport, tourism, construction, and such professional services as relate to research, computer programming and operation, design and other consultancy services, and so on. If these three conditions are satisfied, then the final assessment will be that the entrepreneurial resource in the Arab region at large can without much difficulty or delay play an important role in the generation of self-reliant development, once there are cross-country flows to permit a more balanced allocation of the resources. Finally, the fourth condition is political stability and the rule of law and order in society.

The availability of resources for domestic fixed capital formation and accumulation

What is vital for capital accumulation is not financial resources in terms of the national currency. These can be created by the monetary and fiscal authorities, and may have only a very limited effect on capital accumulation and fixed capital formation in terms of real goods – that is, the creation or acquisition of machinery, tools, equipment, and constructions associated with productive capacity. Financial resources can serve to this end only to the extent that they can become a medium in the generation of national product, part of which would then be used for fixed investment, and/or for the acquisition of foreign exchange resources which in turn can be used for the importation of capital goods. Consequently the enquiry in the present sub-section will address the extent of the availability of the gross domestic product (GDP) or the gross national product (GNP) – as the case may be – part of which is devoted to capital formation. The excess of imports over exports (that is, the import surplus) also contributes to capital formation to the extent that it consists of capital goods for investment. Together with GDP, the import surplus constitutes total resources available (TRA). In the final analysis, it is TRA which determines how much capital formation is possible, within the total allocation or use of resources.

The region's aggregate net trade balance for goods and services combined for 1987 was a deficit of $23,346.3 million for the twenty-one Arab countries (see Table 2). It is worth noting that every country within the group labelled Group 2 in the source – eight non-oil-exporting countries, plus Syria, Egypt and Tunisia, which are modest oil-exporters – had a deficit in its trade account in 1987. (The deficit aggregated for the eleven countries was $13,079.7 million.) Indeed, four major oil-exporting countries in Group 1 also had a deficit in their trade account; the remaining five – United Arab Emirates, Bahrain, Oman, Qatar and Kuwait had a surplus. But this surplus was not large enough in the aggregate to make up for the combined deficit of the four other countries in the group. Thus, together the nine countries in Group 1 had a deficit of $10,266.6 million. Hence the deficit on trade account, or the import surplus, for the whole region of $23.3 billion referred to earlier. Consequently, TRA for the region was $408.8 billion in 1987 (GDP of $385.5 billion plus import surplus of $23.3 billion). The import surplus constituted 6 per cent of GDP for 1987, or 5.7 per cent of TRA. It represents a small but not negligible proportion of GDP and TRA.

Table 2 Expenditure on gross domestic product, 1987, at current prices ($ million)

Country and grouping	*Population 1987 ('000)*	*Private consumption*	*Public consumption*	*Total consumption*	*Investment*	*Exports of goods and services*	*Imports of goods and services*	*GDP at market prices*	*GDP per capita ($)*
Total	202,151	192,680.8	84,355.0	315,754.4	93,130.1	105,874.5	129,220.8	385,534.5	11,907.2
Group 1	63,048	102,396.5	64,434.0	205,549.1	69,732.5	84,922.0	95,188.7	265,011.3	4,203.3
United Arab Emirates	1,432	8,962.5	5,188.9	14,151.5	5,855.0	12,750.2	9,588.5	23,168.2	16,178.9
Bahrain	453	1,516.0	779.3	2,295.2	922.9	3,245.7	2,649.0	3,814.9	8,421.4
Algeria	23,329	34,176.8	11,291.5	45,468.3	21,628.3	11,040.4	13,742.2	64,394.8	2,760.3
Saudi Arabia	13,841	30,557.5	29,535.4	60,092.9	16,690.3	25,820.8	32,460.3	70,140.0	5,067.6
Iraq	16,653	...	...	38,718.6	11,580.8	10,873.1	14,086.8	47,085.8	2,827.5
Oman	1,353	2,967.5	2,236.7	5,204.2	2,197.7	3,474.7	3,152.2	7,724.4	5,709.1
Qatar	381	1,592.4	2,303.9	3,896.3	1,069.7	2,159.4	1,904.5	5,220.9	13,703.1
Kuwait	1,874	9,350.9	5,309.0	14,659.9	3,661.4	9,257.6	8,740.7	18,838.2	10,052.4
Libya	3,732	13,272.8	7,789.3	21,062.1	6,126.5	6,300.1	8,864.5	24,624.1	6,598.1

Group 2	139,103	90,284.3	19,921.0	110,205.4	23,397.6	20,952.4	34,032.1	120,523.3	866.4
Jordan	3,775	3,666.6	1,384.6	5,051.2	1,154.3	2,175.8	3,327.1	5,054.2	1,338.9
Tunisia	7,748	6,369.0	1,556.6	7,925.6	2,256.6	2,980.5	3,596.0	9,566.8	1,234.7
Djibouti	384	532.0	169.6	701.6	204.9	28.0	115.0	819.5	2,134.1
Sudan	22,828	5,833.3	1,333.5	7,166.8	1,137.9	782.3	1,493.5	7,593.5	332.6
Syria	10,969	6,867.8	1,942.4	8,810.2	2,165.1	1,046.9	1,746.4	10,275.9	936.8
Somalia	4,878	1,324.0	171.3	1,495.3	359.1	103.6	418.0	1,540.0	315.7
Lebanon	2,731	408.2	163.8	572.0	36.0	263.3	792.5	78.8	28.8
Egypt	50,742	48,943.8	9,043.0	57,986.9	11,643.1	8,900.2	15,600.3	62,929.8	1,240.2
Morocco	23,356	11,643.9	3,032.5	14,676.4	3,246.5	3,918.2	4,977.5	16,863.6	722.0
Mauritania	2,012	655.3	124.9	780.2	193.7	496.5	566.9	903.5	449.1
North Yemen	7,248	3,360.1	541.3	3,901.5	707.8	167.4	901.0	3,875.7	534.7
South Yemen	2,432	680.4	457.4	1,137.8	292.4	89.8	498.0	1,022.0	420.2

Sources: Population column from Table 2/5; data on GDP per capita calculated from total GDP and population data shown in table above. The rest of the table is reproduced from Table 2/1 in *Unified Arab Economic Report, 1988*, Statistical Appendices. The notes below are my own.

Notes: Until 1987, the grouping of the Arab countries was different. The five groups were constituted as follows:

1 United Arab Emirates (UAE), Bahrain, Saudi Arabia, Oman, Qatar and Kuwait;
2 Algeria, Iraq and Libya;
3 Tunisia, Syria and Egypt;
4 Jordan, Lebanon and Morocco; and
5 Djibouti, Sudan, Somalia, Mauritania, North Yemen and South Yemen.

Information for Lebanon is highly speculative. The extremely small GDP is not possible to justify. Factor payments from abroad are known to be considerable, and the GNP would reflect the inflow. Nevertheless, GDP itself cannot be justified as it appears in the table above.

As Table 2 shows, capital formation or gross fixed investment absorbed $93.1 billion. Thus it constituted 24.1 per cent of the region's GDP, or 22.8 per cent of TRA. These proportions are distinctly smaller than they were on the whole during the years of the oil decade 1973–82, that is, before the crisis in the oil sector had set in. Nevertheless, the proportion of GDP going into investment is still somewhat high compared with that in most Third World countries. It places the countries of the Arab region together at the top of the group considered by the World Bank to have occupied a medium position with respect to the proportion of its GDP allocated to gross investment in 1987. (The proportion was 28.6 per cent for the group of 'high' investors, or 26.7 per cent if China is excluded, and 19.0 per cent for the 'low' investors. The 'medium' investors among whom the Arab group fits had a proportion of 22.6 per cent (World Bank 1989: 27).)

The picture is not as rosy as it looks in its broad, regional contours, if scrutinized at the individual country level, or at the level of country groupings. This can be seen from Table 3 which shows the relative size of investment, compared with GDP, country by country and grouping by grouping. (The grouping applied in Table 3 is the one that used to be applied in *The Unified Report* until 1987, not that applied in Table 2 which has been taken from *The Unified Report 1988*. We feel that the former is better justified and more conducive to useful analyis.)

The data in Table 3 show considerable differentiation, both among country groups and within them. Many factors are at work to bring about such differentiation, but they are not very relevant to our regional approach, although of course they influence intraregional capital flows and therefore the adequacy of the criterion of capital availability and accumulation for the assessment of the feasibility of self-reliant development. But one point needs to be made, and it is that the fact that two countries fall within the same group does not mean that they have the same thirst for investment, or that they can absorb the same amount of capital per capita in sound and fruitful investment, or yet that they have the same access to investible resources to place them alongside the more heavily investing countries within the group, were they to have the same thirst for productive investment.

Two general observations can be derived from the country profiles. The first is that the relatively high ratio of capital formation to GDP for the region as a whole is misleading, since the spread among countries is wide. This means that certain countries like Kuwait, Egypt, Morocco, Sudan and North Yemen (all with a ratio below 20 per cent) cannot fit into the same explanation. No one explanation

Table 3 Investment in 1987 as a proportion of gross domestic product

Group and country	*Percentage of GDP*
Group 1	23.6
United Arab Emirates	29.6
Bahrain	24.2
Saudi Arabia	23.4
Oman	28.4
Qatar	20.5
Kuwait	19.4
Group 2	28.9
Algeria	33.6
Iraq	24.4
Libya	24.9
Group 3	19.4
Tunisia	23.6
Syria	21.1
Egypt	18.5
Group 4	20.2
Jordan	22.8
Lebanon	45.7
Morocco	19.2
Group 5	18.4
Djibouti	25.0
Sudan	15.0
Somalia	23.3
Mauritania	21.4
North Yemen	18.3
South Yemen	28.6
Whole region	24.1

Source: Calculated from Table 2

Note: Data for Lebanon are highly speculative, and have to be understood in the context of the serious political and security crisis from which the country has suffered since the spring of 1975. Furthermore, the GDP seems to be grossly underestimated, even though the economy has been functioning at a very low level. Hence the very high proportion of investment to GDP.

of the reasons for high or low ratios can fit the countries with one or the other relative levels of investment. Thus, Kuwait has no shortage of financial resources translatable into real investment; what is short is rewarding investment opportunities. The case of Egypt is altogether the reverse, with a serious shortage of resources, but immense opportunities. Sudan can be placed in the same category as Egypt with respect to resources and opportunities, but in addition suffers from a serious failing in political stability, efficiency in public administration, skilled manpower, and development policy in general. And so on.

The second general observation to make is that the ratio of investment to GDP for the region as a whole disguises the fact that there are a number of capital-short countries, at the same time as there are some capital-surplus countries, although the oil crisis has caused the members of the latter group to draw heavily on their reserves held abroad since 1983. (Budget deficits for the years 1983–7 have been estimated by a well-informed economist in the Gulf region to aggregate about $70 billion for the countries of the Gulf Cooperation Council (see al-Kawari 1989).) Furthermore, it ought to be pointed out that while the grouping system suggests the sharing of economic characteristics, this is true only in part, not absolutely. Thus, the LDCs in Group 5 include North Yemen whose oil resources have already begun to reduce its past balance of payments hardship. On the other hand, Egypt, though placed in Group 3, suffers from serious balance of payments strains. And Iraq, though a major oil producer and exporter, is heavily in debt and will remain so for many years to come owing to the demands of its war with Iran between 1980 and 1988. Algeria, another important oil exporter, also has a serious foreign debt problem.

However, in spite of the drop in the accumulated reserves of the major oil-exporting countries, they can still contribute handsomely to the development efforts of the less-endowed countries in terms of financial resources. Such contribution would narrow the present wide gap between the two groups of countries, to the extent that the gap is attributable to resource shortages. Understandably, the drop in oil revenues over much of the decade of the 1980s will be brought up by the donor countries and by some analysts as explanation and justification why a larger outflow in aid from the donors cannot be undertaken – indeed that a considerable shrinkage in the present outflow is inevitable.

Without arguing this point at length, since it is warranted to a certain degree, it is sufficient for present purposes only to indicate that the current financial stringency cannot be wholly attributed to the drop in oil revenues. To a considerable extent it is also the product of ill-conceived development plans, excessive consumerism, and permissiveness in spending during the oil boom era. These additional causes of the stringency should be an incentive for a rationalization of public and private spending, and for a much closer scrutiny of arms purchasing policies. Indeed, the incentive has been influential in bringing about a change in attitude with regard to private and public spending, although the conceptualization and pursuit of development have not yet received what they deserve in re-examination and correction.

It is of direct relevance to our enquiry to address the question of the sources from which capital formation is financed. Examination of this question by the present author for the years 1950–70 has revealed that just before the oil boom era, some 85 per cent of capital formation was financed from national sources, that is, by the national GDPs of the countries concerned. Obviously, this is an average, and it hides wide varation in the proportion from one country to another. The balance was provided by international (non-Arab) sources, largely the OECD countries, plus the World Bank and lastly the socialist countries. During the 1970s and early 1980s, much of the balance of 15 per cent – probably no less than 8 per cent – was financed by Arab donor countries, directly from governments, from private investors, or from Arab development funds.[26]

Today, with the oil crisis weighing heavily on the economies of the donor countries, with economic aid from the socialist countries at a low level, and with OECD aid not expanding enough to make up for the shrinkage in the aid from Arab oil-exporting countries, a larger share than before of capital formation depends on individual-country resources – perhaps as much as 90 per cent. The balance is shared by OECD countries and the World Bank, on the one hand (a little over two-thirds), and the Arab donor countries and their development funds (about one-third),[27] on the other. Even if these estimates err somewhat on the side of overestimation of the self-financing of capital formation, they remain valid as an indication of a large measure of national and collective (regional) self-reliant capital accumulation.

However, the largely quantitative findings and/or estimates of the previous paragraphs, and the conclusion that flows from them, are insufficient to suggest the true extent of the region's ability to meet the criterion under consideration. They have to be qualified by a few observations of a qualitative nature. Four of these will be stressed, though briefly. The first is that capital availability is insufficient in itself as an indicator of the feasibility of self-reliant development, other things being equal. It has to be supplemented by other supportive factors that are promotive of productive investment. These include government, manpower, business behaviour, seriousness of purpose, technological change, and so on. Furthermore, the directions of the investment have to be conducive to meaningful development.

In the second place, the outflow from the region, mostly to Western industrial countries, of a large volume of financial resources – a volume which reached a cumulative peak of $374 billion by the end of 1982, as already indicated – seriously diminishes the potential favourable impact of capital availability. This is because a substantial part of the outflow could be invested within the region in the service of development, instead of leaking out to be put into use in already capital-abundant Western countries. Furthermore, instead of acquiring political and economic leverage in their dealings with the West thanks to their huge reserves there, the Arabs have become hostages (they and their reserves alike) to the Western countries. The very rationale and wisdom of the permissive oil production policy adopted in the boom era by OPEC, and particularly by its Arab members, can at least be questioned if not outright condemned. But we need not argue the point as this would take us away from the line of analysis we are pursuing. What is essential to emphasize now is that it is in the long-term interest of the individual countries which own the reserves placed abroad, as it is in the region's interest as a whole, for a large part of the resources to be repatriated and invested in the region, thus adding tangibly to its capital accumulation.

The third observation to make is that self-reliant development in the Arab region requires the existence of a significant and active public sector to own and operate a substantial part of the capital accumulation available to the individual countries and to the region as a whole. It would be largely the joint Arab economic sector, in its capacity as a regional (or collective) public sector, that would own and operate the part of the capital accumulation available to the region. The quality and content of the development advocated within the context of self-reliance (as characterized in the first chapter of the book) justify insistence on the existence of an important, dynamic public sector. But, in addition, it should be recalled that the region's foreign reserves are essentially oil-export revenues. As the oil resource is public property, the disposal of its revenues will naturally be within the jurisdiction of public authorities.

The fourth and last observation is that a far-sighted policy for the utilization of the capital available, and its addition to the capital accumulation of the region, in a manner which is orientated towards the safeguarding and expansion of the economic independence of the region, would move away from the practice adopted by a number of Arab countries to invite and encourage the entry of TNCs as partners in new industrial, financial or touristic enterprises or undertakings. The justification given for this practice is that it enables the host country concerned to acquire expertise at all stages in the establishment and operation of the industries or activities concerned. This expertise – it is claimed – involves planning, design, construction, operation, marketing and every other technological, administrative, economic or accounting aspect.

Apart from the meagreness of the training and expertise imparted by the TNC partners to their national counterparts, since the latter are often kept distant from the really meaningful decisions, and in fact lose the essence of independent decision-making, the TNCs see to it that it is their own interests that determine the technology chosen, the design adopted, the scale decided upon, the markets targeted, and all other matters that form the substance of the decisions involved. Rather than shortening the period of the 'acquisition of technological and administrative capability' by the national partner, the relationship in effect lengthens it. Other formulas can be adopted for such acquisition, like clearly defined service contracts. And, above all, it is not in the interest of the host country to see a cumulatively vast outflow of foreign exchange over the years of the partnership, to reduce the country's volume of capital accumulation and, against that, add to the opulence and strength of already powerful TNCs. Nothing could be further from a true pursuit of self-reliant development than the policies currently pursued.

The availability of development-orientated leaderships

This last criterion of adequacy to examine is more demanding than its shortened title suggests. A fuller specification would contain insistence on the availability of a determined and enlightened development-orientated leadership, not only in the political sphere, but also in the education sector, the business community, the labour movement, the intellectual circles, and the media. It would also indicate that the existence of such a leadership must necessarily be predicated upon the enjoyment by the people of a wide measure of political participation and basic human rights, for them to be able to express their preferences among political and economic choices. Such a 'leadership network' or resource would, if available, ensure the country endowed with it of an imaginative, sound and energetic management of the economy, through the public, the private and the mixed sectors, and thus advance the forces of production tangibly and promote self-reliance.

There are two observations to make right away in connection with the introductory statements just made. First, that the discussion of leadership fits more appropriately into the next chapter of the book, where the dynamics and machinery of self-reliant development are explored. Second, that the qualities and attitudes stated as necessary conditions for the leadership to satisfy are excessively demanding and idealized, and therefore unlikely to be satisfied in a developing country or region. It could be argued that any country, or community of countries, endowed with such a leadership could, almost automatically, be trusted to seek and achieve self-reliant development.

The criticism which would be contained in such observations is not totally unwarranted, but it could be explained away. With regard to the first point, although the substance of the criterion under examination forms a vital part of the enquiry into the dynamics and machinery of self-reliant development, which is the subject of the next chapter, it also legitimately constitutes a crucial aspect of the test for the feasibility of self-reliance in the Arab region. Indeed, it must have become clear by now, from the discussion of the six criteria already examined, that even if these were all met satisfactorily, they would fail cumulatively to establish this feasibility, unless the factor of leadership – as understood and defined above – were in sufficient evidence.

The second observation made seems more difficult to defend, because it arises from the incorporation of overly stringent characterizations of the leaderships considered essential for the establishment of the feasibility in question. This is true. But it must be remarked that these conditions are not expected to be fully satisfied together and right from the start. It is sufficient to have a critical leadership nucleus which is development orientated, determined, aware of the centrality for society of self-reliance, and of the pressure of the politicized public for political participation and human rights, for the leadership-network to become gradually but positively and tangibly influenced through a process of diffusion. To deny such a possibility is to deny the power both of ideas and of social forces in history.

Besides, the process is not expected to happen without effort, pain, and social and political action. And action is expected through parties, intellectual vanguards and popular movements. It is nowhere maintained in this book that self-reliant development is an easy process, or that it can be achieved smoothly and effortlessly, or in a short period of time. Quite the contrary. Furthermore, to argue that because the Arab region is today very far from the pursuit of self-reliant development and that, therefore, it would remain incapable of undertaking such a pursuit, would amount to a harsh, almost racist verdict on the Arabs. It ought to be remembered that at least two countries – Egypt and Algeria, and in addition possibly Iraq – took serious steps in that direction in the 1960s and 1970s, and made tangible achievements within the limited scope of their national economies, before they faltered and experienced setbacks for various reasons. This should be taken as an encouraging indication of the possibility of the endeavour, especially if it is attempted collectively at the level of the region or large parts of it. It also suggests the need for any countries attempting to pursue self-reliance to avoid the mistakes committed by Egypt, Algeria and Iraq. These mistakes were political, economic and institutional.

The question now is: how well endowed with the leaderships characterized earlier is the Arab region today? The answer cannot be clear-cut. Some of the leaderships, particularly in intellectual circles, in a minority of influential periodicals, and among progressive elements in the education sector, are committed to self-reliant development, and willing to stand up and work for it as a priority objective for Arab society. To the other extreme, the business community is hardly moved by this objective – if at all – and largely ignores it or considers it one of the crazy ideas of long-haired intellectuals. The labour movement shows no more concern than the business community, though for different reasons. Foremost among these is labour's all-absorbing concern with employment conditions – job opportunities, pay rates, fringe benefits and the like – rather than some 'abstract' desideratum like self-reliant development. It is the political leadership which in the final analysis is the centre of decision-making in the present context.

Political leadership is quite varied. But although in each country certain elements can be found, in the higher rungs of authority, and among party leaderships, that are development orientated and amenable to conversion to the principles and pursuit of self-reliance, no one country today can be said to satisfy the requirements of the criterion of adequacy being considered. Although five or six countries have strong development-orientated leaderships, hardly any of these are primarily concerned with the pursuit of self-reliance and consistently opt for economic and political priorities and policies consistent with this pursuit. In addition, almost all Arab leaderships in power today are excessively authoritarian and have an undemocratic outlook and style of government. The 1960s and 1970s witnessed some strongly development-orientated leaderships at the highest level of authority, but these have either disappeared or were made by the force of events to change course, or to lower their sights, or else they became autocratic.

The central problem is not the absence from the Arab political scene of development-orientated leaderships – there are several of these, as already indicated – but the fact that the qualification of those that are appropriately orientated and determined is marred by one or more serious failings or adverse circumstances. Among these are the suppression of democracy and human rights, which breaks the lines of communication between the leaders and the people; preoccupation with long drawn-out war or internal strife; excessive 'economism' in the understanding of the nature of development and therefore disregard for political and socio-cultural aspects of national regeneration; narrowness of the leadership base caused by the existence of a wide gap between the political leaders, on the one hand, and social-minded intellectuals, educators, journalists, professionals, and politicized elements in the general public, on the other; and insufficient appreciation of the seriousness of the state of dependence and its implications. But apart from the flaws in the qualification of the leadership resource, there is the low level of adequacy in one or more of the other criteria which puts an early limit to the feasibility of self-reliant development.

To sum up, none of the countries of the region is adequately endowed with a large enough and broad enough development-orientated leadership network which is determined to launch the process of self-reliance with vigour and continuity, even if the satisfaction of the other criteria of adequacy were to be ignored for the moment, or, alternatively, to be assumed satisfied for the sake of the argument. This implies that the whole discussion in the present section has ended on a negative note.

The conclusion is even less reassuring if sought through an assessment of the power of the development orientation of the leadership networks in the various Arab countries, as they set their sights on collective self-reliance and the promotion of Arab development through the instrumentality of complementarity and the joint Arab economic sector. Indeed, almost by definition, the leadership networks would be less determined in their development orientation if this were directed at the whole region than at their individual countries. Table 4 at the end of this section, which contains the matrix that cross-tabulates the individual countries with the extent of satisfaction of individual criteria of adequacy, clearly shows why self-reliant development is not feasible at the present point in time, except possibly and maximally for a few countries acting together, which might at best enjoy a medium/high level of adequacy of development orientation.

But, even in this case, individually, the countries concerned have to contend with a low level of adequacy arising from the present directions and composition of their foreign trade, the insufficiency of their entrepreneurial resource, or the limitations of their internal market – to say nothing of other non-economic preoccupations which weigh heavily on them. Other countries with a score of medium/high in the degree of adequacy of development orientation, like Tunisia, Syria and Jordan, also have serious handicaps, particularly in the smallness of their internal markets and the shortage of domestic capital resources to promote capital accumulation extensively. The pursuit of collective self-reliance at the region's level is much more difficult *a fortiori* if this pursuit is expressed through collective action, from the level of the summits of the heads of state, down to the establishment of joint projects and professional unions. The reason is the low score in most of the countries of the criterion of leadership.

Nevertheless, I do not consider the enquiry as complete and closed, with the negative conclusions just stated. It seems to me that the enquiry should be conducted backwards, so to speak. That is, that we should begin by asking if collective self-reliant development would be feasible at the level of the region, were the appropriate political will and determination to be available and translatable into concern and action for development.

The concern could first operate at the country level, even if only with partial promise, but proceed to an indicative regional level, in harmony and consistency with a pre-formulated regional conceptualization and a regional plan to make it concrete. Such a plan need not be comprehensive or mandatory, but could, at least initially, be restricted to the joint Arab economic sector, with provision and scope for its extension as it gets increasingly and more effectively implemented. It would likewise be essential for the plan to permit the weaving together or the intermeshing of country and regional development objectives, since there are many priority objectives which serve both individual country interests and regional interests.

The rearrangement of the argument as suggested will be attempted in the rest of the chapter. It will be undertaken on the presumption that the political will for the pursuit of self-reliant development could conceivably be generated and nourished among the leadership networks in the region's countries, particularly those leaderships which reasonably satisfy a notable part of the criterion of development orientation through the strategy of self-reliance, and are also supplemented by the other critical criteria.

To serve the purposes of enquiry, we must address a two-part question. (1) Supposing the political will and determination were available in sufficient strength to permit a drive towards collective self-reliant development, owing to the realization that it cannot be sought at the individual country level, would the region in fact satisfy the other criteria of adequacy today, within the prevailing state of political and economic fragmentation? If not, will it satisfy these criteria within a framework of co-operation and complementarity, and the use of the joint Arab economic sector as an effective instrument of collective action? (2) And, if the answer to the latter question is in the affirmative, what would be the priority sectors, activities or programmes to embody the pursuit of collective self-reliant development concretely?

Obviously, addressing the first part of the question must be undertaken before we end the present section. Thus, it is necessary to justify the supposition that the political will and determination could realistically be generated. Otherwise the supposition would remain largely a futile exercise, if the grounds on which it is based are not satisfactorily probed and found to be firm. A brief such probing will be attempted later. The second component of the first part of the question posed above can hopefully be answered by the contents of the boxes in the matrix in Table 4 on p. 172 as explained or qualified by the notes which follow the matrix.

These contents show that the various countries compensate for each other's shortcomings with respect to the criteria numbered 1, 3, 4, 5 and 6 throughout. In other words, the second criterion (the directions and composition of foreign trade) is not adequately satisfied today, even if it were to refer to the region as a whole. (Obviously, it would be much less adequate if considered as relating to individual countries, as shown in the matrix.) This is because the directions and composition of the region's foreign trade can sufficiently change to become a positive factor in the pursuit of self-reliance only gradually, as part of the dynamics of the pursuit of self-interest through regional self-reliance, under the influence of the determination of the leadership networks defined broadly.

On the basis of the assessment of the adequacy of the first six criteria as indicated, what has just been said strongly suggests that gradual self-reliant development at the region's level is feasible only once the seventh criterion begins to be effectively satisfied, through the presence in sufficient strength and spread of a development-orientated determined leadership network, willing to mobilize society behind the pursuit of self-reliance, and capable of doing so. As the matrix shows, this does not have to happen in every single country. It would be enough for it to happen in a number of leading countries acting together. These occupy a central position in the Arab regional system and their leaderships can influence the other countries through a process of diffusion.

Such countries are Algeria, Egypt, Saudi Arabia, Syria, Iraq, Lebanon and Jordan. The diffusion would in this instance be most operative around each of the countries listed, that is, within the grouping to which it belongs. Here it should be noted that the grouping system adopted in the matrix in Table 4 is the one used until 1987 by the four bodies which prepare and publish the *Unified Arab Economic Report*, namely the Secretariat of the League of Arab States, the Arab Monetary Fund, the Arab Fund for Economic and Social Development, and the Organization of Arab Petroleum Exporting Countries. But this grouping is not necessarily the one most suited for the purposes of our analysis, as we shall see later where an alternative system of grouping will be suggested for the purpose of assessing the feasibility of Arab self-reliant development.

Investing hope in the leadership resource in a number of leading countries is justified on the premise that the better-endowed countries could, through their influence in the countries within their grouping, activate the forces that might generate the appropriate leadership network, or put pressure on the existing network to accept a developmental reorientation and a reordering of its priorities. The mechanics of such a process form part of the dynamics and machinery of self-reliance, which is the subject of the next chapter. If the process of diffusion unfolds as expected, then those countries that are better endowed with the leadership resource can in a sense compensate for the shortage where it exists in their neighbourhood.

Where it exists, the rather adequate leadership resource would be capable of achieving two vital functions. The first is the redirecting of development efforts in the countries concerned, and subsequently but gradually in the members of their grouping, to become, at least in certain aspects, less dependent on the advanced industrial countries. Obviously, they would not be capable of achieving a very large measure of self-reliance, because of the deficiencies in certain criteria of adequacy in the individual countries, or, alternatively, because of the inadequacy of the extent to which the second criterion (the direction and composition of foreign trade) is satisfied at the regional level – as already indicated. The second vital function is the preparation of the course of regional (collective) self-reliance, partly by so shaping country development as to be in harmony with the regional desiderata and objectives (as already agreed upon), and partly by intensifying and expanding the process of complementarity within the region, and by energetically and earnestly promoting and strengthening the joint Arab economic sector.

We come, then, to the most vital and crucial question: how can the leadership resource be made to emerge and play its role as a catalytic agent in the operation of the other six criteria of adequacy, thus providing the feasibility of self-reliance with the necessary as well as the sufficient conditions required? It is necessary that I emphasize, without delay, that what is meant by the repeated reference to the leadership resource, or network, is not a literal focusing on a small elite emanating from the various spheres of life: the political, educational, syndical, and so on. As the next chapter will attempt to show, the position underlying my approach to the *problématique* at hand is by no means elitist. The politicized public has a significant and large place in the scheme of things, as seen in this book. The people are the beneficiaries, but also, to start with, the makers of development, and they must not, by logic, commonsense or necessity be ignored or relegated to a minor position. The vanguard assessment in this discussion necessarily consists of a considerable number of people.

In fact, it is the centrality of the people in the whole scheme that holds the key to the process of the emergence and the dynamism of the leadership network. Hence the emphasis in this book, indicated earlier, and to be indicated again, on broad-based political participation, human rights and social justice, which are necessary conditions for the emergence of development-orientated leaderships with social awareness and resolve. The relationship between the two parties that are conventionally designated as the 'leaders' and the 'led' is not a simple one, or a one-way relationship. Socially-conscious leaderships can and are expected to lead the way to popular struggle for the right to political participation, for human rights and for social justice.

But, at the same time, the yearning and the stirring by the people for participation, human rights and social justice in turn activate the leaderships. Often these leaderships are found to be hesitant, or in a semi-dormant state, and it is the people that inject dynamism and initiative into the situation and set the leaderships into action. But, still more importantly, the struggle cannot succeed without widespread, deeply-committed participation by the public at large. The connection between the demand for political participation, human rights and social justice is closely related to the chances of self-reliant development. For, unless the people have and exercise these rights, their voices will remain muted and their true interest in socially-directed development and pressure for it will never be allowed to be expressed loudly and strongly enough. (The apparent possible contradiction between development and its requirements, on the one hand, and the enjoyment of participation, human rights and social justice, on the other, will be examined in the next chapter.)

However, the process needs a great deal of re-education and socialization. Here, the progressive, social-minded intellectuals, educators, journalists and publishers, labour unions and politicians can play a most important role. And they can be more directly and forcefully sensitized to this role the more committed they themselves are to the struggle for the aforementioned demands, and the more involved they are with this struggle directly. The content of the message of re-education should have two components. The first is the clear and simple demonstration of the benefit to the people of self-reliant development. And the second is the clear and simple demonstration of how disastrous it would be for many years to come if such development were not sought and struggled for, within a much wider and more comprehensive civilizational enterprise that involves the whole of society in all aspects of its life.

Once the people are made fully aware of the high stakes they have directly and tangibly in self-reliant development, and of its feasibility within a framework of complementarity and joint Arab action, and once they are made equally aware of the extent of their loss if such development is missed, they can be trusted to press and struggle for it. This will involve explanation and reassurance that regional self-reliance begins with the pursuit of self-reliance, even if only partial, at the level of individual countries, and that national and regional development complement and nourish each other. This can be ensured both through joint Arab economic action and through the promotion of close and far-reaching complementarity among the individual countries. Such complementarity would provide a firm foundation for the pursuit of regional development.

These two avenues of action are not identical. Joint action involves co-operation and communal participation in regional organizations, unions or projects – that is, in institutions and undertakings of the same nature. Obviously, such undertakings can cut across the whole region, or can involve only as many countries as are interested in joining. On the other hand, complementarity involves activities, sectors or undertakings of a different nature which intermesh with each

Table 4 Matrix relating the extent of the satisfaction of the criteria of adequacy to individual Arab countries

Countries and country groupings	*Criteria* *1. The size of the internal market*	*2. The directions and composition of foreign trade*	*3. The natural resource base*	*4. The availability of appropriate technology and man-power skills*	*5. The availability of a sizeable entrepreneurial capability*	*6. The availability of resources for capital accumulation*	*7. The availability of development-orientated leadership seeking self-reliance*
Group 1							
United Arab Emirates	Low	Low	High	Low	Low	High	Low
Bahrain	Low	Low	Low/medium	Low	Low/medium	Medium	Low
Saudi Arabia	Medium/high	Low	High	Low/medium	Low/medium	High	Low/medium
Oman	Low	Low	Medium/high	Low	Low	High	Low
Qatar	Low	Low	Medium/high	Low	Low	High	Low
Kuwait	Low	Low	High	Low/medium	Low/medium	High	Medium
Group 2							
Algeria	Medium	Low	High	Medium/high	Medium	High	Medium/high
Iraq	Medium	Low	High	Medium/high	Medium	High	Medium/high
Libya	Low	Low	High	Low/medium	Low	High	Low

Group 3							
Tunisia	Low	Low	Medium	Medium	Medium	Low/medium	Medium/high
Syria	Low	Low	Medium/high	Medium/high	Medium/high	Medium	Medium/high
Egypt	High	Low	Medium/high	High	High	Low	Medium
Group 4							
Jordan	Low	Low	Low/medium	Medium/high	Medium/high	Low/medium	Medium/high
Lebanon	Low	Low	Medium	Medium/high	High	Low/medium	Low/medium
Morocco	Low	Low	Medium/high	Medium	Medium	Low	Low
Group 5							
Djibouti	Low	Low	Low	Low	Low	Low	Low
Sudan	Low	Low	High	Low	Low	Low	Low
Somalia	Low	Low	Low	Low	Low	Low	Low
Mauritania	Low	Low	High	Low	Low	Low	Low
North Yemen	Low	Low	Low/medium	Low	Low	Low/medium	Low/medium
South Yemen	Low	Low	Low/medium	Low	Low	Low/medium	Low/medium

other functionally. Once again, the intermeshing can take place on a very broad basis involving many other undertakings and/or countries, or on a narrower basis. As it is understood here, complementarity is essentially a relationship involving backward and forward linkages, or one involving the compensation by one or more countries which are well endowed with a certain resource for the shortages suffered by one or more other countries with regard to the resource in question. (Complementarity will be the subject of independent discussion at the close of the present section.)

In the light of the differentiation made here between joint action and complementarity, the two avenues must be opted for together for collective self-reliance to become possible. The extent of 'collectivity' cannot be determined in advance in the abstract, because the unfolding of the pursuit of self-reliance in practice may show more promise in some directions than in others. Consequently, the pursuit may be much more energetic and earnest, and fruitful, in some country groupings than in others. Any success, no matter how partial, must be welcomed and built upon, so long as it does not pre-empt or negate the unfolding of the process in some other part of the region.

We need not go any further here into a discussion of the development-orientated leadership network necessary for and capable of embarking on the pursuit of development as characterized in the present study. All that is needed, by way of conclusion to the present section, is to emphasize, first, that the task will be better undertaken, the more squarely it is shouldered by political parties, labour unions, progressive movements committed to social transformation, and intellectual circles, rather than by isolated individuals or small elites; and second, that the task will not be a pleasant picnic but a harsh, costly and long struggle that cannot be shifted or shirked. My final contention is that the task ought and also can be discharged effectively and decisively – though it will necessarily require considerable effort and resolve over many long years.

Several explanatory notes are called for to make the matrix in Table 4 clearer and more meaningful for the purpose of the assessment of the feasibility of self-reliance. The overall conclusions which can be drawn from the matrix have already been recorded.

As indicated earlier, the country grouping is made in accordance with the *Unified Arab Economic Report 1986*. This grouping divides the twenty-one Arab states on the basis of national income, population, the significance of the oil sector, and the extent of economic diversification, into oil countries (Group 1); quasi-oil countries, that is, countries rich in oil and gas resources, but which have other important resources or activities apart from oil and gas extraction and export (Group 2); countries with some oil production though it does not make the major contribution to the national product owing to the existence of other important sectors, and with a reasonably satisfactory economic performance (Group 3); countries without oil resources, but with economies that have a creditable economic performance by regional standards (Group 4); and the least developed countries, LDCs, with a low economic performance and serious social handicaps (Group 5). There is evidently some overlap among the groups. Furthermore, the last group will probably have to be redefined, now that Sudan, North Yemen and South Yemen have been proven to have hydrocarbon reserves of important commercial value. (Since then, the grouping has been altered, as can be seen in Table 2 which relates to 1987 in the *Unified Arab Economic Report 1988*. The old grouping has been retained for the matrix and for Table 3, as it is more expressive of common features within groups.)

A scale with five positions has been used for scoring the degree of adequacy, with three basic positions (low, medium and high) and two intermediate positions (low/medium and medium/high). The scoring has been undertaken on the basis of my cumulative research on and close familiarity with the Arab countries and economies stretching back for over three decades and continuously brought up to date, and, to a lesser extent, upon reference to scanty evaluations of relevance in the works of some other Arab economists. No attempt has been made to quantify the extent to which the criteria of adequacy are satisfied. This is not only because there are no sufficient data to permit quantification and numerical grading for criterion numbers 3, 4, 5 and 7, but also because I shy away from 'misplaced concreteness'.

A proper reading of the overall situation of any one country with respect to its ability to pursue self-reliant development should take into account its score or position with regard to all the criteria. It is arguable that the last four (numbers 4 to 7) are particularly significant.

The adequacy of the criteria can also be assessed group by group, in order to see how well endowed each group is with the resources and capabilities essential to self-reliance. It would seem from the matrix that groups 2 and 3 are the best endowed, taking into account the scoring they have been accorded. Were these two groups to be adjacent, they could seek self-reliant development through their joint efforts, largely apart from the efforts of the other groups, except in so far as the other groups constitute an important component of the region's market. However, given geographical reality, some other more satisfactory grouping system will have to be explored for sub-regional feasibility. This will be attempted in the section to follow.

The scoring should be read in the context of the discussion of the individual criteria of adequacy presented earlier in the present section.

The scores relate to the present situation – say from the early 1970s to the very late 1980s – not to any remote future possibility or potential. This is of particular relevance to the availability of natural resources, technological capability and manpower skills, entre-preneurial talent, domestic capital resources for investment, and, above all, development-orientated leaderships stressing self-reliance.

The caption of the first criterion in the matrix (The size of the internal market) is ambivalent. Since the market deals with individual countries explicitly, the word 'internal' should relate to the countries one by one. On the other hand, in our earlier discussion of this criterion we dwelt on the regional market as an entity, in order to show its size and potential for the absorption of a sizeable part of the region's production, in case collective self-reliance were sought earnestly. What the column under reference suggests now is that, one by one, all the countries of the region suffer from the extreme limita-tion of the absorptive capacity of their individual markets, except Egypt, and Saudi Arabia. However, looked at together as one market, the country markets constitute a large regional market which deserves a high rating.

The rating of all the countries with regard to the second criterion, 'The directions and composition of foreign trade', is consistently low, without exception. This means that every country's foreign trade with regard to imports and exports is skewed, with very strong bias in favour of OECD countries. However, unlike the situation with regard to the criterion referred to in the note immediately before, adding up the foreign trade of all the Arab countries does not change the situa-tion, since the region as a whole comes up with the same trade bias and heavy dependence on the industrial countries of the West. This suggests a very wide scope for the diversification and exansion of production under the impetus of self-reliance, complementarity and joint economic action. The only qualification necessary here is that some individual countries have substantially more intra-Arab trade than some others, but that does not alter the overall outcome of very modest intra-Arab trade for the region as a whole.

Natural resources include mineral (underground) resources as well as land and water. Hydrocarbons feature very importantly in groups 1 and 2. (And they have great promise for North Yemen, South Yemen and Sudan, once the hydrocarbons sector has been adequately developed.) Natural resources are an endowment to contend with in countries of Group 3, and phosphates and iron ore are also very important in some of the other countries. Although several other minerals are known to exist, and a number of these are under commercial exploitation, they are far from being significant enough to serve as a launching pad for development. (Land and water have received specific mention earlier on in the section. They are of special significant where they abound, and where the land is cultivable.)

The availability of technological capability and manpower skills, as of entrepreneurial talent, relates to the nationals of the country. Where collective self-reliance is considered, the availability of these resources in other Arab countries which are willing to allow the outflow of the resources to meet shortages in other countries is not only allowed for but considered a positive factor in the context of regional self-reliance. Foreign (non-Arab) resources are excluded from consideration.

The criterion relating to the availability of internal resources for fixed capital accumulation includes Arab assets placed in foreign money markets and investments in foreign economies, in addition to resources available within the individual countries themselves.

It is useful to emphasize that the last column, relating to the availability of development-orientated leadership, involves more than just that. Almost all countries have a development-orientated leadership, but the content and quality of the development advocated vary widely from country to country. Furthermore, the development in question should be sought as far as possible through a strategy of self-reliance for it to feature as one of the criteria being assessed. In addition, though many leaders are development orientated, only few of them meet the other specifications suggested earlier, such as respect for human rights, and concern for a wide base of political participation and social justice. This explains the pattern of scoring in column 7 in the matrix.

The last observation to make with regard to the assessment of the level of adequacy of the various prerequisites for Arab self-reliant development, as reflected in the matrix contained in Table 4, relates to the pattern of complementarity among the countries of the region that the matrix reveals. This pattern is crucial because the pursuit of *collective* self-reliance would be fruitless if the economies concerned have failed to achieve, or to show potential for, meaningful complementarity. Such failure could be the result of the similarity of their endowments and/or their products, or else the failure of the decision-makers to seek and achieve complementarity even if their endowments and products could logically lead to complementarity. Such failure could be caused by lack of interest, the adoption of inappropriate policies, or ignorance of the merits of complementarity. It would not be feasible without meaningful complementarity for the Arab countries to attempt collective self-reliance as a group, since it would not be possible for them to bring about a regional reallocation of resources and endowments – whether human, natural, or man-made – between those that have a surplus or an advantage, and the others that have a shortage or a disadvantage. In other words, the presence of meaningful complementarity, or the potential for it, is an essential precondition for collective self-reliance.

The matrix reveals that individual Arab countries have different profiles of resources and endowments, and of the economic performance associated with them. The differences are in fact longer if the various economies are examined in greater detail than the matrix permits. Furthermore, there is much greater scope for complementarity than has been achieved so far, although the oil decade 1973–82 has brought out a number of clear instances of this scope, as the preceding discussion has pointed out with respect to manpower movements and financial flows among several countries (with manpower and financial resources generally moving in opposite directions), and with respect to the establishment of a large number of regional organizations and joint projects and companies. The measure of complementarity achieved has been expressed both in horizontal and in vertical complementarity. The former refers to identical or similar products or activities which are aggregated or combined to meet internal (regional) or external demand. This is expressed, among other things, by joint projects or programmes. The latter refers to different products or activities which together constitute integrated processes of production or of end products, thanks to the pattern of backward and forward linkages which bind the processes or phases of production together. The case of vertical integration can be seen clearly in manufacturing industry – within individual industries, or among a group of interconnecting industries. It can also be seen among sectors which are interrelated.

The question of similarity between resources and endowments, or between products, and how this impedes complementarity, and, instead, encourages competition, needs to be discussed and qualified. For, even where different countries produce the same agricultural crops, for instance, a closer look at the specifications of these crops often reveals a scope for complementarity and exchange. Thus, while both Egypt and Syria produce cotton, Egypt's cotton is essentially of a long-staple variety, while Syria's is short- and medium-staple. This fact leads to potential and actual trade in cotton between the two countries. Another illustration relates to wheat, of which Egypt produces a hard variety and Syria a soft one – with the former more suitable for the manufacture of macaroni, and the latter for bread. A third illustration relates to a number of similar vegetables which both Jordan and Lebanon produce. But the Jordanian crops ripen several weeks before their Lebanese counterpart, owing to the fact that the former are grown in the Jordan valley which enjoys a much warmer climate than the areas where the latter are grown. The variation in ripening seasons also leads to trade in vegetables between the two countries. In short, the similarity is often superficial; underneath it lie differences in quality, timing of seasons, or in specifications of nominally the same crops.

There is need to distinguish between the outward or nominal instances of similarity, and therefore the presumed absence of possibility for complementarity, and the more basic differences underneath outward appearances. This can be seen in the broad field of manufacturing industry, as in the field of agriculture to which reference has been made. Thus, seemingly similar industries can be and often are at different technological levels or capable of different levels of performance, and their products can be quite different. In such cases, the logic of comparative advantage dictates co-operation and co-ordination, where this seems beneficial, and therefore the adoption of an appropriate pattern of division of labour and specialization. In extreme cases the reallocation of capital is called for, in such a manner as to enable the less efficient industry to seek other fields of production where the capital involved can be more efficiently and profitably invested.

But manufacturing industry presents an even more promising scope for complementarity than the one just referred to. This is the siting of industries across the region (or at least within sub-regions) in accordance with comparative advantages. This would necessitate preplanning before the allocation of capital for industrial development. Indeed, such a scope is enormous, and embraces the more traditional, established industries, which in their own interest should submit to a rational plan of resiting, as it embraces more appropriately new industries that are just emerging or are being considered. Both horizontal and vertical integration ought to be sought. The former would involve the grouping of industries or industrial establishments that produce similar products, while the latter would involve close linkage between industries or industrial establishments designed to produce different but inter-connected or inter-linked products within one manufacturing process. Those parts of an industry concerned in vertical integration could thus be sited where the input and/or the marketing situation is most appropriate for them, and the different components or units lying in different countries can then co-operate in the chain of production. As the Arab region is still at a relatively modestly developed level of industrialization, it can achieve a large measure of complementarity through intelligent and far-sighted division of labour and specialization and, thus, achieve complementarity.

Without going any further in showing the enormity of the scope for complementarity by providing specific illustrations, it will be enough at this point to list certain additional categories or areas of possible (or already emerging) complementarity. These include the following:

- Food production constitutes the most urgent need for joint Arab economic action and complementarity. Thus, Sudan, Morocco, Syria and Iraq – to name the countries with the most promising potential for agricultural development – can produce most of the food products now being imported at very high cost. The countries with large financial reserves can provide capital funding, and the whole region will provide an extensive natural market for the crops. Agro-industries can be developed within, but also outside, the group of countries enumerated, thus expanding the scope for complementarity.
- Mineral resource development will also promote complementarity, since there is diversity in mineral resource endowment, as Table 5 shows. Apart from potash, phosphates and hydrocarbons, which have received considerable exploration, the development and commercialization of most other resources are yet to be achieved. The variety of minerals will promote intra-regional exchange and complementarity.
- Tourism is a relatively prosperous industry in several countries. But the touristic appeal varies from one country to another. Thus, it is essentially beautiful scenery, moderate climate and attractive beaches in Morocco, Algeria, Tunisia and Lebanon, while it is historical sites and monuments in Egypt, Jordan, Syria and Iraq, and pilgrimage in Saudi Arabia that draw millions of Arabs and non-Arabs annually to the countries listed for holidays. (Some countries combine more than one attraction.) Here again there is an obvious pattern of complementarity within the region.
- A limited scope for complementarity exists in the joint use of rivers

running from one country to another, such as Sudan and Egypt with respect to the Nile river, Syria and Iraq with respect to the Euphrates river, Syria and Jordan with respect to the Yarmouk river, and Lebanon and Syria with respect to some tributaries of the river Jordan, which flows southward between Israel and Jordan, into the Dead Sea.

- The energy sector provides a major area of complementarity and co-operation. The Arab oil-producing countries – thirteen of which already produce crude and export it, and two more of which are developing their oil resource – co-ordinate policies and undertake oil-related studies and research through the instrumentality of OAPEC. OAPEC's studies also involve gas production and use in petrochemical industries, and the development of energy sources other than hydrocarbons. Another area of complementarity in the field of energy is already emerging in electricity production. There are a few programmes at an advanced stage of planning involving co-operation in the utilization of power between countries with shared borders.
- The expansion of much wider networks of intraregional roads, railroads, airways and sea routes is an essential facility for greater exchange and complementarity, as well as a prominent manifestation of it. Once again, present planning for such expansion is much more ambitious than achievement, in spite of the demonstrable benefits that the networks bestow.
- The last scope for complementarity to mention is a very significant one, not only because it has extensive potential, but also because the oil decade 1973–82 made possible the translation of much of this potential into actuality. As indicated earlier on in the present chapter, the decade witnessed large-scale movement of skilled (and some semi-skilled) workers from a number of countries (notably Egypt, North Yemen, Syria, Jordan, and the Palestinian community both in the Diaspora and in the territories of Palestine occupied by Israel in 1967). The numbers involved are estimated at 3–4 million, who mostly sought work in the Gulf countries and Iraq in the Mashreq, and in Libya in the Maghreb. A second flow of considerable magnitude took place in the reverse direction: it was the flow of remittances by the expatriate workforce constituting the first flow (estimated at about US $1,000 on the average per worker, or between $3 billion and $4 billion annually). In addition, the major oil-exporting countries have, since the mid-1970s, supplied the needier Arab countries with economic aid, in the form of grants and long-term loans on concessionary terms.

Table 5 The variety and distribution of mineral resources in the Arab region[a]

Mineral resources	*Proven reserves[b] and their location*	*Possible or probable reserves and their location*	*Remarks*
Petroleum	OAPEC members[c] plus North Yemen, Oman and Sudan	South Yemen	Production in process, except in South Yemen where the resource is being developed
Natural gas	OAPEC members	Morocco	Proportion of utilization is 75%, plus 22% used for injection
Coal	Morocco, Egypt and Algeria	Oman	Production capacity developed in Morocco and Egypt
Shale	Jordan	Morocco, Egypt, Syria and Palestine	
Uranium and thorium		Morocco, Algeria, Somalia, Egypt, Saudi Arabia, Mauritania and North Yemen	On the basis that phosphate deposits contain uranium in a ratio of 1:10,000
Iron ore	Mauritania, Algeria, Egypt, Saudi Arabia, Morocco and North Yemen	Iraq	Minor deposits in Jordan. Production now in Mauritania, Egypt, Algeria, Morocco and Tunisia
Copper	Mauritania, Oman, Algeria, Palestine, Jordan, Saudi Arabia and Morocco	Sudan, North Yemen, Egypt and South Yemen	Productive capacity now in Morocco, Algeria, Palestine, Oman and Mauritania
Manganese	Morocco, Egypt, Sudan, Somalia and Jordan	Mauritania and Tunisia	Minor deposits in Oman and Syria. Productive capacity now in Morocco, Egypt and Sudan
Lead and zinc	Tunisia, Algeria, Morocco, Saudi Arabia and Egypt	Sudan and Mauritania	Productive capacity now in Tunisia, Algeria and Morocco
Tin		Egypt and Morocco	
Chrome	Sudan and Oman	Egypt and Mauritania	Productive capacity now in Sudan. Minor deposits in United Arab Emirates

Molybdenum		Egypt and Somalia	
Nickel	Morocco, North Yemen and Egypt	Mauritania	Productive capacity now in Morocco
Titanium	Egypt	Somalia, Saudi Arabia, North Yemen, South Yemen and Mauritania	
Tungsten	Egypt	Morocco and Mauritania	
Cobalt and antimony	Morocco		Productive capacity now in Morocco
Silver	Tunisia, Algeria and Morocco		Productive capacity now in three countries
Gold	Saudi Arabia	Egypt	Productive capacity now in Saudi Arabia
Potassium	Jordan	Morocco, Libya and Tunisia	Productive capacity now in Jordan
Phosphate	Morocco, Jordan, Egypt, Syria, Iraq, Tunisia, Algeria and Palestine	Mauritania	Productive capacity now in all countries with proven reserves
Sulphur (natural)	Iraq	Saudi Arabia, Morocco and Mauritania	Owing to serious environmental hazards associated with its extraction, it is currently obtained from petroleum and gas in Saudi Arabia, Iraq, Kuwait, UAE, Qatar, Bahrain, Syria and Libya

Source: *CAUS 1988*

Notes: *a* A few insignificant minerals have been excluded.

b The extraction of proven reserves is feasible, given technical and economic conditions prevailing in the mid 1980s.

c OAPEC members are: Saudi Arabia, Kuwait, Iraq, Qatar, Bahrain, United Arab Emirates (UAE), Syria, Egypt, Libya, Tunisia and Algeria.

The average such aid over the perion 1975–87 has been $5.6 billion a year.

The preceding discussion of complementarity has on several occasions dwelt on the distinction between existing instances of and potential for complementarity. It must be pointed out that there is an enormous gap between what is and what can be. The modest translation of potential into actuality can be related to several factors. These include insufficiency of co-ordination and planning among the region's countries with a view to achieving complementarity; the narrow country-focus of political and economic decision-makers, who have yet to realize the economic advantages both to their own and to the other countries involved, of co-ordination and the promotion of development which benefits from complementarity; and insufficient awareness of the enormity of the opportunities and advantages foregone because of insufficient complementarity.

However, there is growing awareness of the lessons even of the minimal effective co-operation already experienced, in the design and pursuit of development during the oil decade. These lessons are most visible in the Gulf area, where vast investments were made in the establishment of a wide range of petrochemical industries. Many of these were duplications of each other. Each industrial complex had been designed (as to productive capacity) as though it was the only one in the region. The resulting excess capacity is now visible and is seen as wasteful and costly to all concerned. It has led the six members of the Co-operation Council for the Arab States of the Gulf to opt for a course of much more co-ordination and co-operation in the future.

The overall lesson for the countries of the region as a whole is that self-reliant development cannot be sought purposefully and intelligently unless the political will is there for co-operation, co-ordination and planning, and unless these processes are pursued in such a manner as to express close and large-scale complementarity among the various economies. If there is the political will for political complementarity, then economic complementarity will be the other side of the coin and can become attainable, considering the fact that the resource and endowment profiles of the various countries are conducive to it. This lesson is particularly essential as the development of many industries and activities cannot be undertaken optimally except at the regional level. And the more extended the complementarity, the more diversified the regional economy can become, and the larger the range of goods and services produced and the wider the scope for exchange. The process has every promise of becoming cumulative and positive in its impact on complementarity and development.

PRIORITY AREAS OF ACTION FOR ARAB SELF-RELIANT DEVELOPMENT

It was argued in the last section that even though no single Arab country can by itself meet all the criteria of adequacy for the feasibility of self-reliant development, the region as a whole, or at least some groups of closely related countries within it, could do so in a gradual manner. The basic condition was that the constituent countries of the region, or of the groups singled out, should share a number of broad objectives which they would seek with determination and consistency, through joint action and within a framework of complementarity. In the more limited case of two or three groups making the pursuit of self-reliance by themselves, the condition was that they should together meet several of the basic criteria at a reasonably high level of adequacy.

The maximum case, namely the pursuit of self-reliance by all the countries of the region together, is clearly defined. It is in the second, more limited case that identification of the countries best suited for joint action is needed. Earlier on, the countries most satisfactorily endowed were listed as Algeria, Egypt, Saudi Arabia, Syria, Iraq, Lebanon and Jordan. These seven countries belong to three of the five groups according to the grouping system of the *Unified Arab Economic Report 1986*. But while Egypt, Saudi Arabia, Syria, Iraq, Lebanon and Jordan, which are in the eastern part of the region, are not only close to each other geographically but, in fact, border on each other, Algeria is situated in the Maghreb or the western part of the region.

A more practical system of grouping would be to divide the region into four sub-regions or groups: the Maghreb (Morocco, Mauritania, Algeria, Tunisia and Libya); the Nile Valley (Egypt, Sudan, Somalia and Djibouti); the Fertile Crescent (Lebanon, Syria, Jordan and Iraq), and the Arabian Peninsula (Kuwait, Bahrain, Qatar, United Arab Emirates, Oman, Saudi Arabia, North Yemen and South Yemen).[28] In view of the impracticality of binding association among all twenty-one Arab states at the present moment, it would be more realistic and fruitful to suggest such association among a smaller number of countries with obvious promise for the feasibility of self-reliance among them. Such a nucleus would include Egypt, Lebanon, Syria, Jordan, Iraq and Saudi Arabia.

This group of six involves three sub-regions in the system suggested presently on the basis of geographical proximity or even contiguity. The six form a continuum geographically, but also command other advantages. They have diverse – therefore complementary – resources and capabilities. This is particularly so if the nucleus of six countries were also to bring into closer interaction with itself the remaining oil-exporting countries of the Arabian Peninsula. In effect, then, the pursuit of self-reliance would be undertaken by Egypt (in the Nile Valley), the Fertile Crescent countries, and the oil exporters who are the members of the Gulf Cooperation Council (GCC). Egypt, Jordan, Lebanon, Syria and Iraq could provide Saudi Arabia and the other oil-exporting countries with skilled workers, entrepreneurial capability and a large scope for investment in agriculture, industry and tourism.

On the other hand, the oil-exporting countries have capital-surplus economies but a very narrow resource base. Consequently, their rational choice would be investment in the neighbourhood, rather than placing substantial reserves in deposit accounts, bonds and stocks in Western financial markets. Furthermore, the small oil-exporting countries suffer from the shortage of skilled workers and entrepreneurship, and, apart from Saudi Arabia, have small internal markets that cannot match their production and export capacity in refined oil products, petrochemicals and fertilizers. Egypt and the Fertile Crescent countries, and some of the Maghreb countries further away, are a natural market for these oil- and gas-based products. This last point is of special significance in view of the import restrictions being imposed or threatened by OECD members. Finally, the economic performance of Egypt, Jordan, Lebanon, Syria and Iraq is creditable in terms of the region's standards, while the economies of the oil-exporting countries in the Arabian Peninsula are still at a less advanced level if their own performance is to be considered, not the vast input of TNCs operating within them. Here again there is scope for co-operation and complementarity with Egypt and Fertile Crescent countries.

Admittedly, this scope is not as large and promising as that provided by the region as a whole, which in its entirety provides strategic economic depth to any of its constituent members. But it is more feasible to design, create consensus around, and implement effective complementarity among a limited number of countries – a nucleus of six – than among the twenty-one states with their diversity and the vast distance that separates one periphery of the region from another. The political problems involved in bringing together the Mashreq countries (that is, Egypt plus the Asiatic Arab countries) into some institutional framework within which to co-operate in joint action and to seek complementarity, are less formidable and intractable than those involved in bringing the twenty-one states of the region into some such framework. This is particularly so as the oil-exporting countries in the Peninsula are already members of the GCC which functions increasingly as an integrating body in economic and politico-security matters. It is the members of the Fertile Crescent that still need to be brought nearer together within a reasonably well-functioning political system, even if a very loose one. (The formation by Egypt, Iraq, Jordan and North Yemen of the Arab Co-operation Council in February 1989 falls short of the qualifications that the nucleus of six described here enjoys.)

Whether the whole region is considered, or sub-regions within are considered, the primary and most essential area of action to be targeted is political: the building up of some formula of association. One thing is certain: the present state of political and economic fragmentation will not permit any serious steps in the direction of self-reliance as conceived in this book. On the other hand, a drive towards close integration of all the member states of the region is not on the political agenda for the foreseeable future, since it would involve too wide a jump from the present fragmentation and 'parochialism' (in Arabic *qutriyyah*, that is, excessive isolationism within the confines of the single state, away from a sense of and loyalty to Arab nationalism). This leaves one rather realistic option open, namely sub-regional association on the basis of some loose federation (or even confederation), with the major decisions only assigned to the federal authority. The broad objective of self-reliant development, and the broad policies to serve it, would be among such decisions, in addition to the general orientation of foreign policy and external security.

An even more realistic option exists that could conceivably be preferred, because it is less ambitious than the association of the members of the Fertile Crescent parallel with that of the members of the GCC. This is co-ordinated co-operation between members of the Fertile Crescent and the GCC, which could be horizontal or vertical, or a mixture of the two. The former means that co-operation would revolve around similar activities or involve joint membership in organizations serving the same clearly defined function. The Arab region has many such organizations and activities, though a large proportion of them are sluggish. Judging by the energy with which the GCC conducts its activities, it is reasonable to expect joint horizontal organizations and activities between the Fertile Crescent and the GCC to be more seriously and effectively run and conducted than those that bind together all or most of the twenty-one Arab States.

Co-ordinated co-operation could also be vertical, in the sense that it would involve the complementarity of different activities, like division of labour in the undertaking of different processes of a certain large industry, or the assignment of different stages or phases of an industry of different countries, according to a pre-set plan. On the sectoral level, it would mean specialization according to comparative advantage, or the flows in different directions of different resources, like manpower and entrepreneurship on the one side, and capital on the other. It would also comprise the provision by GCC countries of capital for investment within the scope provided by Egypt and the Fertile Crescent countries.

If Egypt, the Fertile Crescent and the GCC, that is, the Mashreq countries, have been emphasized here, this is not because there are no other sub-regions capable of co-operating horizontally and vertically, within some framework of association. Indeed, the Nile Valley and the Maghreb groups are coherent enough within themselves to undertake such co-operation. However, neither of them alone, nor the two together, have the advantages that endow them with the capability of being the nucleus which the Mashreq countries could be. The twelve Mashreq countries have had close political, cultural, social, commercial and general economic relations for generations. Their populations have a closer familiarity with each other than with the other states of the region. Finally, the feasibility of self-reliance among the six Mashreq countries singled out as a nucleus is much higher than that among the members of any other group or combination of groups, in the rest of the region. Table 4 brings this out clearly. Yet, despite all this, the twenty-one states of the region should ultimately all be involved, for a more meaningful drive for self-reliant development, under some politico-economic formula or another.

So much for a discussion of broad political frameworks involving association among several countries within the region. There is still need for a more probing discussion of the leadership network or resource within each of the countries than has so far been provided. But for the present we are assuming such networks are available (or potentially available), and that they have a strong orientation towards and commitment to self-reliant development. In fact, the same outlook, motivation and impetus that make for close politico-economic association, in some sub-regions or in the region as a whole, can be counted upon to be promotive of self-reliance. Consequently, all we need to emphasize here is that the two-pronged political factor of association among countries, and the development orientation of the leadership networks within countries, are together the primary prerequisite for the feasibility of collective self-reliance in practice. Indeed, without this factor there can be no self-reliant development in the Arab region. Yet more will be said about leadership networks in the context of the dynamics and machinery of self-reliance to be dealt with in the next chapter. We move on, therefore, to a discussion of more specific priority areas of action into which the pursuit of self-reliant development ought to be translated.

Though meant to be specific, the discussion to follow ought to be put in its proper broader perspective, without which the identification of areas of action will be erratic and non-directed. The guideline directing such identification is the selection of areas of action consistent with the determination to seek self-reliant development, and the causality between the selection made and the materialization of such development. It is hardly necessary to emphasize that a selection that meets these qualifications can be made only if society is in the process of being restructured with respect to its values and outlook, priorities, and the locus of real power in it. In turn, the restructuring necessarily involves the formulation and implementation of democratic principles and modalities of government, along with an earnest move towards Arab co-ordinated co-operation, if not outright integration. For such profound transformation to be possible, society will have to be re-educated in harmony with the objectives sought, and therefore the leadership network and the socially-aware elements of the people will have to struggle against the values and forces which have a vested interest in blocking the transformation. With this perspective in mind, the specific areas of action to be suggested will now be presented.

The first priority is for a close, if not identical, perception of what development means for society – and, more specifically, of the objectives of development and their interaction and intermeshing. This is essential for the harmonization and co-ordination of national development plans and programmes, for the initiation of joint projects among some or many of the Arab countries, and finally for the design of activities and patterns of division of labour within the region (or the sub-regions) which are necessary for the achievement of complementarity. Harmonization and co-ordination among country plans is the most modest target. At a later stage, the drawing up of a plan for the joint Arab economic sector will have to be undertaken, and finally and ideally a development plan for the whole region's economy will have to be drawn, even if on an indicative basis.

A number of institutions can contribute to the process of identification of regional development objectives. The most prominent among them would be the Economic and Social Council of the League of

Arab States, the Council for Arab Economic Unity, the Arab Fund for Economic and Social Development, and the Arab Planning Institute – all official institutions. Three important private bodies can be added: the Federation of Arab Economists, the General Union of Arab Chambers of Commerce, Agriculture and Industry, and the Centre for Arab Unity Studies.

The development of human resources and manpower should be society's topmost concern within planned harmonization and co-ordination. We need not discuss here the objectives and ideal content of education and training, and how they can best serve the broader objectives of a society that is determined to bring about its own regeneration. Such discussions can be found in the many books and documents in existence that address the philosophy and purpose of education in the Arab region. Our concern at this point is rather to stress these aspects of upbringing, education and training which are of direct service and relevance to the formation of citizens as an end in itself, if the regeneration is to be brought about. But the aspects concerned must also be of service and relevance to the pursuit of self-reliant development. As these desiderata can optimally be sought within the context of close Arab political association, with what they involve in institutions, programmes and outlays, they must form central components in the value system around which the upbringing, education and training of Arab youth are to be built. It is therefore obvious that the development of Arab human resources and manpower should contain not only economic but also other inputs relating to the political, social, cultural, scientific and technological aspects of the individual's, and of society's life, and his/its preparation for the future sought.

Two further observations must be made in connection with the area of action being discussed. First, that regional or sub-regional activities and programmes should be designed and undertaken in line and in harmony with their national counterparts, and vice versa. This is in order to facilitate the exchange of cultural, economic and technological capabilities among the countries, with a view to achieving a better allocation of manpower and cultural output on a regional basis. The second observation is that the design of programmes – both national and regional (or sub-regional) – for human resources and manpower development should provide, or at least allow scope for, future needs. This would be based on the expectation of growing and diversified needs, changing conditions in the world at large, especially in science and technology, and a greater determination to achieve a large measure of national and regional security along all the fronts where security is exposed or threatened.

The leading regional institutions that could provide important inputs to human resources and manpower development would be the Economic and Social Council of the League of Arab States, the Arab League Educational, Cultural and Social Organization, the Arab Labour Organization, the Arab Fund for Economic and Social Development, the Council of Arab Ministers of Education, and the Union of Arab Universities.

The acquisition of appropriate effective technological capability is the third urgent area of action that the region ought to concentrate on if its extreme technological dependence is to be reduced or qualified at a satisfactory pace, and its technological self-reliance is to be promoted earnestly. Among other fundamental considerations, this view of acquisition means caution that society does not take the line of least resistance by sliding into uncritical imitation and mere importation of the hardware and software of technology, and does not become obsessed with the need for fast change in the technologies in use, simply because the much better endowed Western industrial countries do so. In fact, there is much to criticize in these countries themselves in this respect, like the artificial encouragement of technological obsolescence and the resultant waste of resources, and the obsession with gadgetry and the multiplication of goods the differentiation between which does not justify the effort and resources going into their production.

We have already referred to the widespread practice of large corporations to create wants not spontaneously felt, through the power of the media and aggressive marketing, and subtly and effectively to nurse these wants to become thought of by the large consuming public – in the North and the South alike – as pressing needs. But while the countries of the North can largely afford such waste of purchasing power, those of the South can ill afford it. It ought to be remembered also that a substantial part of aggregate purchasing power in Third World countries comes from the well-to-do who are influenced by the desire to imitate the better-off in rich industrial countries. Thus the rich or nearly rich in Third World countries in this fashion reduce capital accumulation in their economies, and divert the disposable income in their hands away from developmental uses.

As in the case of education and training, it is necessary to realize that the process of acquiring appropriate effective technological capability can be intensified more through a regional (or at least sub-regional) approach than through a narrow country approach. Collective effort is not only necessary, but in many cases vital and indispensable, for certain programmes aimed at promoting science and technology. And this will be all the more true, the more industries and other activities become promoted and developed at a regional or subregional level. Again, as in the case of education and training, country and collective efforts should be harmonized so that they can benefit from mutual feedback from each other's experience, initiatives and creative ideas. In addition, collective programmes will constitute a net saving in outlays, as many components of these outlays which are duplicated in country programmes can be reduced or minimized thanks to the establishment of collective programmes. Such programmes can be so designed as to serve the particular interests and needs of particular countries, and need not be monolithic in content and design.

The Arab region has not yet fully developed enough institutions concerned with the promotion of technological capability, although a couple of projects for that purpose have been under consideration for a number of years. In addition to the setting up of a regional centre for technology under one or another of the projects drafted, the Union of Arab Universities and the Union of Arab Scientists can be instrumental in providing assistance in ideas and modalities of work.

The next area of concern which needs immediate and massive action is agricultural and rural development. This is crucial because the exposure of Arab food security has become critical, as already indicated, and the extent of dependence on the major Western food producers has become so excessive that the Arab region imports more than half its total requirements. The development considered vital is very wide-ranging. It is not merely economic and technological, but also social and above all political, so that the rural population may acquire the political leverage that it ought to have by the right of its weight in the society and economy.

The programmes that are urgently called for include rural and technical education and training, infrastructure in the form of roads and means of transport, a diversified system of co-operative societies, extension services, as well as storage and refrigeration facilities, grading centres, research and experimentation centres, irrigation and drainage networks, clinics – in fact there is hardly any aspect of life or activity which is adequately equipped at present.

We must single out here four other areas of action associated with rural and agricultural development. Three of these are purely economic in nature. They are sound, non-discriminatory pricing policies which do not amount to a subsidy by the countryside to the cities; energetic and enterprising marketing institutions and programmes; and agricultural credit through banks and credit co-operatives in combination. The fourth is of mixed nature. It is the reform of the land tenure system – a reform which will not be insufficiently thought-out like the ones which were put into effect in the 1950s and 1960s. Appropriate institutions were not then built up and equipped in order to replace the large landlords who were dispossessed. As a result the functions of the landlords remained unfulfilled, and agricultural production not only stagnated, but in many instances dropped down.

Collective action, whether at the level of the exchange of ideas, experiences, or design of institutions and programmes, or yet at the level of financing and the undertaking of joint programmes, can be of immense value to rural and agricultural development. Indeed, all the countries with immense agricultural potential, except Iraq, need the support and co-operation of other countries. In the present instance, the peoples of the whole region have a stake in the development in question, whether as consumers of food, producers of agricultural equipment and chemicals, suppliers of agricultural skills, or yet as suppliers of investment capital. There are many modalities for co-operation, and we have here an ideal case of optimal complementarity. So far the exemplary field for the institution and application of such complementarity, which is Sudan with its immense land and water resources, and the AAAID – the Authority for Arab Agricultural Investment and Development ('Triple AID'), set up in Sudan by the Arab Fund for Economic and Social Development (AFESD), have both failed to fulfil the expectations invested in them. The basic cause for the failure has been the irresoluteness of the political will of the countries involved (and they were many), and the poor political management of the economy within Sudan itself. However, an analysis of the problems involved will take us far afield beyond the limits of our immediate task.

Apart from the Economic and Social Council, the Arab Organization for Agricultural Development, AFESD and Triple-AID can make the basic contributions to design and institution building for rural and agricultural development, including the setting up of programmes and projects. The last two bodies, AFESD and Triple-AID, can also provide finance from their own resources, and be catalytic agents in attracting finance from governments. The General Union of Arab Chambers of Commerce, Agriculture and Industry has also recently involved itself deeply in agricultural development, and is promoting the setting up of a large joint programme for the purpose worth $2 billion.

Another priority area of action is the development of basic and engineering industry, in order to build industrialization on a firm foundation capable of facilitating the phases and stages that are to follow. The foundation involves intensive recourse to science and technology, and therefore experimentation and research, rational calculativeness, and industrial entrepreneurship – all for the inculcation and spread of the spirit of 'industrialism' (see Kerr *et al.* 1960). The example of Third World countries that have moved into advanced lines of industry, like Brazil, Mexico, India, Taiwan, Singapore and South Korea – to name the most notable cases – is often quoted as one worth emulating. It is added that the Arabs lack neither the finance, nor the trained technicians, nor yet the market for accelerated industrialization.

The case that I will try to make here is that the Arabs must walk firmly first, before trying to run. It should be enough for many years to come if the Arab region attempted jointly to develop many or most of the manufacturing industries which the TNCs have developed in part or are developing within the region, or whose products they are exporting to the region. The industries easiest to go into, and for which the regional market is quite adequate at present, include durable household goods, food products, engineering equipment, equipment and furnishings for hotels, machines used in banks and other rather simple electronic equipment, machinery and equipment for public works and contracting, hospital and educational supplies, and building industry requirements. In all these industries the demand is large enough, and the skills available are adequate enough, to launch the industries listed, if the countries with available investment capital were willing to enter into joint projects. It would be wasteful for individual countries to attempt to set up a wide range of industries singly. With the necessary far-sight and sound analysis, they could undertake joint programmes and projects which would be viable and profitable, in addition to being politically advisable.

The institutional framework for industrial development is available to a large extent, with the Economic and Social Council providing an umbrella institution (as it does for manpower and agricultural development, and for plan co-ordination), and the Arab Organization for Industrial Development providing the specialized knowledge required. AFESD could help with financing, and, in addition, country funds (like those in Kuwait, Saudi Arabia and Abu Dhabi – the most active presently) could also be counted upon to provide funds. Private enterprise would also be interested on the basis of regional or sub-regional enterprises, directly or through the General Union of Chambers of Commerce, Agriculture and Industry.

The sixth priority area of action is the development of infrastructure across national borders, on a sub-regional basis in certain instances (like the management of shared water resources, the linkage of electricity networks among groups of countries for a more even flow of power, or the building of road and railroad networks), or on a regional basis like the supply of aviation services and sea transport. It is much easier at present to make connections by sea or air with Europe or the United States than with many other Arab capitals than one's own. Indeed, there are many cases where connections between Arab cities are much more frequent via European airports and seaports, than directly.

This area of action is all the more essential for the effective widening of the regional market, for the reduction of the cost of intra-regional imports, and for the movement of Arabs across national frontiers. Some intraregional road networks are already designed, and some projects for operational linkages and airline amalgamations have been under discussion for years, but not much concrete work has yet been done. It ought to be added that a much more intensive exchange of visits by Arabs to each other's countries, for the purpose of tourism, business or education, would be extremely useful for solidifying the ties between the Arab peoples, and for making integrative moves or measures more binding and lasting. It should not be left to intergovernmental agreements and institutions to forge such ties: they would be much more dependable and reassuring if they grew at the grassroots level.

Arab oil and gas policies are supposed to receive abundant thought, analysis and formulation through the instrumentality of three bodies. The first, both historically and in terms of real power, is OPEC, but this organization has Arab and non-Arab oil exporters, although the former are slightly more numerous and have far more oil resources. The second is OAPEC, the all-Arab OPEC, but this organization is much more a research and publication body than a policy-formulating body. The third is the GCC which has been rising to prominence of late among the oil-exporting countries of the Arabian Peninsula.

This seemingly large framework should not conceal the fact that there are other aspects of the management of the Arab hydrocarbon resource than those normally dealt with by OPEC, OAPEC and GCC that need examination and appropriate policies. A sound, comprehensive view of the resource in general seems to require policies that can achieve balance or equilibrium among a number of outwardly contradictory or conflicting positions. Such positions relate to pricing; the volume of production, export, and domestic consumption or domestic industrial use; conservation; the earning of revenues; the use of oil revenues internally and externally – to name a few issues. There seem to be at least two stands to take with respect to each of these issues. For instance, the desire for conservation works against the expansion of production beyond a certain point, and also against the desire to maximize revenues, and so on.

The search for a reconciliation of the various possible conflicts is further complicated by two factors. First is the absence of consensus among most producers as to the nature of real country interests with respect to each of the issues concerned. Consensus is especially necessary if a long-term perspective is to be taken into account, and if account is also taken of the regional dimension in the formulation of policies. There is great intellectual and some political pressure to include the region's fundamental causes and interests among the determinants of oil policies. The second unbalancing factor is the oil crisis that erupted in the early 1980s. This crisis has been generated by a drop in world demand for oil among energy sources, and of Arab oil particularly among all oils. Hence the drop in prices and exports, and consequently in oil revenues. The drop in revenues has had serious repercussions nationally, regionally and internationally.

Still broader than purely economic developments, serious issues of a social nature have arisen in association with the brief affluence experienced in the oil era in the decade 1973–82. These issues related to the accrual of unearned income (or pure rent) which has caused a separation in the minds and behaviour of many oil-country nationals between effort and reward, and has damaged an already insufficiently established work ethic. On the political level, the sudden financial affluence has led to the intensification of national identification (*qutriyya*, as indicated earlier), at the expense of identification with Arab national entity. And at the cultural level, the new patterns of consumption largely shaped by external forces have represented serious incursions into the national culture and upset many of its values, thus causing considerable dislocation and loss of direction.

The economic and non-economic issues involved, which are matters of direct and significant relevance to the whole region, though of particular relevance to the oil-producing countries, and which are causes for concern for the present as well as the future, deserve to be considered carefully and responsibly by OAPEC members, and possibly also within the framework of the Arab Economic and Social Council. The purpose of such consideration would be to identify the issues that arise from the management and exploitation of the hydrocarbon resource, in all their economic, social, cultural, political and security implications; to elaborate the optimal policies called for in the service of national and regional causes and interests, and to design instrumentalities for action, or provide the ones in existence – most notably OAPEC – with the power and the means to implement the policies.

The repatriation of the maximum amount possible of Arab financial resources placed in the industrial countries abroad is the next priority area of action to consider. The purpose would be to use the repatriated resources for investment in development work in the Arab region. It can be stressed that these resources are very marginal in volume compared with the vast domestic resources available to the industrial countries which host Arab funds today, while they can have a massive impact on the factor of capital availability in the Arab region. Besides, it is both ironical and humiliating for certain Arab countries to seek foreign economic aid under stringent terms, and with tough political strings attached, when Arab capital can be made available. Obviously, great care ought to be taken that the repatriation of Arab reserves does not constitute an encouragement to the countries which own these reserves to adopt yet more permissive policies for the importation of yet more non-essential goods and services, or yet for more conspicuous investment from which the peoples do not derive any real and lasting utility.

The capital-needy countries, on their part, will have to make sure that they can provide a healthy and safe climate for the investment of borrowed funds from the capital-surplus countries. Furthermore, the former group will have to make the investment in well-prepared projects and programmes which promise to pay the loans back, if not directly then through the benefit to external economies which they are expected to bring about. Obviously, there will be other uses to which repatriated funds can be put, like participation in joint projects of a regional or sub-regional nature, or for the import of vital consumption goods and services, or yet for the current expenses of development-orientated programmes in science, education and technology. What should be very carefully guarded against would be the use of the funds for yet more arms purchases, merely in order to appease the military establishment, or the appetite of arms manufacturers always seeking expanded sales outlets, or arms dealers ever-hungry for commissions, or merely the fascination with ever-renewed arms systems that look alluring and pride-satisfying in military parades.

Between them, the Arab Monetary Fund and the Arab Fund for Economic and Social Development can be useful instruments in the management and utilization of the funds repatriated, as agents for the countries that own them. But here, once again, the first priority area of action, namely the harmonization and co-ordination of plans, as well as the elaboration of a common perception of development and its objectives, would be a vital input in the optimization of the use of the repatriated funds. This is because such use should submit to rigorous principles and guidelines that meet the priority system initially established for investment.

The last priority area of action to refer to is foreign trade and its policies. In this respect, attention should first be directed to the overall expansion, diversification and improvement of Arab productive capacity. This is essential so that many more, and better, goods and services can be put into trade flows. The first task here should be the satisfaction of the maximum possible number of basic needs from Arab production. The next objective would be a dual attempt to replace as many as possible of the goods and services imported, and to expand exports – both to other Arab countries and beyond to non-Arab markets. The expansion in the volume of production within the region, along with diversification and quality improvement, will widely enlarge the region's internal market, and gradually cause a considerable redirection of the region's foreign trade, and a radical change in the composition of the region's imports and exports. The reader is reminded in this context of the discussion undertaken in the preceding section of the chapter, in connection with the first and second criteria of adequacy – namely, the size of the region's internal market, and the directions and composition of its foreign trade. Serious concern and action along the priority lines suggested in the present section can be trusted gradually to achieve the objectives set for the purpose of the satisfaction of both criteria.

The institutional framework to serve the promotion of intra-regional trade has been drawn but is still being utilized most insufficiently. The Council for Arab Economic Unity, the Arab Common Market, the Economic and Social Council, and two basic agreements entered into for the facilitation of intra-Arab trade and settlements, have all been in existence for many years. Unfortunately, not all Arab countries have adhered to the first-named Council, and fewer have adhered to the Common Market. As to the agreements, they remain largely ignored, subject to arbitrary freezing or outright violation, even without decorous legislation by the countries that decide to flout some of their clauses. But, most importantly, they are consistently made the victim of the violent ups and downs of inter-Arab politics.

A number of conclusions can be drawn from the discussion in this chapter in its entirety. Some of them have emerged explicitly, while others are largely implicit.

1 The region's endowments, as expressed through the assessment of the criteria of adequacy, make the pursuit of self-reliant development feasible, if the latter is undertaken by the region as a whole through a well-prepared collective effort. The feasibility has also been established, though conditional on co-ordinated co-operation undertaken by the Mashreq countries, especially the six described as a nucleus for self-reliance. But in either case a development-orientated leadership network should be available in enough strength and should be committed to self-reliance as a strategy. Furthermore, the materialization of self-reliance must be expected to be gradual, and must be aimed at soberly and with a good measure of realism, away from absolutism.
2 Collective self-reliance is no substitute for national development efforts, even if the degree of self-reliance possible will be small at the one-country level. In fact, collective and single-country development efforts ought to proceed together: the dynamics of one supports and activates the dynamics of the other, provided the efforts of both are so designed as to be complementary and to permit mutual feedback.
3 The nature and content of the priority areas of action examined indicate clearly that a large measure of development work must be undertaken by the public sector in the individual countries co-operating together, and by the joint Arab economic sector acting as an entity – indeed as a public sector at the regional level. However, spacious room should also be provided and maintained for the efforts of the private sector, within a broad structure of division of labour. This would ensure the Arab economies of the dynamism, capabilities and enterprise of the private sector.
4 The priority areas of action suggested in the present section are not listed according to any scale of significance. It would be very difficult to apply such a scale, since the areas interact and intermesh closely, and supplement each other.

5 There is no serious shortage of regional organizations, accords or instruments generally eligible to be vehicles for collective action. Some new such vehicles are no doubt necessary; but the basic need is first for the individual governments, acting through the summits of heads of state and the many regional ministerial councils, to provide regional institutions, programmes, projects and agreements with the necessary earnestness, leaderships, direction and guidance, and the financial means and authority to proceed with their functions and tasks.

6 The clear, consistent and continuous emphasis on internal forces and action for the pursuit of self-reliant development does not mean that external forces and actors are absolved from their role – historical and contemporary – in blocking such development. The emphasis here should not conceal the fact that behind many of the obstacles to action lie certain external causes, in addition to the internal. However, at this stage in the book, we are in a position to concentrate on internal forces.

7 The most important of these internal forces is national will and determination at the level of the leadership network in each country, and that of the regional leadership network. The latter is represented not only by the summits of heads of state, the regional ministerial councils, the League of Arab States, and the many regional organizations, but also by all the other elements in our definition of the national network that have influence at the regional level. We emphasize in particular those elements whose voices are heard through political, economic, educational, professional, intellectual and syndical channels – in addition to parties and popular movements with an Arab national dimension on their platforms.

8 The designations of the criteria of adequacy, and the tone of the discussion, might together seem excessively economistic to some readers. However, in reality they all have close and substantial aspects and implications of political, social and institutional nature. Indeed, the all-important seventh criterion – the availability of a development-orientated leadership – is probably more political and cultural in content than economic.

9 Finally, the spirit in which this chapter has been written strongly suggests the message that economists and other social thinkers and historians in the Third World have done enough excavation in their colonial past, and have drawn a long enough bill of charges against dependence. The time has certainly come for a determined and focused look forward at the functions and tasks which development

would need when sought through the strategy of self-reliance. There is enough challenge in such a forward look to absorb a great deal of the imagination, capability and resolve of society so as to forbid continued return to past accounts. Even then, and given the best circumstances, self-reliant development can only be approached slowly and painstakingly. All the more reason, therefore, why it should demand and receive our fullest and undivided attention.

5 The dynamics and machinery of Arab self-reliant development

INTRODUCTION

The first three chapters of the book addressed these three questions. Why develop? For whose benefit is development? What kind of development is needed? These questions dealt with the pressing need for development, the beneficiaries of development in an order of priority, and the content and quality of development considered capable of responding to the needs of the social groups at the top of the priority ladder among all beneficiaries. The discussion led to the conclusion that self-reliant development, as characterized in Chapter 3, had the content and quality deemed capable of meeting the specifications that had been evolved during the examination of the three questions stated.

As a result of the conclusion reached, Chapter 4 has been devoted to the enquiry as to whether self-reliant development in the Arab region is feasible, and has come up with an affirmative, though strongly conditional reply. The reason why the reply is qualified relates specifically to the present inadequacy of the factor of leadership – its misdirected orientation, its lack of purposefulness in the pursuit of self-reliance, its narrow social and political base, and the inadequate framework from which it springs and within which it operates. It becomes necessary, therefore, in the light of the assessment made in the last chapter of the degree of feasibility of Arab self-reliant development, to address the last question which is considered in the book: how can development be undertaken?

Stated more precisely for the purpose of this chapter, the question becomes: how can self-reliant development be undertaken? Within what political and socio-economic framework appropriate to Arab society and conditions can this development be attempted, and through the instrumentality of what dynamics and machinery?

Although some general aspects of the possible answer to the components of the question just stated have been touched upon briefly on occasion in the past chapters, it remains for this last chapter to deal with them more fully. This is necessary because of the reach and depth of the political, social, economic and structural transformation which the Arabs will have to be able and willing to bring about, if the pursuit of self-reliant development is to be undertaken seriously, and with a reasonable promise of success.

In this connection, it must be admitted that any kind of meaningful development attempted by the Arab social forces *now* in the seat of power, cannot rise to the level and quality of the development whose main specifications I have tried to characterize in the earlier chapters. These social forces are unable, and clearly unwilling even if able, to rise to the challenge, judging by their self-centredness and their narrow horizons – whether political, social or economic – within which the realization of the expectations of the Arabs has been imprisoned since political independence. Any exceptions to this generalization witnessed between the mid-1950s and the early 1970s have been partial, few and far between. Consequently, to have rosy expectations regarding the possibility of self-reliant development within the political and social conditions prevailing today, at the start of the 1990s, would be not only unrealistic, but overly idealistic and utopian. Hence the urgency and criticality of the endeavour to bring about far-reaching social change if the search for self-reliant development if not to remain an intellectual exercise which is most unlikely to be translated into concrete reality, under present circumstances.

The discussion to follow is conducted under three headings that deal with the framework, the dynamics and the machinery of self-reliant development, respectively. However, these three focuses overlap and the strands of the analysis pointing to them interact and mutually determine each other. Their separation into three sections in a sequence is justified basically by practical considerations, that is, to make the presentations easier to handle.

THE POLITICAL AND SOCIO-ECONOMIC FRAMEWORK

The identification of the political and socio-economic system suggested as a framework, within which Arab self-reliant development could possibly be launched, is necessary for the identification, in its turn, of the dynamics and machinery capable of initiating and sustaining the motion towards such development. The connection between the system, on the one hand, and the dynamics and machinery, on the other, will become clearer as the discussion proceeds.

However, the attempt to undertake the identification of the suitable framework should not proceed in the abstract. It has to take account of the culture, the mainstream outlook, the past experience and the future expectations of Arab society. Understandably, to tie the nature and content of the system and framework to the objective conditions presently governing in society – that is, to the past, the culture, and the future expectations – would be pre-emptively to restrict the system to what already shapes it and makes it what it is. No doubt this would seem to contradict the insistence that deep and far-reaching social change is needed if self-reliant development is to be sought. However, this contradiction can be explained away once it is realized that the governing conditions are no more than a launching pad from which to start, one within which it would be necessary to engineer fundamental changes, if the system is to become a suitable framework for self-reliant development and for other significant and pressing changes in the economy, the society and the polity.

The Arab countries have gone through a great deal of experimentation with economic, social and political systems during the past decades since the end of the Second World War and political independence. The system-map of the region can show a wide range of choices, including extreme forms of greatly uncontrolled market economies, heavily regimented forms of state capitalism (often designated as socialism), Marxism, liberal parliamentary democracy, one-party systems, absolute monarchy, theocracy, anarchy, highly centralized personal rule robed in republican garb – not to mention rudimentary modernization wrestling with tribalism. The labels just cited do not constitute comparable categories; some refer essentially to the economic aspects prevailing in the system, others to the social and cultural aspects, while others still refer to the political aspects.

What justifies the listing together of all the portraits enumerated is probably that they are all on a transmission or conveyor belt of transition, of change. Indeed, the observer can rightly complain of excessive experimentation with 'systems', even if in reality the changing features remain not much more than skin-deep. Thus, a free market economy in many countries coexists with a large and strong public sector (state capitalism); parliamentary elections coexist with one-party, one-candidate systems – even with the rule of an autocrat; and post-*coup* 'new' classes break bread, after an appropriate period of uneasy adjustment, with the old established classes. Furthermore, these contradictions are not frozen, as there is movement across economic, social and political lines over relatively short periods of time.

This is possibly, even probably, all a sign of energy, acceptance of change, mobility and dynamism. (However, some may attribute it to insufficient profundity in thought and fickleness in character.) For our present purposes, it may also seem to suggest a greater degree of openness to yet more change in some more clearly defined directions. But whatever the assessment of the merits or disadvantages of the mosaic of systems just referred to, this mosaic still reveals some fundamental underlying similarities in the generally prevailing trends in the economic, social and political life and outlook of the region's countries, which make it possible also to discern broad features that characterize the region as an entity. This justifies generalizations about the Arabs, in spite of the particularities of the individual independent countries among which the 200 million Arabs are divided, in North Africa and West Asia.

This is not the place to examine the broad, shared features and the particularities. But it would be useful, for our discussion of the framework appropriate for self-reliant development, first to identify and take stock of the main governing features – the mainstream features – underlying and cutting across the many varied aspects of systems prevailing. This would help us in assessing the rationale and the outlook for the system favoured by us as a framework for the desired development.

I venture to suggest nine such mainstream features. These have not been identified through formal personal research and field work, but from close observation and the perusal of a large number of careful studies, seminar proceedings, scholarly field work, newspaper coverage, and also from extensive participation in Arab conferences and symposia.[1] This build-up of the sources spans the past three decades, but most notably it began in the early 1970s when intra-Arab intellectual contacts intensified greatly, in relation to the examination and discussion not only of economic, social and political issues but also of cultural and scientific issues.

1 After much experimentation with systems and system (or sub-system) permutations, the region's countries are moving away from identification with or adoption of 'pure' forms of social (including economic and political) organization – 'ideal types' in the Weberian sense – no matter how superficial, marginal or partial the identification or adoption. The movement has been towards some variation of capitalism. The only exception to this generalization is South

Yemen, whose inclination is mainly Marxist. (However, the Gorbachev Reforms in the USSR, and subsequent profound system transformations in the other European socialist countries, will no doubt leave their mark on the Marxism of South Yemen very soon.)

2 The vast majority of the region's countries are sunk in a gripping state of dependence on the advanced capitalist countries, but a few of them are heavily dependent on the USSR in the areas of military supplies, and political and diplomatic support. The dependence reaches well beyond economic and technological fields to include advanced education, consumption patterns, and cultural orientation. The last-named aspect of dependence is one of the causes for the growing religious fundamentalism and advocacy of a return to the 'authentic' Islamic/Arab cultural heritage. Other causes relate to the current political identification with and leaning on powerful capitalist or socialist countries.

3 There is greater diversity in the forms of government prevailing (and their sources of power and legitimacy) than in the forms of economic organization. However, in all countries there are rather narrowly based elitist governments, in spite of the entry of considerable numbers of middle-class men (but very few women) into the privileged circle of authority. The elitist aspect can be seen no matter how old or recent the coalescence of the source of power, and whether the grounds for elitist status are military take-over, tribal hierarchy, established monarchy, party ascendancy, bourgeois predominance, or even direct lineage from Prophet Mohammed's descendants. All can be found in the region's experience.

4 There has been notable social and economic mobility, thanks essentially to three factors: mass education; energetic (even if often misdirected) development efforts, with what they create in economic and social opportunities; and obligatory military service in virtually all the countries. The mobility can be witnessed across and between classes, strata and sectors. Even if political power and social influence and pre-eminence had not been initially associated with economic power, they end by permitting the possession of great economic power as well by a minority in each country. On the other hand, wealth does not necessarily lead to political power for those who opt, or are forced, to remain outside the privileged circle of the politically powerful, whether these are party elites, the officer class, or the branches of ruling dynasties.

5 There are today immense numbers of educated, middle- and lower-class men and women who are outside the narrow circle of political influence and power, though many of them are politicized. They

constitute a reservoir of considerable potential power, once widely based political participation through the enjoyment of democracy and basic freedoms and rights becomes possible, and a large measure of social justice is realized through fairer distributive policies, and more widely spread economic and social opportunities.

6 However, the potential just mentioned in the preceding point is largely aborted through the widespread repression practised by narrowly based political leaderships, and the denial by virtually all political systems of the rights of the citizens to meaningful and true democracy and basic freedoms and rights, and in many instances to an adequate measure of social justice. The repression is possible owing to the immense build-up in all countries of a large and well-equipped apparatus of internal security, whose allegiance to the ruling elite is assured through generous economic and political favours.

7 The preceding two points explain the noticeable and fast-expanding expression of a desire for democracy in all the Arab countries where it is still possible to articulate the desire. The expression is not restricted to the intellectuals, though spearheaded by them in their writings, as well as by the more daring journalists and editorialists. It is also a recurrent theme in conversations in clubs and sermons in mosques. For the past decade or so a significant phenomenon has come to be experienced. This is that virtually all seminars and conferences, whether they centre around issues within the field of the social sciences or the natural sciences, history or the arts, express the need for democracy and human rights as a priority need for the individual and for society. While the political leaderships have not yet shown a concern and a positive response commensurate with the growing feeling for democracy and human rights, they cannot remain for much longer immune to the insistence of the pressure. So far, the demand for democracy has been contained through a mix of a great deal of repression with some appeasement – a sort of 'carrot and stick' policy.[2]

8 Besides the demand for democratic and other human rights and freedoms, there is a strong demand, though with limited articulation, for some form of Arab unity – generally characterized as a federal or at least confederal form by the more articulate intellectuals. These advocate unity as capable of embodying the salvation of Arab society from many of the serious ills from which it presently suffers.[3] Here again, the very limited extent of political participation is presented as the reason why the innate yearning for

unity is not articulated loudly, insistently and widely enough to influence the policies and behaviour of political leaders. It must be admitted that the word 'unity' is used here as a blanket expression of the demand for much closer co-operation or 'togetherness' among the Arab peoples and countries, for co-ordination, for closer and wider complementarity in the economic and political areas of action, for integration, or else, finally, for unity.

However, the last form, which constitutes the peak of ambition, is increasingly seen as very difficult to achieve, and in practice as necessitating a graduated march over many years, beginning with effective co-operation and the expansion of the joint Arab sector (in the areas of politics, external security, and economics), before the stage of unity through federation can be sought. In other words, the demand for unity is much more realistically expressed now than it had been in the 1950s, when, under the leadership of President Gamal Abdel-Nasser, Egypt and Syria merged into a unitary state in February 1958.

It is much more fully realized at present that unity must grow from the base upwards in the area of economics, through immensely increased and invigorated joint projects and programmes; the movement across national frontiers of more dollars in expatriate investment; and the intensification of joint Arab action in all important areas of life. The advocates of unity no longer consider the presence of a popular and charismatic leadership, like Nasser's, as enough assurance for the entry by the Arab states into binding and sustainable unity arrangements. Much more would be needed by way of institutions, a fuller Arab circuit of life, and, above all, a much clearer realization by all concerned that political fragmentation is as harmful and dangerous for the individual states as unity is beneficial and reassuring.

9 Although there is a small but firmly devoted nucleus of socialists in most Arab countries, and one country that has officially adopted a Marxist social system, nationalism is the ideology most in evidence in the Arab region. Nationalist loyalty can be said to be directed mainly to the individual nation states (the feeling which is called *qutriyya* or *wataniyya* in Arabic). But there is a substantial proportion – many analysts say a majority – of politicized Arabs whose nationalism embraces the Arab nation in its entirety, namely the inhabitants of the whole Arab region or Arab homeland (a feeling which is referred to as *qawmiyya* in Arabic) (*Ibrahim 1981*).

In brief, the predominant ideology is one of Arab nationalism, even though the content claimed for this ideology varies from one school of thought to another. Furthermore, not all Arab nationalists demand the same things from their concept of nationalism: some believe that it would not be worth striving for unless it allowed basic freedoms, democracy and human rights; others want Arab nationalism embodied in Arab unity even if the social system under unity were harsh or repressive.

However, there are indications that most Arab nationalists would, after serious consideration, say that Arab unity as an embodiment of Arab nationalism would lose its value unless the social system were progressive, participatory, respectful of human rights and freedoms, concretely attentive to the requirements of social justice, and distinctly development orientated.

This is my reading of the mainstream features and contours of the political and socio-economic map of Arab society today. Whatever expectations may be entertained for the further future, the fact remains that for the present, and for the immediate future, what is most likely to be desired and worked for by most segments of the leadership network (as defined broadly earlier), and by the many intellectuals and politically concerned educated, would be a system based on nationalism. But the various segments of the network and the intelligentsia part ways when they come to their definition of the contents of the system.

As far as I am concerned, the content that would satisfy the requirements of the pursuit of self-reliant development, and contribute to the regeneration of Arab society in the many aspects of its life, would have to include certain characteristics as fundamental and mandatory. Thus, the orientation of nationalism should be progrssive, in the sense that nationalism should be supportive of the struggle for liberation and for social justice; it should respect human freedoms and rights and allow meaningful political participation for the broad masses; it should motivate the people to protect Arab territory from external incursion and to liberate areas already usurped; it should be a force in the struggle to free the economy as well as society and the polity of dependence as fast and as far as possible, and therefore to adopt a strategy of self-reliance in development; and it should involve the design and sustenance of an economy where ownership of the means of production is broad-based, with a strong public sector, alongside a sizeable and active private sector and a wide-reaching co-operative sector, within a pattern of division of labour which is not tampered with arbitrarily and irresponsibly. Above all, the social system opted for should allow for the change of government in response to popular will expressed in an orderly way and within the confines of legitimacy, and should provide the machinery and modalities for accountability of the political leadership.

There is no need to characterize rigorously and at length what the system that is meant to provide the appropriate framework for self-reliant development should *not* be sought to be, given the mainstream features of Arab society today, and the limited absorptive capacity of this society for change within the short and medium term. Stated briefly, the system should not embody a market economy enjoying unlimited freedom in relation to essential and strategic industries and activities, where it is the 'laws' of supply and demand all by themselves that determine what should be produced, for whom this production should be targeted primarily, the level of the returns to the factors of production, pricing policy, and other central economic issues and decisions.

This brief statement should not be understood to mean that the dictates of supply and demand ought to be violated and disregarded out of hand. What it means is that profit expectations should not be the *only* determinant of what is produced; nor should effective demand be the *only* determinant of the direction of the national output. In other words, social considerations should also be invoked in the determination of the selection of goods and services produced, and in the satisfaction of the basic human needs of the lower-income strata of the population. Furthermore, concern for self-reliance should run through all economic, social and political policies. It is only thus that society will have an optimal mix of concern for the dictates of social need, fair returns, and the satisfaction of the norms of human dignity and a decent level of living.

It is maintained here that neither pure capitalism – textbook capitalism and free enterprise, perfect competition, and all the rest – nor pure Marxism – textbook Marism of the orthodox type – can meet the specifications contained in the last paragraph. These specifications provide a good fit for what would be demanded of the system with respect to political, social and economic desiderata. To meet them would involve a reasonable degree of disruption in the current outlook, priorities and ways of life of Arab society, a degree which would not vastly exceed society's ability to absorb change. Those who ask for vast radical or revolutionary change in a very short time often project their own desire for such change, and their own absorptive capacity for it, to the population at large. This sort of projection or extrapolation is quite dangerous to indulge in, since it violates reality and realism, and can only lead to hardship for the people, confusion, and possibly violence – but invariably to the frustration of excessive expectations.

But, having warned against a dosage of excessively sweeping radical change which cannot be sustained within too short a span of time, I must hasten to indicate why neither pure capitalism nor pure Marxism can satisfy the desiderata suggested earlier. This is because the predominance of the private sector in an economy, within a social and legal framework designed essentially to serve this sector, with its nearly total submission to the profit motive and its excessive disregard for social welfare, cannot lead to self-reliant development or the satisfaction of basic human needs. On the other hand, a system of pure Marxism would strangle the initiative and dynamism of the private sector, and also drastically ration political participation and basic freedoms and rights for the masses, though – admittedly – it would provide a notable measure of distributive justice.

The assessment just made of the two systems in juxtaposition is certainly brief to the point that it contains only the basic essentials, and in very condensed form. It is also to be admitted that neither system unfolds today in its 'pure' form, or in its 'ideal type' specifications. But the qualifications that have been introduced over the past half century into the capitalist system – social welfare, much greater involvement by government not only in the formulation and implementation of economic policies, and the pruning of a part of the excesses of profit accumulation, but also in economic activity through the instrumentality of the public sector, to name leading instances – still fall short of what in the present context is demanded and expected of a nationalist–progressive system geared to the pursuit of self-reliant development with the objectives and the content specified in this book. Likewise, the qualifications which are currently being introduced to an extent in China but especially in the Soviet Union, with respect to the expanded role of the private sector, or to the recourse to profit as an indicator of the level of performance, or yet to the enjoyment by the population of a much larger degree of political participation and basic rights and freedoms, are not yet far enough advanced for the observer to take complete comfort in them.

At yet another level of discussion, the framework to be drawn involves concern for the many more circles of potential decision-making than the top rung of leadership in government or business. An appropriate framework ought to take account of the interest, the needs and the demands of people at the grassroots level: in remote as in close villages, in the rural as in the urban sector, within small associations of craftsmen, labourers or clerks as within powerful business groupings, national labour federations or influential economic societies. In short, local and provincial groups must share with their national counterparts the right and the duty of the moulding of decisions and the pressure for a share in decision-making.

Obviously, the nationalist-progressive system offered here as optimal for the conditions of Arab society is not one in existence, or even in the making, but only one in hope and expectation. Consequently, we cannot go far in piling praise on it, or claiming special merit for it, since we have not yet established that it is feasible to launch and maintain. The next two sections of this chapter will attempt to show whether it is realistic to expect the system to have the dynamics and machinery that can make it a reality in Arab society and life.

THE DYNAMICS OF ARAB SELF-RELIANT DEVELOPMENT

What, then, would be the dynamics of self-reliant development which could with good reason be expected to activate society to move in the direction of such development? It would be natural for individual Arab countries that are relatively large and well endowed with a wide natural resource base and appropriate manpower and capital resources to aim in normal conditions at a certain limited measure of self-reliance. Some of the countries included in my designation of 'the nucleus of self-reliant development' – namely, Egypt, Saudi Arabia, Iraq, Syria, Jordan and Lebanon in the Mashreq, and Algeria in the Maghreb – could conceivably make the attempt. Indeed, Egypt and Algeria, and to a lesser extent Iraq and Syria, sought self-reliance between the mid-1950s and the 1970s, but changed course for various internal and external reasons. My assessment of the feasibility of self-reliance in individual countries, undertaken in the last chapter, showed that no one country by itself, whatever its resources and capabilities, could pursue self-reliance and achieve a large measure of success. What is at issue, therefore, is the identification of the dynamics of self-reliance at the individual country level as a beginning, no matter how partial and marginal the result might be, and then to move on to make the identification for the well-endowed countries of the Mashreq listed earlier and, *a fortiori*, for the region as a whole.

It seems warranted to consider that the dynamics are generated by two basic components. These are vision or perception, and action. This division is made for the purpose of explanation and on the grounds of conceptual differentiation, to facilitate the analysis. The qualification is necessary inasmuch as the two components are not unrelated, but influence each other and interact in an energetic dialectical manner. In the process, they enrich each other, and the outcome of the interaction is an improvement in the clarity of perception, on the one hand, and in the soundness, orientation and effectiveness of action, on the other.

Perception consists, first, of the ability of the 'forces of change' or the 'agents of change' in society, which will be identified in the section to follow, to comprehend the nature of the *problématique* which Arab society would face in the pursuit of meaningful development, and in the desire for liberation from the grip of distorted and dependent development. The comprehension should be possessed by the forces constituting the machinery of development, and projected by them to as large a part of the population as possible, to the effect that the development experienced so far is distorted, dependent and niggardly in its rewards and unfair in their distribution among different social strata. The logic of this comprehension would show the forces of change, and, by extension, the population at large, that distorted and dependent development can lead nowhere but to the failure of Arab society to rise to the many economic, social, cultural and political challenges which it faces today.

The second aspect of perception would be a natural outcome of the first. This is the advocacy and spread of a counter-comprehension, namely, that self-reliant development is the antidote to distortion and dependence, and that it enjoys credibility because it can be shown to be feasible in the Arab context. The two components together call for a wide measure of social re-education inside society as a whole, irrespective of the level of conventional or formal education of the various social strata, the extent of their affluence, or the degree of their politicization.

The third aspect would certainly be the most difficult to provide and involves the highest risk to the agents of change. It is their ability to elaborate and crystallize a philosophy and course of action for the liberation of society from lethargy, dependence and misdirection, in order for it to be able to resist the condition of dependence and struggle to pull out of it. This would be a most demanding task, since it involves resistance to the forces and interests, both internal and external, which have a stake in the persistence of dependence.

This resistance invokes the second component of the dynamics: action. It necessitates the formulation of a national political stand for a response to the challenge, as well as the formulation of the policies and the strategies, then the programmes; and finally it involves creating the institutions and evolving the modalities, all of which, in combination and interaction, are necessary for the response to the challenge of distorted and dependent development, and the pursuit of self-reliant development. And the intensity of such action would rise under the pressure of the process of action itself. As it does, it would become more demanding in effort, struggle and sacrifice, if it is to be effective and of long-standing corrective influence.

At this point, the close interconnection and interaction between perception (or theory) and action (or experience) through praxis must have become clear. It has probably become evident that the first two aspects of the dynamics would certainly fall short of the necessary transformation in society by themselves, unless there is action and struggle, within organized avenues of action such as parties, unions and other associations capable of channelling action for greater effectiveness, continuity and more coherent direction. Nevertheless, the criticality of the dual aspect of comprehension must not be underestimated. Today, many intellectuals and thinkers, and some political and labour leaders, recognize the serious danger for Arab society of erosion in national will and resolve, extreme lethargic dependence on external powers and forces in many aspects of life, complacency in the face of external threat to national territory and interests, and cultural alienation.

This perception must be made crystal clear to the broad leadership network, particularly to the political leadership which is less aware of it than the other elements in the network (or else less interested in acting in line with the perception). The perception is a prerequisite for the imparting of a clear appreciation of the criticality of recourse to independence in decision-making to the extent reasonable and possible, of concern for basic human needs, of awareness of the urgency of harmony between the social and physical environment, and of recognition of the pressing need to pursue an inner-directed and an inner-driven and motivated development. The task of the absorption of all these aspects of comprehension is enormous and very demanding. And the values and implications of the comprehension should be internalized by the social forces that constitute the machinery of self-reliant development, and to the extent possible by society at large.

So far I have focused on the dynamics of self-reliant development as it could unfold in individual Arab countries. The same components – comprehension and action – can be identified as equally necessary for an attempt by the various Arab countries and their integration-orientated institutions and leaders to make an energetic and persuasive advocacy of self-reliant development within the Arab region at large. The difference between what applies to individual countries and what applies to the region as a whole (or some groupings within it, like the Mashreq countries) can be seen more clearly in the discussion of the machinery of development, as I will have occasion to indicate further down.

Indeed, the argument can be offered that what is harmful and dangerous for individual Arab economies and societies, is *a fortiori* harmful and dangerous for the region looked at in its entirety. This is because individual countries are expected to look after their own particularistic interests more seriously than those of a somewhat abstract entity – an entity which constitutes one economy and one society in the eyes of the 'believers' in Arab nationalism and unity. At best, the Arab region can be considered one economy and one society in the making, or in the remaking if the historical perspective is to be invoked. If so, then it is all the more reason that the agents of change referred to earlier, especially those with an Arab nationalist orientation and commitment, should expend more effort and attempt more persuasiveness than they need to in their advocacy of self-reliant development within their individual countries.

Perhaps the key to success in such advocacy which targets the whole region is the ability of the intelligentsia (as intellectuals possessing political initiative) among Arab nationalists from all walks of life to convey the message, strongly and clearly, that individual Arab countries stand to suffer if they ignore the necessity and urgency of self-reliance at the regional level, and that they stand to gain if they commit themselves actively to regional or collective self-reliance. In other words, concern with the region's interests is not a burden on individual countries, or a favour they would be called upon to confer on the community of Arab countries without benefit to themselves. In fact, the contrary case can be made. Individual Arab countries can neither successfully stand in resistance to dependence, nor seek self-reliance successfully, each by itself, no matter what any one country has by way of endowments and capabilities.

Before I turn to a discussion of the machinery of self-reliant development it would be useful to point to a factor that has been developing in recent years, which could add to the strength of the dynamics of self-reliance at the regional level. This is the experience of the Arab region since the early 1970s and the onset of the oil era with the financial affluence it brought with it to many Arab countries. Although the region has been going through a reversal (or at least a freezing) of experience since the early 1980s, with a drop in world demand for Arab oil, and a drop in prices, exports and revenues, the expansionary effects of the decade 1973–82 have not been erased. On the contrary, the lessons, both of the expansion and of the subsequent shrinkage, are being increasingly absorbed; and they are of relevance to the point at issue.

The experience in question involved massive movement of workers across national frontiers within the region – somewhere between 3 and 5 million strong,[4] according to the more knowledgeable estimates. There have also been massive capital transfers. One prominent component of these has been labour remittances, estimated at $6.8 billion at their peak in 1984,[5] more or less in the opposite direction to labour flows. The other prominent component of capital flows has been concessionary assistance by oil-exporting governments, a considerable part of which has been non-reimbursable grants. At its peak in 1975 this assistance is estimated to have exceeded $18 billion[6] to Arab and non-Arab recipients – governments and national and multinational institutions. Over three-quarters of this sum went to Arab countries. (The average of the assistance provided over the decade 1974–83 was $7.7 billion.)[7] In addition, over 390 joint projects were established,[8] each bringing together few or several countries in shared undertakings – some with private sector participation. Scores of specialized regional organizations and professional associations have been established, several of them combining all the Arab countries. Many industries have been set up, which increasingly need the Arab regional market for their output, specially with protectionist policies by the Western industrial countries becoming menacingly visible. And immense food imports from non-Arab, advanced industrial countries, threaten the food security of the region and therefore call for joint Arab action.

These are not isolated events or developments. Their significance in the present context is that they have shown even the least unity-orientated Arab leaderships that complementarity among the region's economies is natural, necessary and beneficial to all those concerned. They have shown some of the most externally-orientated countries that the Arab market is the prime natural outlet for their manufactured goods. The economies that need expatriate labour but have surplus capital, and those that need expatriate capital but have surplus labour, have seen how much they need each other. Furthermore, the dangerously considerable demand for foreign food and for foreign technology (whether in capital goods or expertise) has shown that only if the Arab countries co-operate closely and extensively in the joint development of their agricultural and industrial skilled workforce can they reduce the costliness and danger brought about by the exposure to external suppliers, markets and skills. Only the most short-sighted leaderships can withstand the weight of evidence, that the region has to resort increasingly to self-reliance, and that this can optimally be approached on a collective basis. Finally, while the recent adverse developments of the Arab oil industry serve as a strong supplementary component of the dynamics of self-reliance discussed earlier in this section, they also underline the role of the leadership network at the regional level which is already in existence and reasonably motivated, in spite of the frustration born of its bitter experience in the 1980s.

THE MACHINERY OF ARAB SELF-RELIANT DEVELOPMENT

What I mean by 'machinery' is something much wider than conventional institutional set-ups for planning-cum-development purposes. These are usually small groupings of economists, statisticians, and engineers and technicians. Furthermore, in ordinary usage, the word 'machinery' in the present context refers only to institutions in the public sector and government engaged directly in economic development. On the other hand, the expression as used in this book relates to a much broader base, one which is considered the rightful engine for the mobilization for and the promotion of self-reliant development, and for the moulding of decision-making to that end. The wide reach of this engine will become evident further down during the discussion. The justification for the adoption of a very wide angle of vision in the examination of the machinery is that it would be impossible otherwise for the drive for self-reliant, socially-orientated development to take off with a good prospect of success. No other instrumentality is likely to have such a prospect.

The association of the composition of the machinery of self-reliant development with the locus of decision-making suggests that this machinery has a political, in addition to its economic and social, function. Johan Galtung is right when he discusses this connection under the heading of 'the politics of self-reliance' (Galtung 1980). Thus, the drive for self-reliance has at least as much a political as an economic rationale and motivation, and its feasibility and chances of success are causally tied to the ability of politically aware social forces to influence the process of decision-making to bring the drive into being and sustain it. The broad-based purposefulness to be involved in the pursuit of the type of development advocated in this book can spring only from certain socio-cultural values and a political stand which together emphasize self-reliance as a value and as a strategy for the development desired. It is only with this background that action could be expected in the appropriate direction.

The development sought so far in the Arab region has no doubt emphasized certain social objectives, as can be seen from its declared aims and the financial allocations directed to education and health services, and the policies formulated for a somewhat better distribution of wealth and income. However, the initial intentions have been left without appropriate political, legal and institutional safeguards capable of sheltering them against powerful particularistic interests, within and outside the sphere of government. Thus it was not long in the Arab experience since independence before development efforts turned disproportionately towards the service of the interests of governing elites, and ended by leaving the broad masses only slightly better off, while the powerful, the rich and the influential have become much more powerful, much richer and much more influential.

Many of the social groups enjoying privilege have changed in identity over the decades, as 'new classes' have emerged, but each new class in its turn has appropriated the privileges without much delay. The reason for the dilution of the initial good intentions, and the frustration of broad, popular expectations, lies essentially in the powerlessness of the people at large, and their absence from the decision-making process. The power elites that were supposed to represent them and serve their interests have largely defaulted, without much delay and with only marginal consideration for the cause of the masses. This was to be expected, since the Arab masses, by and large, have had very little say in the political management of the economy, which in turn is because they have had very little say in political decision-making. It is precisely this state of affairs that needs change urgently, for self-reliant, socially-orientated development to be at all possible to pursue.

Two questions arise in this respect. How can such change be brought about? And in what relationship do the agents of change – broadly defined – stand with regard to the social groups that specifically constitute the machinery of development? While the first question is undoubtedly interesting and relevant, there will be no direct attempt to answer it here, since the focus of this chapter – indeed, of the whole book – is on socio-economic development. Though this development is an integral part of an enterprise for the broad regeneration of society, the claim cannot rightly be made that development is the whole of that enterprise. However, as we shall shortly see, the machinery of self-reliant development comprises the major agents of change that in large measure would be expected to be active in shouldering the responsibility for formulating and putting in motion the broad social enterprise. To this extent, therefore, the first question will not be ignored in substance, but will receive attention through the examination of the second question.

In identifying the social forces that can and are rightly expected to shoulder the responsibilities which the drive for meaningful development calls for, I will try to steer carefully between two possible dangers. The first is to proceed from an elitist stand, since the act of singling out certain groups may suggest leanings towards certain elites, whether political, social or economic. The second danger is to adopt an economistic approach under which the drive for development will be seen to devolve upon what might be called 'the professional developers', namely the ministers of national economy, planning and finance, and the various agencies connected directly with development activities in government. If the private sector is allowed any room at all in the thinking and formulations of the professional developers, it would be more through the expression of certain expectations of the business sector than through the formulation of specific policies likely to serve as the guidelines of indicative planning, and to embody incentives capable of encouraging this sector to move in the directions desired.

But businessmen are not the only or major social group left out of account in the perceptions and formulations of conventional, economistic planning. The majority of the beneficiaries targeted, irrespective of the size and significance of the programmes and projects meant and/or planned to serve their interests, have hardly any say or voice in the determination of development objectives and priorities. This generalization is all the more true, the poorer the would-be beneficiaries and the deeper their settlements in the countryside, far from urban centres. As stated earlier in this book, much of the rural population and the poor urban population suffers from political weightlessness when it comes to economic as well as political decision-making. There is no need to emphasize once more that the cause for this weightlessness is the extreme restrictiveness and marginality of political participation in the Arab countries. As little commitment can be expected where there is little participation, the development efforts so far made have not succeeded in mobilizing the fervour and sense of community and sharing of the masses. The desire to avoid both elitism and economism determines the course of the identification of the social forces considered likely to be adequately and forcefully concerned with self-reliant development. This concern can be expected once the nature and implications of such development are widely expounded and related to the needs of the people, without rhetoric and exaggeration and with simplicity and objectivity.

The machinery suggested here as potentially capable of promoting self-reliance comprises three social forces.[9] The first consists of the leaderships in the main aspects of society's life and structure, that is, in politics, education, culture and thought, information and the media, labour, business, and the professions. The leaderships belong in fact, though not formally and institutionally, to the leadership network described in Chapter 4. The network has many rings which interconnect closely or loosely, and which therefore have a potential ability to achieve mutual influence. Political leaderships have a particularly prominent role: they must be understood to include men and women in positions of responsibility in government and representative bodies, as well as political parties and popular movements. However, crucial as the role of the various leaderships may be, none of them could constitute an effective component in the machinery unless its members in general distinguished themselves by possessing a clear and strong comprehension of society's concerns and interests, and unless the membership enjoyed cohesiveness and evolved broad consensus around the basic themes connected to the concerns and interests. Furthermore, the leaderships must be strongly mobilized in the service of the causes they advocate.

The second component of the machinery consists of those non-affiliated, activist intellectuals and thinkers – the intelligentsia – who have a clear nationalist-progressive orientation, and therefore feel engaged in the service of the causes of liberation and self-reliance, within their broad concern for society's regeneration. The social force under consideration does not include only the specialists in economics, engineering, sociology or political science – the areas of close and direct relevance to development – or only the holders of university degrees. It also includes all those citizens who are deeply concerned with and contribute to intellectual and cultural causes and pursuits of relevance to society's regeneration, provided they are politically sensitive and ready to take an initiative in influencing the direction of society's movement, and to accept sacrifices in the process of struggling in the service of their convictions.

The intelligentsia have an elevated status in Third World countries, and more particularly in the Arab region where historically they have always enjoyed respect and wide influence – both among the people and in rulers' circles. However, their role and function are today menaced by considerable loss in their weight, status and effectiveness. This is because the intellectual conflicts which divide them are numerous, and they themselves are frequently characterized by absolutism and excessive abstraction, with very little readiness to seek broad consensus around the issues generally agreed upon. Often, marginal differences overcome the weight of the more important aspects of the issues which are the subject of conflict or controversy.

The Arab intelligentsia would no doubt have much more influence in the orientation of development policies formulated by the leadership, were they to practise more mutual accommodation and less absolutism in their views.

The third component consists of those citizens of each Arab country who are not included in either of the two components already identified, but who are politicized enough to be constructively concerned with self-reliant development, within a broader concern with society's regeneration. The citizens in question constitute a broad-based vanguard, which could provide solid ground (or a potentially solid ground) of critical significance for the drive for self-reliant development. The significance springs from the likely strong impact which this vanguard would have were it to enjoy political participation commensurate with its size and intellectual power. Once it is duly sensitized to the meaning of self-reliance, thanks to the operation of the dynamics discussed in the preceding section of this chapter, the vanguard could be a potent factor in the mobilization of the population at large, and the creation of a wide popular awareness of the rewards, as of the tasks, of self-reliant development.

This mobilization would be more meaningful and effective if achieved through organized institutional channels – political, economic and social – for the intensification of the drive for development and the provision of greater safeguards for its sustenance and continuity. To attribute such a significance to the third component of the machinery runs counter to a widely held view that ordinary citizens have only a modest political education compared with the members of the first two components discussed so far. Yet the attribution is justified inasmuch as the members of the broad-based vanguard, being largely outside the circle of power and privilege, become aware of society's concerns through personal experience and suffering daily and directly. It is natural for them to long for, and whenever possible to seek, political participation.

Before we discuss the relationship and interaction between the three components in the machinery in their operation, we need to go into an examination of the place of political participation in the scheme of things as envisaged here. This is necessary because of the obvious connection between political participation and the power it would impart to ordinary people in making their voices heard, in pressing for the protection of their interests through the pursuit of self-reliant development. For, unless this pursuit were sought by the public at large, there would be the danger that the influential and rich minority in every Arab country would refuse to see (or admit) the public interest in self-reliant development. Indeed, guided by their long-standing experience, the privilged would probably see their interest only in some form of dependent development, within which only marginal benefits would accrue to the mass of the people.

The question of participation raises three areas of doubt for some well-meaning, development-orientated intellectuals.[10] The first centres around the nature and place of the role of political participation, or democracy, in the dynamics of development. The second suggests that participation is not essential for development, and suggests an antithesis based on the experience of the Soviet Union and other socialist countries which have registered notable developmental achievements *in spite of* the absence of political democracy. (In its extreme form, the argument says that the achievements materialized *because of* the absence or very limited enjoyment of democracy.)

The third area of doubt derives from the position that it would not be realistic, under conditions of democracy, for the political leadership (as well as the circles involved in the formation of public opinion) to ask the people at large to exercise strict discipline in consumption, for saving more domestic resources for investment purposes, which discipline would be necessary under the orientation of self-reliance. It is claimed that this would be particularly difficult and unrealistic, after the populations of virtually all the Arab countries had been offered very generous promises that many more goods and services would be made available for consumption under the impact of the development processes launched since independence. The failure of the leaderships concerned to make good on most of these promises would severely curtail their freedom to take firm positions with respect to belt-tightening. It is thus argued that the people's refusal to observe injunctions for strict discipline in consumption would be natural and logical.

These three areas of doubt are worthy of serious consideration, and I will try to deal with them.[11] It can be said, with respect to the first, that without the ability of the people to exercise political participation and enjoy their rights as citizens, they would remain unable to submit the various economic options available, freely and responsibly, to criteria of preference, and to make their choice in the light of their interests. In consequence, they would be unable to make a proper comparison between the costs and returns expected with respect to each option available. Furthermore, it is appropriate at this point to emphasize once again the causal connection between participation and commitment to the objectives, the tasks and the burdens involved in the pursuit of development, since commitment reflects the extent and meaningfulness of participation.

In this connection, it would be useful to bring back into focus the experience of the Arab region over the years stretching from the late 1950s to the late 1960s, with respect to the perception of democracy. These years witnessed the formulation and wide circulation of the thesis that political democracy was necessarily related to and incumbent upon socio-economic democracy as a prerequisite, within the framework of some sort of a phase sequence. Thus, it was maintained,[12] the citizens would be unable to exercise political democracy and enjoy it in a meaningful way, if this had not been already preceded by their enjoyment of economic and social restructuring permitting economic development, the provision of educational opportunities and health services for the whole population, and improvement in the pattern of distribution of wealth and income to make it less discriminatory.

The thesis was based on the conviction that poor, illiterate and underprivileged citizens were exposed to exploitation and manoeuvring as voters in any election, and therefore would in effect lack the freedom and the discernment to choose the political option which would best serve their real interests. The thesis was sound in large part as it applied to the conditions of most Egyptians, in whose country it was first expounded, and also of most other Arabs. Buts its soundness and relevance could be, and in effect were, grossly exaggerated. However, what is more serious is that the thesis could be, and was, used as an alibi for withholding the right of people to enjoy political democracy in a true manner. (Various formulas were devised over the years, in several Arab countries, for the opening up of democratic options, under some modality of representation. But as all these involved one-party systems – where party life was allowed at all – even the *outward form* of democracy was not kept, let alone the substance. Where personalized, authoritarian rule was in force, even the cosmetics of democracy were not applied.)

Withholding political democracy until the people would become capable, through first having economic and social democracy, properly to exercise political democracy treated the people as minors who had to wait until they were considered by the rulers to have come of age before the reward of political democracy could be released. This form of reasoning also implied that only the rulers were mature, and they alone could exercise political choice, not only for themselves but for the whole population. Those who stand sharply in disagreement with the thesis being considered, and I fully share their position, believe that the exercise of political democracy freely, and learning how to do so through a process of trial and error, is the only way to acquire the necessary awareness and capability of the exercise, with responsibility and on the basis of merit. Indeed, to submit the people to a period of guardianship is only to delay the day when they can acquire the capability and the worthiness for the exercise. In other words, the imposition of the guardianship is counter-productive and constitutes a policy that will only produce exactly the opposite of what it is purported to produce.

There is little doubt that the availability of freedom and political participation would enable the society to choose political leaderships with a developmental orientation, and empower these leaderships to discharge their responsibilities with confidence, but also with discernment and within the framework of legitimacy, since democracy provides the scope for accountability. (The corollary of this statement is that the deviation of the leaders from the course of action wanted by the people at large would justify a change of leadership through the working of the democratic process.) Yet the emergence of leaderships which the pursuit of development would call for would not be restricted to politics alone, but would expand to include those areas comprised in the notion of the leadership network. This would further develop social organization, and broaden the base of leadership along with the broadening of the base of participation. The broadening of the base, and the emergence of an alert and sensitive public opinion, would add considerable legitimacy to decision-making and decision-taking processes.

Finally, with respect to the first questioning now being discussed, it is reasonable to expect the development orientation and commitment of the leadership network to become continuous and sustained, rather than intermittent and fickle, and furthermore, to be expressed in an atmosphere of voluntary and creative political stability. What is witnessed today in the Arab region instead is stability which is enforced by diktat and the iron fist of security agencies. Such enforcement is hostile to the evolution and crystallization of national resolve in the pursuit of development, and would only succeed in the mobilization of a small proportion of society's resources, capabilities and commitment.

The response to the second area of doubt, which suggests that broad-based and meaningful and political participation is not essential for the purposes of development, and which uses the experience of the Soviet Union and the other socialist countries as evidence, calls for recourse to deduction and the application of value considerations. Thus, it can also be supposed, though it will not be possible to prove this empirically, that the Soviet Union would probably have been able to register greater and more encompassing achievements in the area of development, achievements more satisfying to the needs and requirements of its people, had the people succeeded in appropriating a larger area of political participation and thereby had reason and scope for greater economic motivation. Furthermore, with respect to values, this issue raises the counter-suggestion that development that is achieved with restricted participatory rights remains lacking in the fundamental human right to freedom. Such a deficiency means that the citizens will be unable to achieve a significant dimension of self-realization.

The third area of doubt, it will be recalled, was about whether the political leadership could realistically ask the people to curtail their consumption in order to mobilize more domestic resources for the purpose of investment, after having lavished promises on them during the decades of modern independence of a greater availability of goods and services for consumption. Here again the answer can come in two parts. The first is that sound development requires attention primarily and basically to the satisfaction of the basic human needs of the broad masses. As indicated earlier, these needs rise in quality and broaden in coverage and quantity, as the satisfaction of one 'generation' of basic needs after another is achieved. Consequently, since sound development in its essence involves a responsible concern for the needs of the population, it follows that population would not resent the obligations of development under a regime of political participation, so long as basic physical and human needs were being satisfied.

The second part of the answer is that by far most of the sacrifice to be called for in order to meet the requirements of self-reliant development would be asked of the better-off strata of the population – whether as individuals or business concerns – not essentially of the urban and rural poor and under-privileged. But, in any case, it would be necessary to combine the call for discipline in consumption with wide-ranging effort to broaden the awareness of the people of the long-term gains that would derive from development, and of the need for more domestic resources for self-reliant development. A campaign of education of this sort would have to stress how the medium- and long-term benefit expectations shold not be aborted for the sake of short-term, short-sighted, non-sustainable benefits. Furthermore, the campaign would have to point clearly to the political, economic and socio-psychological dangers of putting primary emphasis on foreign financial aid instead of domestic resources.

Some observations are now in order with regard to the likely operation of the components of the machinery of self-reliant development, after the comments just made on political participation in its relevance to development. The first and probably the most pertinent observation is that the intelligentsia, because of their status and the esteem with which they are held in Arab society, would have a central role in the operation of the whole machinery. This is because it is they who would be expected to bear a major share in the responsibility for the activation of the dynamics and the mobilization of the people behind self-reliance, as indicated in the preceding section.

The significance of the role of intellectuals refers essentially to their ability to promote general awareness of the defects and dangers of dependent development and its narrow social focus, and of the benefits that self-reliant development could bring about. Furthermore, it is they who would of necessity serve as a conveyor belt between the leadership network and the politicized segment of the population. While a part of the network – the educators, the media, the labour leaders and some politicians – would also be instrumental in widening the perception or comprehension of the defects of dependent development, and of the merits of self-reliant development, it is the intelligentsia whose central function it would be to convey this dual comprehension, and to prepare the atmosphere for action, which is the second component of the dynamics after perception.

The function of 'connecting' the leadership and the vanguard or the broad base of politicized citizens is particularly essential, as there is very little contact between these two groups. The leaderships rarely attempt to identify with and understand the concerns of the people directly, and the people rarely manage to convey to the leaderships their concerns and needs, except when matters reach boiling point. Furthermore, there is a great deal that the leaderships could learn from the popular base before they design development objectives and policies.

The second observation relates to the social transformation which it would be necessary to engineer and carry through for self-reliant development to be seen as desirable and worth pursuing. This transformation would require considerable and sustained inputs by all three components of the machinery. Social re-education would be essential for revealing the urgency of the transformation, and in promoting general readiness for the acceptance of change. The urgency would need to become internalized by the broad base of the politically and socially aware segments of the population, before action could be hoped for. However, the social re-education called for would remain of limited reach and impact unless it was conducted through organizational and institutional channels, such as parties, labour syndicates, co-operative societies, professional associations, and the like. The central theme of the social re-education would have to be the crystallization of a mental attitude and a political stand with which the pursuit of self-reliant development would be in harmony.

In spite of the centrality of the role of the intelligentsia, standing as they do between the leaderships and the broad base of politicized citizens, and often interpreting one side to the other, and influencing both through their function as the main carriers and advocates of the dynamics of self-reliance, it is the leaderships that in the final analysis would take the decisions crucial for the pursuit of self-reliance. This is the third observation of relevance to the operation of the machinery. It is the leaderships, especially the political segment among them, that would be responsible for translating the adoption of the cause of self-reliant development into strategies, policies, institutions, programmes and concrete action. This responsibility is naturally theirs, because they are the final depository of organized power.

During the discussion of the feasibility of self-reliant development in Chapter 4, seven criteria were identified for testing the extent of feasibility. They were labelled 'the criteria of adequacy'. It is only logical that every Arab country should assess the adequacy of the manner and extent of its satisfaction of the criteria, in order for it to act in the fashion that would have the greatest promise of bringing the adequacy nearer to the level required in the pursuit of self-reliant development. This is the fourth observation to make. However, we need not specify what policies, programmes, institutions and measures would have to be considered with respect to each of the criteria, to bring its level nearer to the optimal level called for, if the feasibility is to be transformed from a potential into a reality.

Much has been said in Chapter 4 which provides the specificity that is lacking here. This is particularly true of the seventh criterion, briefly labelled 'the availability of development-orientated leadership seeking self-reliance'. Because of the extreme importance of this factor, without which the satisfaction of the other six criteria would remain insufficient for the successful pursuit of self-reliant development, it received rather full examination. But the other criteria were also examined, even if more briefly. No more need be said here, therefore, about the channels through which the decisions, taken by the leaderships for the pursuit of self-reliant development, have to be translated into concrete action.

The fifth observation relates to the role and function of the third component of the machinery, namely the politicized citizens who provide, or could be made to provide, a solid base for the movement towards self-reliance, thanks to the power of its message. This message is essentially what the intelligentsia would be capable of diffusing in order to mobilize the population. The young, politicized, nationalist-progressive Arabs would be well placed to respond favourably to the efforts of the intelligentsia, to explain the damage that dependence inflicts on society, and the benefits that self-reliance could bring about. Being a significant segment of the population of each Arab country, the politicized young could contribute extensively to the persuasiveness of self-reliance, once converted to its cause.

The presence of the politicized young may not be readily evident to the casual observer, especially when the political system is reactionary and repressive. But their presence can be ascertained from some indicators. These include the spread of books and periodicals carrying the message of liberation, Arab unity, social justice, democracy and self-reliant development; their spontaneous reaction to calls made in some other Arab countries for the support of causes that form part of the message just referred to; and the notably increased advocacy in Arab media, conferences, symposia and other gatherings, as well as in Pan-Arab parties, of the message and the causes it upholds. It is thanks to this large body of citizens that the identification of the social forces, which constitute the components of the machinery of self-reliant development, does not reflect an elitist approach. Instead, the emphasis laid on the third component now being discussed arises from the fact that it is a broad front, not a narrow-based and elitist vanguard. In its absence, the emphasis on the intellectuals and the leaderships, which in comparison would form a relatively narrow base numerically, would justify the accusation of elitism.

This vanguard would be essential to the pursuit of self-reliance for two reasons. First, its conversion to the cause of self-reliance would generate enormous pressure on the political leadership to adopt similar orientation and to move on to the formulation of policies and programmes consistent with the orientation. Secondly, it would provide the support and energy which the policies and programmes would need in the process of being carried out. The vanguard would not only themselves be directly involved in action, but would also have the power to influence the rest of the population to provide their own input in the action called for.

The sixth and last observation relates to the movement or operation of the machinery as a whole. It has probably become clear that the operation starts from the central role of the intelligentsia, and their influence on the leaderships on the one hand, and the broader vanguard on the other. As indicated earlier, the intellectuals can now find some readiness within the leadership circles, thanks to the lessons derived from the cumulative experience of the Arab region over the past decades of independence, but more particularly from the oil decade 1973–82, when the oil industry prospered with breath-taking speed, and in the years since then, when the oil crisis developed, also with breath-taking speed. The implications of the boom and the crisis together are becoming clearer for a part of the leaderships. The leading thinkers who had foreseen the crisis at the very peak of the boom, and who were then considered prophets of doom by most political leaders, today find their earlier message accepted, even repeated by many leaders. Though painful, the irony is also gratifying to the intellectuals and thinkers concerned.

The overall result of what has just been said is that some elements in the political leadership are becoming aware, even if slowly and not painlessly, of the need for greater self-reliance in their pursuit of development. Even though most leaders have consistently found comfort in dependence as it has nourished their private interests and agreed with their political orientations and alignments, some do not fail to see how urgent it has become to be more self-reliant in the production of food, the acquisition of technological capability, and generally the promotion of a larger Arab regional market for Arab products. To achieve all this, the case for an inner-motivated, inner-powered and financed development is becoming clearer and more forceful, at both the country and the regional level.

If the message of the intelligentsia today seems to meet weaker blockage on its way to the leaderships, as just suggested, it finds distinctly ready acceptance by the broad vanguard, or the politicized, progressive–nationalist citizens. While many political leaders still conceive their interests as falling more in the fold of dependence, the vanguard much more readily see their interests in self-reliant development. The intellectuals could make their message more persuasive and effective within the leadership network, both through addressing the leaderships directly, and also indirectly through cementing the conversion of the vanguard, which in turn could exert more pressure on the leaderships to act consistently with the demands of self-reliance, since self-reliance can be proved to mean long-term self-interest. As this process expands and intensifies, and as the base of political participation gets widened, the leaderships could be expected to become readier to get into direct contact with the vanguard and, beyond them, with the people in general. If, and when, this point is reached, there would be communication in all possible directions and combinations. This would be the point when it could be said that a national resolve behind self-reliant development was coalescing.

The preceding observations should not be taken as an expression of unqualified optimism. They point to what could happen, under favourable assumptions and circumstances. But this need not necessarily happen in the way described. Every advocate of self-reliance should remind himself that there is no guarantee that each of the three social forces designated as components of the machinery would act as expected or hoped for. Furthermore, there is no guarantee that each would keep its position, attitude and role, or that positive and constructive interaction between the two parties in each of the three possible pairs or among all three parties would materialize. And there is no guarantee that power and influence would not corrupt the leaderships after seeming to acquire the appropriate development orientation; or that the intellectuals might not lose their idealism, clarity of thought and perspicacity, and public-spiritedness, if and when they were invited to walk in the corridors of power; or yet that selfishness, short-sightedness and obsession with short-term private interests might not blind the citizens at large to the broad objectives of society and to their very own long-term interests and expectations, which they might have possessed at some phase in the process of interaction with the other agents of change.

All these setbacks would be possible, and could abort the hope for self-reliant development. Perhaps the only guarantee, if there was one, would be the hope that spreading and deepening awareness of the dangers of dependent and essentially distorted development, and conversely spreading and deepening awareness of the advantages of self-reliant development, thanks to social re-education pointing in that direction, might well act as an incentive for insistence on self-reliance. Furthermore, hope could be entertained that the efforts by the people to capture their basic rights and freedoms and to enjoy meaningful political participation might deter the political leaderships from aborting the drive for self-reliant development, and encourage the intellectuals to stand by their initial convictions, and to stand up to any efforts of the authorities either to repress them or to bribe and corrupt them.

In addition to the possible setbacks that could beset the operation of the machinery of self-reliant development from within the machinery itself, there is serious danger that the drive to self-reliance might be blocked by enormous external obstacles. These could be referred to as constituting a counter-machinery, in the sense that they would be obstacles placed by external forces and interests in the course of the drive. They would obviously be hostile to any serious effort in the Arab region – as indeed in any other Third World region – to strive to liberate itself of dependence and seek self-reliance instead.

External vested interests have a high (and remunerative) stake in the preservation of the status quo, and in keeping Arab society 'immune' to radical transformation – economic, social and political. The centre countries – the advanced industrial countries – make immense gains out of the dominating state of dependence. These arise from the export of many goods and services which the Arab region has a potential capacity itself to produce, with particular emphasis on food supplies, as well as capital goods, technical skills, and armaments that are not highly sophisticated, and from the cultural and political affinity with, not to say subservience to, the leading Western countries (especially the United States), an affinity which has a material and a strategic value to the West. Once again, the reality of these external obstacles underlines the need for serious and sustained action by the Arab region to free itself of the state of dependence, even if the initial cost were high.

So far we have been considering the dynamics and machinery of self-reliant development at the level of individual countries, and we have ended by referring to likely setbacks and obstacles to the unfolding of the dynamics and the operation of the machinery. Careful thinking about the dynamics and the machinery would show that much of what has been said relates also to self-reliance at the regional level, or at the level of groupings of several Arab countries. Yet while there is not much to add to what has already been said with respect to the dynamics needed for the movement towards regional self-reliance, there are some points to be made relating to the machinery.

As already indicated, the machinery that could be capable of operating in favour of self-reliance at the regional level consists, first, of the Arab heads of state acting through their summit meetings. The only such meeting in the long history of Arab summitry (first started in 1964) that was totally devoted to broad economic issues was held in November 1980 in Amman, Jordan. Its central concern was the consideration of a newly prepared Strategy for Joint Arab Economic Action, the documents relating to which included, among other things, a Five-Year Plan for the joint Arab economic sector, and a budget proposal for financing the programmes included in the plan. The strategy and documents had been prepared for the Secretariat General of the League of Arab States (which serves as the secretariat of the Summit) by a large group of Arab economists.[13]

The Strategy and the Plan are still the only formal institutional framework for the operation of the Arab joint sector, although very little has been done to implement the Plan and its programmes, basically because financing has not been forthcoming as undertaken.

The main concern of the Strategy was the extension of the reach of Arab economic complementarity and the intensification of commitment to regional organizations, institutions and joint projects, as well as the expansion of intra-regional trade. But liberating the Arab economy from dependence was also an objective of joint economic action, although it received less attention than complementarity.

Further down from the apex of the pyramid of authority in the regional machinery for self-reliant development are ministerial councils, most notably the Arab Economic and Social Council of the League of Arab States. Some of the councils (which include economic affairs, finance, planning, agriculture, industry, labour, education and communications, to name those most relevant to development) have commissioned the specialized agencies under them to formulate strategies for the development of sectors within the area of their authority. These strategy documents suggest a number of policies of relevance. Self-reliance can be said to be a central theme in all the strategies and policies. The League of Arab States Secretariat and the Council for Arab Economic Unity are the two main bodies that try to co-ordinate the policies laid down by the ministerial councils, and to provide a co-ordinative input in the activities of the various regional organizations. The Arab League and the Council for Economic Unity both put self-reliance as a high objective in the list of priorities of these organizations and of their own activities.[14]

There are a large number of organizations, dealing with agriculture, industry, communication, labour and other sectors or activities. Of special significance are four institutions whose objectives and work have a promotive value for self-reliance. These are the Organization of Arab and Petroleum Exporting Countries, the Arab League Educational, Cultural and Scientific Organization, the Arab Fund for Economic and Social Development, and the Arab Monetary Fund. There are also several professional associations (of economists, engineers, and so on). Finally, as far as official and semi-official components of the regional machinery are concerned, there are nearly 400 joint projects and companies the top managements of which are orientated towards development, Arab economic complementarity and collective self-reliance. And, parallel with the official or semi-official components, there are private organizations, associations and joint projects, which also promote the development of many economic sectors and, by extension, overall development.

The discussion in the last few paragraphs has focused on the machinery which is specifically regional in scope. To this must be added those elements in the country leaderships who have a voice and respected status at the regional level, that permits their advocacy of self-reliance to be heard not only at home but across national borders as well. Likewise, political parties and movements (whether regional in scope or operating only in individual countries) which assign a prominent place in their platforms for regional concerns and causes qualify as part of the machinery for regional self-reliance. And finally, the intelligentsia in the various Arab countries comprise elements of regional status and influence. As these are committed to the cause of self-reliant development, they can potentially constitute an important part of the machinery. To sum up, it can be seen that the drive for Arab self-reliance could have an extensive and potentially powerful machinery. What is needed for this machinery to be active is for its various components to become fully persuaded of the merits of self-reliance, firmly committed to its pursuit as the most effective strategy to serve the interest of the Arabs, and ready to act in union and thus put the machinery in motion.

It is appropriate at this point to bring together the strands of the discussion so far conducted in this chapter, and the book as a whole. The last two chapters have examined the meaning and significance of self-reliance as a strategy for development, and specified how the quality and content of this development can serve the long-term, legitimate socio-economic interests of the Arabs. Then, the feasibility of self-reliant development was explored and found to be promising, but with certain conditions relating to regional political co-operation and economic complementarity, and to the availability of development-orientated leaderships seeking self-reliance. This fifth and final chapter has moved on to address the question: what would the dynamics and the machinery of the hoped-for development be, for it to be likely to be pursued successfully?

The consideration of this question has indicated that the national resolve to seek self-reliance must be formed firmly – both at the level of individual countries and of the region as a whole – in order for the Arabs to establish a strong base for the pursuit. This resolve needs six conditions to be satisfied, for it to bear fruit:

1 Realism in the setting of the objectives, and acceptance of the necessity of graduated movement towards them, owing to the fact that the roots of dependence are deep, and the internal obstacles to self-reliance are enormous.
2 The enjoyment by the people of each country of broad-based political participation, through modalities that make this participation

real and create meaningful democracy. Through democracy, the largest possible proportion of the people would take part in the examination, discussion, formulation and making of decisions, even though it would ultimately be the political leadership (including the elected representative bodies) that would take the decisions. Participation is essential for commitment to the tasks, the shouldering of the burdens and the making of the sacrifices that would necessarily be involved in the pursuit of self-reliant development. Most importantly, it would ensure the people of their fair share in the rewards of development, which is the most persuasive incentive for commitment. The democratic right is but one of the basic human rights, but it would be a prerequisite to the ability of the people to capture their other rights and their freedoms.

The connection between democracy and self-reliant development is very close and direct. It is only thanks to the democratic process that the people can express their economic (and political) choices and make their voices and their pressures not only heard and felt but also taken proper notice of. The political leadership and the people can thus have two-way communication. This would be especially true with the broadening of the political base of the leadership.

Finally, in the present context, the key to the prospect that self-reliant development would be pursued, to its feasibility if and when pursued, and to sustenance of the drive for it, resides in the power of the democratic process. At the present, most of the political leaderships would be unwilling – assuming they were able – to resist dependence and to work for self-reliant development. Democracy would provide the only course which could bring about the political change necessary for the process.

3 The forging of a politico-economic system for society which is nationalist *and* progressive. This system would provide the various Arab countries with an appropriate framework within which they could elaborate and develop an understanding and a conceptualization of self-reliant development at the country level, and would also enable them to seek far-reaching regional political co-operation and co-ordination and political complementarity. It is only thus that the political and economic circuit of life within the region could flow and be optimized, and finally lead to benefits to all the parties involved.

Ideally, the politico-economic system appropriate to the present conditions and likely to be in line with the general political orientation of the Arabs, and also potentially capable of serving the cause of self-reliant development among broader social and political goals, would have to meet a number of specifications. These can be briefly suggested as follows:

- The adoption of a progressive philosophy and an outlook that reflect the belief that the people should enjoy their basic rights and freedoms and put them into effect.
- The presence of governments that submit to the dictates of justice and the rule of law in the conduct of their duties and the exercise of their powers, and that direct the civil service and the armed and security forces, as well as the other parts of state apparatus, consistently with the principles of justice and legality.
- The presence of a dynamic and large, though not all-pervading, public sector, alongside a strong private and a co-operative sector. The proviso must be added that the public sector would have to submit to considerations of efficiency while retaining its central concern with social considerations, and that the private sector, in turn, would have to submit to social considerations as a framework that sets the frontiers of its activity, while retaining its intensive concern with efficiency and profitability.
- Opennness in each of the politico-economic systems in the various Arab countries to some political formula that would enhance intraregional co-operation and co-ordination, as first steps that could, when conditions matured, permit closer association and finally a federal form of unity among the countries that accept it. The political formula referred to must be flexible rather than dogmatic, in order to embrace sub-regional associations as a start, if necessary. In the present context, the Mashreq countries could to great advantage be one such association because they qualify as a viable nucleus for self-reliant development, as indicated earlier in Chapter 4.

4 Determined, enlightened and sustained effort to achieve the utmost possible degree of independence in economic decision-making in the service of national interests, essentially through the effort to possess the capability for independent political decision-making, to the extent possible. Without such independence, and without cultural authenticity and self-reliance, the perception and the model of development resorted to would continue to be imported and to remain alien. The aspects of capability just cited could be acquired only within a politico-economic system like the one stipulated in the previous specification, and within a framework of regional political co-operation and co-ordination and of economic complementarity.

5 Social justice sought through the achievement of a distinctly less inegalitarian pattern of the distribution of wealth and income, and of opportunities, among both social groups and individuals. A notably improved pattern would likewise allocate burdens and sacrifices more equitably, and would bring these more into line with the rewards of development. Furthermore, the presently under-privileged and powerless would, through better distribution and its political implications, acquire greater say and influence in the formulation and making of economic (and political) decisions. Needless to add, better distribution would generate a positive feed-back from which the drive for and process of development would benefit, and commitment to the cause of development would be strengthened and sustained.

6 Realization that any deep and extensive transformation in the outlook and behaviour of society that would necessarily be called for if self-reliance is to become earnestly sought would meet with daunting problems and obstacles, and would therefore call for struggle and sacrifice. The magnitude of the transformation would become evident once it is remembered that it involves the areas of politics, economic and social organization, but first, and above all, values and attitudes.

Consequently, the task of transformation must not be viewed with excessive optimism, facile assertions or oversimplification. This warning is particularly necessary as the problems and impediments in the course of transformation would be both internal and external, and probably more covert and skilfully camouflaged than overt and crudely revealed. To face them and to launch the drive for self-reliance would therefore call for the acceptance by its advocates of the necessity for hard work, struggle and sacrifice. The struggle may even necessitate far-reaching social and political restructuring – indeed, 'creative destruction'.[15] The people would need to have become convinced that the returns would well justify the costs for themselves and for years to come. Such conviction could be acquired only after intensive social re-education. This is a task for which the intelligentsia, parts of the leadership network, and the broad-based vanguard would have to accept responsibility. But the responsibility would be more effectively discharged if it were channelled through political parties and movements, and other social and economic organizations.

But, having said all this, some burning questions remain. Would Arab society act in the way considered necessary and desirable in this chapter? Would the enormous task of transformation, which is crucial if self-reliant development were to become both feasible and viable, prove too daunting to the social forces that are expected to be the agents of change and transformation? Would the analyst, the policy-maker and the operative, and finally society as a whole, end up with anything better than elusive development for their hopes and expectations? These are pertinent questions to pose, but no answer can be ventured except the placing of trust in the politically aware young Arab men and women. Their restlessness and concern for human rights, democracy and development are a powerful motive force for action to bring about appropriate political change. They can hopefully be relied upon to undertake what their fathers and mothers in their vast majority have failed to attempt. There is reason to believe that the young will refuse to inherit the gloomy future that the present, if not radically changed, would bequeath to them.

Notes

The designation 'processed' describes 'works that are reproduced from typescipt by mimeograph, xerography, or similar means; such works may not be catalogued or commonly available through libraries, or may be subject to restricted circulation' (definition of *World Development Report 1989*: 136).

CHAPTER 1

1 The most noted contribution to the formulation of 'pattern variables' is that of Parsons (1951). See also Parsons and Smelser (1965), Hoselitz (1960) and Lerner (1958), among others, also use Parsons' typology or pairing of attributes.
2 The noted exception is Gerschenkron (1962), which probes deeply into the background of development. However, even Gerschenkron does not attach the importance it should have to the network of historical relations between what are today developed and underdeveloped countries, and the implications of these relations. Essentially, his focus is on the Western world.
3 For a characterization of the 'universalist outlook' see Eisenstadt (1983).
4 The reader who is interested in the matter can refer to my own writings, the more relevant of which are listed in the bibliography.
5 The basic statistical indicators and the analyses that support the statement about the shortcomings of the developmental performance in the Third World, can be found in, among others, the annual reports of the World Bank, *World Development Report*, and also in the relevant part of the *Handbook of International Trade and Development and Statistics*, published annually by the United Nations Conference on Trade and Development, Geneva. However, the latter publication contains no analysis. Galal Amin (1974) is highly relevant in the present context.
6 The reader will probably find Hirschman (1981), Stigler (1982) and Boulding (1984) not only relevant but also intellectually provocative.
7 I use the terms 'mainstream' and 'counterpoint' orientation or analysis after the manner in which they are used in Hettne (1982: ch. 1).
8 According to a report published recently in a leading Arabic daily in

Beirut. However, perusal of the annual reports of The International Institute for Strategic Studies, *The Military Balance*, between 1983 and 1988, suggests that the proportion is distinctly higher than just indicated for the Third World. It is not possible to check the overall average since data are not available for a number of countries, and a weighted average will have to be made anyway if it is to be meaningful to refer to an average.

9 A table I prepared for the years 1972–87 for the twenty-one Arab states (based on data in the relevant issues of the IISS annual report, *The Military Balance*, and on United States, Arms Control and Disarmament Agency, *World Military Expenditures and Arms Transfers 1972–1982*, Washington, D.C., April 1984, and subsequent issues) shows that average annual spending by the Arab states is about 4 per cent of GDP. However, the data include only published information. There are good reasons to believe that this information underestimates the actual expenditure considerably, as a few countries hide their purchases inside a thick cloud of secrecy. The countries in question are the largest Arab importers of armaments and spend heavily on defence systems installed by foreign countries. Therefore the proportion may well exceed 5 per cent of GDP per annum on average.

10 Reference here in the context of Arab thought is to Ismail Sabri Abdalla's paper in *CAUS 1987*.

11 The International Foundation for Development Alternatives (IFDA) 'was set up in 1976 to contribute to the movement towards another development and towards a genuine international cooperation' (from a leaflet issued by the IFDA dated 15 April 1986). The Foundation is located in Nyon, Switzerland; it has a steering committee, and its president is Marc Nerfin. The IFDA publishes the *IFDA Dossier*, which 'represents the network in its widest sense, receiving papers and information from those who have something to offer and making them available to all' (also from the pamphlet).

12 As Hettne (1982) was familiar with Nerfin and Galtung (to judge by his inclusion of their works under reference in the bibliography of his own book), we must surmise that the judgement made by him and quoted in the text must apply to both.

CHAPTER 2

1 For a thorough and well-balanced review of the background and content of the dependency paradigm, see Blomström and Hettne (1984). This book also ends with a very useful bibliography of the most relevant works.

2 Apart from references indicated later in this section, I have benefited from the writings of a number of economists and sociologists, whose works are included in the bibliography, even though they are not specially referred to or perused in the text.

3 Seers (1963) is enlightening in this context.

4 The familiarity of Arab economists with Keynesian theory, as embodied in Keynes (1949), became noticeable only after the middle of the 1940s. Subsequently there was widespread 'conversion' to this theory.

5 The reception by a vast majority of Arab economists of Rostow's *The*

Stages of Economic Growth (1960) was highly approving, and the book was translated into Arabic without much delay. Even today, the dissenting voices are still largely submerged under the approval, although the latter is not as overwhelming as in the early 1960s.

6 Parsons' influence can be traced in several subsequent works by sociologists but also by some economists (like Hagen and Rostow, to whom reference has already been made). See, in addition to the authors and works listed in Note 1 of Chapter 1, Moore (1963) and Hoselitz and Moore (1963).

7 Because of the vastness of the literature on modernization and the process of transition through which societies pass, including the Arab society, fuller bibliographical information can be found in the bibliography.

8 The relevant works of the authors listed, and of several others, particularly concerning modernization in the Arab region, are listed in the bibliography.

9 I have benefited in preparing this section from the following works: Seers (1983a) (especially the chapters by Palma and by Seers himself); Bernstein (1979); Foster-Carter (1973) and (1984); Chilcote (1977); Nugent and Yotopoulos (1979); Hettne (1982); Hettne and Wallensteen (1978); Oxaal *et al.* 1975; Palma 1978; Roxborough (1976, 1984); and Taylor (1983).

10 See Palma (1983) for a summary of the ECLA's analyses and their evaluation.

11 The specific references relate to the following works: Viner (1952); von Haberler (1954, 1959); Johnson (1958, 1962) and Kindleberger (1962).

12 For an examination of structuralism see Chenery (1975a). See also Blomström and Hettne (1984: 17–19, and the relevant parts of chs 2 and 3); Myrdal (1957), and Seers (1963) for an identification of leading structuralists.

13 Published in *Third World Quarterly* 2 (1), January 1980.

14 Paul Baran was a forerunner in the introduction of political factors into the analysis of economic development, and of neo-Marxism. Before his book of 1957, referred to in the text, he wrote 'On the political economy of backwardness' in 1952. His work was a major tributary to dependency thought as it developed some years later.

15 Of special relevance are Furtado (1957, 1964, 1983).

16 Of special relevance are Sunkel (1969, 1979).

17 Though writing within two widely different ideological perspectives and outlooks, Bauer (1981, 1984) and Warren (1973, 1985) uphold the point that development is posible under conditions of dependence. Samir Amin's paper in *CAUS (1987)* takes a more cautious position with respect to the experience of the 'Four Little Tigers' of the Far East, in which he neither praises uncritically nor criticizes indiscriminately.

18 Only a limited number of writings of André Gunder Frank will be listed here, as he is probably the most prolific among dependency theorists (1966, 1969, 1972a, 1972c, 1978 and 1982).

19 Cardoso, in addition to co-authoring *Dependency and Development in Latin America* (1979) with E. Faletto, authored three works which are of direct relevance to the present study (Cardoso 1972, 1973, 1977b).

20 For a careful and balanced summing-up of the main components of the analysis of dependency theory, see Blomström and Hettne (1984: 76).

This book is of immense value to readers interested in the evolution of dependency analysis in the context of development theory.

21 The concept of 'unequal exchange' is a recurrent theme in Samir Amin's work (see, especially 1976, 1977b and 1974). Most recently, the theme appears in a series of articles published in 1987 in *Al-Mustaqbal Al-Arabi* (*The Arab Future*), a monthly published in Beirut by the Centre for Arab Unity Studies, under the general theme of 'Ishkaliyyat al-Ishtirakiyya wa ma ba'd ar-Ra'smaliyya' ('The *problématique* of socialism and post-capitalism') (*Samir Amin 1987a, b, c, d*).

22 The concept of 'unequal exchange' can also be encountered in André Gunder Frank's work. For some of Frank's writings, refer to Note 18 above.

23 Immanuel Wallerrstein's treatment of 'unequal exchange' occurs notably in his works on the 'world-system' (Wallerstein 1974, 1979, 1980). A more recent work uses the notion of 'unequal exchange' as an input (Wallerstein 1984: ch. 3).

24 Blomström and Hettne (1984) give this impression, especially when referring to André Gunder Frank. But such an impression cannot be obtained from Limqueco and McFarlane (1984). This book is unremittingly critical of neo-Marxists.

25 An earlier article by Bill Warren (1973) upholds the same basic ideas contained in this later work (first published in 1980).

26 See Note 21 above for a reference to Samir Amin's articles published in Arabic in 1987, as well as the full details in the bibliography. Furthermore, his paper in *CAUS (1987)* contains the gist of the ideas to which the text refers in several paragraphs. See pp. 149–90 for the full text of the paper, but especially pp. 168–78.

27 My treatment of the issue raised can be seen in the items included in the bibliography; see especially Sayigh 1979 and *Sayigh 1982*.

28 The most notable disagreement with Amin's presentation of his proposition that *dawlanah* (*étatisme*) could in effect be a stage between capitalism and socialism came (though not pointedly directed at Amin) in a paper by Ismail-Sabri Abdalla in *CAUS* (*1987*: 25 56).

29 The volume edited by Dudley Seers (1983a) is of close relevance here, especially the chapters by Palma, Lamb, Seers himself, and O'Brien. For a few of the many other evaluations of the work of a number of dependency theorists, see also Foster-Carter (1973, 1976, 1984) and Chilcote (1977).

30 In this connection, it is useful to quote Dudley Seers, with whose position on the usefulness of dependency analysis I largely identify. He wrote:

> We, especially Manfred Beinfeld and David Evans, point out that while the [dependency] school has not yet provided answers which are as correctly framed or as universally applicable as the theorists concerned may think, it raises the right questions – much more relevant ones than those derived from neo-classical economics. Our purpose is not to praise dependency theory, but not to bury it either, rather to raise constructive criticisms that might lead to its improvement and greater acceptability.
> (Seers 1983a: 16)

31 Palma, Cardoso and Sunkel stand out in their insistance that detailed specific situations ought to be studied, as against abstract theorizing or 'intuitive assumptions' or assertions (see Seers 1983a: 18).

32 Writing in Arabic, Galal Amin has been in the forefront among Arab economists upholding the necessity of delinkage, see *Amin 1984*.

33 See Hiba Handousah's paper in *CAUS 1987: 365–411* for a careful assessment of the South Korean experience within the framework of what dependency theorists call 'dependent development'.

34 I have dealt extensively, and in several works, with the serious and basic shortcomings of Arab development and Arab oil policies, as experienced in the era of political independence. (See Sayigh 1979, 1980, 1982, *1982*, 1983, and *CAUS 1987*.)

CHAPTER 3

1 Of direct relevance with regard to Arab history are works by *Amin (1984)* and *Sa'id (1984)*.

2 The generalization was likewise substantiated by my search in the library of the United Nations Conference on Trade and Development (UNCTAD), Geneva, and in several of the libraries of colleges and institutes within Oxford University, where I spent the academic year 1984–5 undertaking research on dependence and self-reliance.

3 Two other books that deal with some aspects of self-reliance, though with less concentration and a narrower coverage, are Erb and Kallab (1977) and Nerfin (1977).

4 The statement in the text applies also to *CAUS (1987)* as well as to Kuitenbrouwer (1975). Works in Arabic to which the statement is also applicable include: *al-Hamad (1987)*, *Zalzalah (1987)*, *al-Khauli and al-Jammal (1987)*, and *Mas'oud (1987)*. These four small books are part of a series of eight centring around self-reliance in the Arab context and form part of the intellectual output of the Arab Planning Institute in Kuwait.

5 I am indebted to the author, the editors and the publishers (Institute for Development Studies, Geneva) of Galtung *et al.* 1980 for permission to reproduce the headings of the thirteen points, which occupy pp. 27–34.

6 The core of points 1 to 7 in the text, which take up the remainder of the section in Chapter 3, are an expanded and revised version of a part of my paper given at the seminar on 'Independent Development' already referred to. See Sayigh in *CAUS (1987: 907–30*; the part under reference can be found on pp. 908–13).

7 In this connection, see Wemegah (1980) and Mishan (1979). Schumacher (1984) is in fact of direct relevance, though the author's angle of vision is much broader. See also Sayigh (1979): 323–41), for an examination of the deleterious social and economic impact of certain major oil policies in the Arab region.

8 The notion of 'embarrassment' within the context in which it is mentioned in the text is borrowed from Enayat (1982: 1–17).

9 Andriamanjara (1984) is comprehensive, in spite of its brevity. The literature on foreign aid is voluminous. The following works constitute a limited sample of analytical studies, some of which are critical or wary of foreign aid: Little and Clifford (1965), Ohlin (1966), Arnold (1966), Payer (1974), Lord Lever of Manchester *et al.* (1984), Hayter and Watson (1985) and Little (1982).

CHAPTER 4

1 The following works in Arabic are of direct relevance to the critical judgment of Arab development experienced since the Second World War: *Fergani (1980)*, *Biblawi (1987)* and *Abdul-Fadheel (1987)*. Of direct relevance also are Sayigh (1979, 1980, 1982, *1982*, 1983) and *CAUS (1987)*.
2 The states (arranged alphabetically) are: Algeria, Bahrain, Djibouti, Egypt, Iraq, Jordan, Kuwait, Lebanon, Libya, Mauritania, Morocco, Qatar, Oman, Saudi Arabia, Somalia, Sudan, Syria, Tunisia, United Arab Emirates, Yemen (North) and Yemen (South).
3 The seven single countries dealt with were: Egypt, Algeria, Saudi Arabia, Libya, Jordan, Tunisia and North Yemen.
4 The 'joint Arab economic sector' comprises all the economic institutions and activities undertaken jointly by the public and/or the private sector of two or more Arab countries. The coverage of this sector is referred to at some length in the present chapter.
5 The Secretariat General of the League of Arab States, the Arab Monetary Fund, the Arab Fund for Economic and Social Development, and the Organization of Arab Petroleum Exporting Countries, *The Unified Arab Economic Report 1988*, hereafter referred to as *The Unified Report (At-Taqreer Al-Iqtisadi al-'Arabi al-Muwahhad)*, Table 2/5 in 'Statistical Appendices'.
6 The following few paragraphs are based on material in Sayigh 1982: i–ix.
7 The volume of economic aid in 1987 was $3.3 billion. It was largest in 1980 at $9.5 billion. See World Bank, *World Development Report, 1989*, Table 19 in 'World Development Indicators' (hereafter referred to as 'Indicators'). For more recent estimates of the capital of the joint sector, see *S. Mas'oud 1987b*. See also *S. Mas'oud* 1987a.
8 *The Unified Report 1982*, Table 2/2 in 'Statistical Appendices' for 1981, and *The Unified Report 1988*, Table 2/2 in 'Statistical Appendices' for 1987.
9 For 1980 and 1981, see OAPEC (1982: Table 2.1); for 1987, see *The Unified Report 1988*, Table 4/3 in 'Statistical Appendices'.
10 See UNCTAD (1989: Tables 1.1 and 1.2) for world exports and imports for 1987. For population data see the World Bank, *World Development Report 1989*, Table 1 in 'Indicators'. For the Arab region see *The Unified Report 1988*, Table 2/1 in 'Statistical Appendices' for foreign trade, and Table 2/5 for population for 1987.
11 *The Unified Report 1988*, Table 6/5 for Arab intraregional trade.
12 Calculated from *The Unified Report 1988*, Tables 2/1 and 2/5 in 'Statistical Appendices'. World Bank data are somewhat different, and anyway they refer to GNP per capita. (See World Bank 1989, Table 1 in 'Indicators'.) But the difference does not disguise the reality of the wide gap in GDP per capita among the most and the least affluent countries.
13 *The Unified Report 1988*, Table 2/1 in 'Statistical Appendices'.
14 See OAPEC (1983). No estimates more recent than those for 1982 are available.
15 World Bank (1989), Table 1 in 'Indicators'. For growth of consumption and investment, ibid., Table 8.
16 I have depended to a certain extent in this sub-section on the analysis and

tables of Part Eleven, 'Foreign and Intra-Arab Trade', in *The Unified Report 1986*. (The 1988 issue of the *Report* does not refer to the matter under consideration.)

17 *The Unified Report 1986*, Table 11/3 in 'Statistical Appendices'.

18 *The Unified Report 1988*, for composition of foreign trade, see Part Six, and Table 6/3 in 'Statistical Appendices'.

19 See FAO 1989, vol. 42, Table 4, 'Food Production Indices' for 1988. World Bank 1989, Table 4 in 'Indicators', records the indices for food production per capita for 1987.

20 Data referred to here are contained in a table I prepared on the basis of material in sources detailed in Note 9 of Chapter 1. As indicated earlier, only published estimates are included.

21 The present sub-section draws on (and quotes from) Sayigh (1978b: 46–8). Minor alterations, cuts and editorial changes have been made in some instances, but none alters the meaning or the context. The direct quotations are indicated as such; (However, a few quotations in the sub-section come from another source, which will be pointed out at the appropriate time.)

22 The data recorded are supported by the *FAO Production Year Book 1988*, Table 1. Comparison has been made between the data for 1988 and those for 1972 as recorded in the same Yearbook. No significant change has been registered with respect to cultivable and irrigated areas.

23 A more recent work (1987) refers to a French study that spoke of the value of 'imported' consultancy services in 1979 alone as being $23 billion, but I consider this estimate as exaggerated. (See *CAUS 1988*, and Note 24 below.)

24 See, for instance, *Hilbawi (1989)* and *Committee for the Strategy of the Development of Sciences and Technology in the Arab Homeland (1988)*.

25 Samih Mas'oud (1987a and 1987b), and his references to his own earlier work.

26 The OPEC Fund for International Development (OFID) and the Islamic Bank for Development are two important sources of economic aid which do not fall in the categories mentioned in the text. However, the largest members of the Fund and the Bank with respect to capital participation are Arab governments, and by far most of the aid emanates from them, and is therefore already accounted for.

27 World Bank (1989), Table 20 in 'Indicators'.

28 This classification is also adopted in a major study undertaken by the Centre for Arab Unity Studies, Beirut, in which a few dozen Arab social scientists and computer experts were engaged for over five years. The Study involves a 'Project for Prospecting the Future of the Arab Homeland'. The supervisor and team leader of the project was Khair ed-din Ḥaseeb. It was completed in the autumn of 1987 and the report has since been published by the Centre (CAUS 1988). The final product consists of four volumes. Three of these address the following themes: Arab Development, Society and State, and The Arabs and the World. The fourth volume is the Final Report and is entitled *The Future of the Arab Nation: Challenges and Options*. It integrates the findings of the first three volumes, and describes the methodology used. For full bibliographical notation, and transliteration of the Arabic titles, see bibliography.

CHAPTER 5

1 Of special relevance and significance in the present context are many of the publications of the Centre for Arab Unity Studies, Beirut, and several of the seminars it has held since its foundation in 1976. Though less active, the Federation of Arab Economists has also made notable contributions to the understanding of the contemporary Arab economy. Much of the research work and publication of the Arab Fund for Economic and Social Development (Kuwait), the Organization of Arab Petroleum Exporting Countries (Kuwait), The Third World Forum (Cairo) and The Arab Thought Forum (Amman) bear directly on the identification of the common features of, and the trends discernible in, Arab society and economic life. The 'Project for Prospecting the Future of the Arab Homeland', to which reference was made in Note 28 for Chapter 4 above, contains the richest and most comprehensive examination of Arab society, economy and polity.

2 However, the 'flowering of democracy' in the socialist community of countries, beginning with the drive for *glasnost* and *perestroika* in the USSR in 1985, and culminating in the far-reaching political and economic reforms in the other European socialist countries late in 1989, has left the process of democratization in the Arab region pale and hesitant by comparison.

3 For a study on attitudes to Arab unity based on extensive field work in ten Arab countries, see *Ibrahim* (*1981*). See also the volume entitled *Society and State* (*Al-Mujtama' wad-Dawla*), and the Final Report entitled *The Future of the Arab Nation: Challenges and Options* (*Mustaqbal al-Umma al-'Arabiyya: At-Tahaddiyat wal-Khayarat*), referred to in Note 28 of Chapter 4.

4 Four papers presented in two seminars within one week (28 November to 2 December 1987) contain varying estimates. Hence the range between low and high estimates in the same paragraph in the text to which this note relates. The papers are: Riadh Tabbara 'Development of human resources and its demographic dimension in the Arab world' (English and Arabic versions), and Mahdi Elmandjara 'Human resources: the weight of science and technology'. Both these papers were given at a seminar on 'Human Resource Development in the Arab World' held in Kuwait, 28–9 November 1987, organized by the Arab Fund for Economic and Social Development, Kuwait Fund for Arab Economic Development, the Arab Institute for Planning, and the United Nations Development Programme.

The last two papers – Abdelatif Al-Ḥamad 'Implications of oil for Arab development, financial and investment issues and options for the future', and Taher Kan'an 'Economic complementarities within the Arab world: optimizing resource use for development' – were given at a seminar on 'Prospects for Oil and Future Development in the Arab Countries' held in Amman, 1–2 December 1987, organized by the Ministry of Energy and Mineral Resources (Jordan), Arab Thought Forum (Jordan), Arab Fund for Economic and Social Development (Kuwait), Organization of Arab Petroleum Exporting Countries (Kuwait), and the Beijer Institute (Sweden). All four papers processed.

5 The paper by Al-Ḥamad referred to in Note 4 above.

6 The paper by Al-Ḥamad, p. 9, quoting OECD data. This paper is also the source for the average indicated for the decade 1974–83.

7 The paper by Tabbara, referred to in Note 4, cites $100 billion as having been transferred by Arab oil-exporting countries to other Arab countries during the years 1975–87, quoting The World Bank, *World Development Report 1987*, pp. 244–5.

8 The paper by Kan'an referred to in Note 4, p. 12.

9 Yusif Sayigh's paper in *CAUS (1987)* was taken as the basis for the discussion of the machinery of Arab self-reliant development in the present text, but with considerable expansion of the material in the paper.

10 The questionings and doubts referred to in the text were voiced also in the paper cited in the preceding note.

11 An earlier examination can be found in *Sayigh (1982)*. The text in the present book introduces some new nuances into the discussion in the paper.

12 Reference here is to United Arab Republic (Egypt), Information Department, *The Charter* (Cairo, June 1962; Arabic, English, and French editions). The proposition under discussion received wide acceptance among the radicalized, nationalist elements of the Arab intelligentsia, after President Gamal Abdel-Nasser announced it and elaborated on it.

13 I was asked by the Secretariat General of the League of Arab States to head a small team, which included Mahmoud Abdul-Fadheel and George Corm, to prepare a draft 'Strategy for Joint Arab Economic Action'. The draft constituted the core of the document which was finally approved by the Arab Heads of State at the 11th Arab Summit in late November 1980 in Amman, Jordan. I was then asked to serve as the co-ordinator of the project, involving the preparation of twenty-six studies by twenty specialists, which constituted basic and supplementary material in support of the Strategy document; I was also asked to be the editor of the studies. In addition, I prepared the *Principal Paper* which contained the overview of the central themes dealt with by the basic and supplementary papers. The whole project consisted of three volumes in addition to the *Principal Paper*. The Plan mentioned in the text (which was one of the basic papers) was prepared by Mohammed Mahmoud al-Imam, a noted Arab planner. The material in its entirety has appeared in two editions, the second under the imprimatur of the Secretariat General of the Arab League. See Secretariat General of the League of Arab States, Directorate of Economic Affairs (1980).

14 Special credit must be given to Abdul-Hassan Zalzalah, for many years Assistant Secretary General of the League of Arab States for Economic Affairs, for his deep concern with the pursuit of Arab economic complementarity and of self-reliant development. The ambitious enterprise described in Note 13 above was under his general leadership.

15 This is Schumpeter's apt designation. Though coined in a different context, it fits the present discussion.

Bibliography

WORKS IN ENGLISH (OR FRENCH)

Abdalla, Ismail-Sabri (1980) 'Arab industrialization strategy based on self-reliance and satisfaction of basic needs', *IFDA Dossier*, no. 16, March–April.

Abdalla, Ismail-Sabri, Abdallah, Ibrahim, S.E., Abdel-Fadil, Mahmoud and Nassar, Ali (1983) *Images of the Arab Future*, trans. Marissa Talaat, London: Frances Pinter.

Adelman, Irma (1975) 'Development economics – a reassessment of goals', in *American Economic Review – Papers*, vol. LXV, part 2.

Alavi, Hamza and Shanin, Teodor (eds) (1982) *Introduction to the Sociology of 'Developing Societies'*, London: Macmillan.

Almond, G.A. and Coleman, J.S. (eds) (1960) *The Politics of the Developing Areas*, Princeton, NJ: Princeton University Press.

Ameri, Anan (1981) *Socioeconomic Development in Jordan (1950–1980): An Application of Dependency Theory*, Ann Arbor, Michigan: Wayne State University, Ph.D. Dissertation, University Microfilms International.

Amin, Galal A. (1974) *The Modernization of Poverty: A Study in the Political Economy of Growth in Nine Arab Countries 1945–1970*, Leiden: E.J. Brill.

Amin, Samir (1974) *Accumulation on a World Scale: A Critique of the Theory of Underdevelopment* (2 volumes), New York: Monthly Review Press.

——— (1976) *Unequal Development: An Essay on the Social Formations of Peripheral Capitalism*, trans. Brian Pearce, London: The Harvester Press; New York: Monthly Review Press.

——— (1977a) 'Self-reliance and the new international economic order', *Monthly Review* 19 (3).

——— (1977b) *Imperialism and Unequal Development*, New York: Monthly Review Press.

Amin, Samir, Arrighi, Giovanni, Frank, André Gunder and Wallerstein, Immanuel (1982) *Dynamics of Gobal Crisis*, London: Macmillan.

——— (1986) *La déconnexion: pour sortir du système mondial*, Paris: Cahiers Libres 413/Editions la Découverte.

Andriamanjara, Rajoama (1984) 'L'aide étrangère vue des pays récéveurs', *IFDA Dossier*, no. 43, September–October.

Apter, David E. (1965) *The Politics of Modernization*, Chicago and London: University of Chicago Press.

Arnold, H.J.P. (1966) *Aid for Development: A Political and Economic Study*, London: Bodley Head.

Baran, Paul (1952) 'On the political economy of backwardness', *The Manchester School*, January.

—— (1957) *The Political Economy of Growth*, New York and London: Monthly Review Press.

Bauer, P.T. (1981) *Equality, The Third World and Economic Delusion*, London: Weidenfeld & Nicolson.

—— (1984) *Reality and Rhetoric: Studies in the Economics of Development*, London: Weidenfeld & Nicolson.

Bernstein, Henry (ed.) (1973) *Underdevelopment and Development: The Third World Today*, Harmondsworth: Penguin, especially the following essays: 'Introduction: Development and the social sciences'; 3, T. Dos Santos, 'The crisis of development theory and the problem of dependence in Latin America'; 9, F.H. Cardoso, 'The industrial elite in Latin America'; 14, J. Gray, 'The economics of Maoism'; 15, I. Wallerstein, 'The state and social transformation: will and possibility'; and 19, R. Cruise O'Brien, 'Colonization to cooperation? French technical assistance in Senegal'.

—— (1979) 'Sociology of underdevelopment versus sociology of development?', in David Lehmann (ed.) *Development Theory: Four Critical Studies*, London: Frank Cass.

Blomström, Magnus and Hettne, Björn (1984) *Development Theory in Transition – The Dependency Debate and Beyond: Third World Responses*, London: Zed Books.

Booth, David (1975) 'André Gunder Frank: an introduction and appreciation', in Ivar Oxall, Tony Barnett and David Booth (eds) *Beyond the Sociology of Development*, London: Routledge & Kegan Paul.

Boulding, Kenneth E. (ed.) (1984) *The Economics of Human Betterment*, London: Macmillan.

Caporaso, James (1974) 'Methodological issues in measurement of inequality, dependence, and exploitation', in Steven Rosen and James Kurth (eds) *Testing Theories of Economic Imperialism*, Toronto: Lexington Books.

Cardoso, Fernando Henrique (1972) 'Dependency and development in Latin America', *New Left Review*, no. 74, July–August.

—— (1973) 'The industrial elite in Latin America', in Henry Bernstein (ed.) *Underdevelopment and Development: The Third World Today*, Harmondsworth, Penguin.

—— (1977a) 'Towards another development', in Marc Nerfin (ed.) *Another Development: Approaches and Strategies*, Uppsala: Dag Hammarskjöld Foundation.

—— (1977b) 'The consumption of dependency in the US', *Latin American Research Review* XII (3).

Cardoso, Fernando Henrique and Faletto, Enzo (1979) *Dependency and Development in Latin America*, Berkeley, Los Angeles and London: University of California Press.

Cassen, Robert, Jolly, Richard, Sewell, John and Wood, Robert (1984) *Rich Country Interests and Third World Development*, London and Canberra: Croom Helm.

Chambers, Robert (1984) *Rural Development: Putting the Last First*, London: Longman.

Chase-Dunn, Christopher (1975) 'The effects of international economic dependence on development and inequality: a cross-national study', *American Sociological Review* 40, December.

Chenery, Hollis B. (1975a) 'The structuralist approach to development policy', *American Economic Review-Papers*, vol. LXV, part 2, May.

—— (1975b) 'Restructuring the world economy', *Foreign Affairs*, no. 2.

Chenery, Hollis and Syrguin, Moises, with the assistance of Hazel Ellington (1975) *Patterns of Development: 1950–1970*, Oxford: Oxford University Press for the World Bank.

Chilcote, Ronald H. (1977) 'Dependency: a critical synthesis of the literature', in Janet Abu-Lughod and Richard Hay, Jr (eds) *Third World Urbanization*, New York, London and Toronto: Methuen.

Cifuentes Espinoza, Malva (n.d.) *Self-Reliance and Dependence: A Latin-American Perspective*, 45 pp., Oslo.

Cockcroft, James D., Frank, André Gunder and Johnson, Dale I. (1972) *Dependence and Underdevelopment: Latin America's Political Economy*, Garden City, NY: Anchor Books, Doubleday & Co., especially the following essays. 'Introduction'; 2, André Gunder Frank, 'Economic dependence, class structure, and underdevelopment policy'; 4, Dale L. Johnson, 'Dependence and the international system'; 5, James D. Cockcroft, 'Last rites for the reformist model in Latin America'; 11, André Gunder Frank and Arturo Bonilla, 'Declaration of Latin American economists'; and 14, André Gunder Frank, 'Who is the immediate enemy?'.

'Culture et Développement', *Revue Tiers-Monde* 25 (97), January–March 1984. Sous la direction de Lê Thành Khôr (avec plusieurs collaborateurs).

Dag Hammarskjöld Foundation (1975) Report on Development and International Cooperation, *What Now?* (Report prepared on the Occasion of the Seventh Special Session of the United Nations General Assembly. Appeared as a Special Issue of the Journal *Development Dialogue*, 1975).

Development Centre, OECD (1977) *The Development of Development Thinking*, Liaison Bulletin No. 1, Paris: Organization for Economic Co-operation and Development.

Dos Santos, Theotonio (1970) 'The structure of dependence', *American Economic Review-Papers*, vol. LX.

—— (1973) 'The crisis of development theory and the problem of dependence in Latin America', in Henry Bernstein (ed.) *Underdevelopment and Development: The Third World Today*, Selected Readings, Harmondsworth: Penguin.

Dowidar, M.H. (1979) 'La stratégie de type 'self-reliance' et l'ordre economique international', *Mondes en Dévéloppement*, 1 (26).

Eisenstadt, S.N. (1983) 'Development, modernization and dynamics of civilizations', *Cultures et Dévéloppement*, 15 (2).

Elgabaly, N.M. (n.d.) 'Agricultural development and land management in relation to environment and food supply needs in the ECWA region', in United Nations Economic Commission for Western Asia (ECWA) and the United Nations Environment Programme (UNEP), *Development Problems and Environmental Issues in Western Asia*, Proceedings of the Regional Seminar on Alternative Patterns of Development and Life Styles in Western Asia, convened jointly by EWCA and UNEP, Beirut, Lebanon, January 1980.

Emmanuel, Arghiri (1972) 'White-settler colonization and the myth of investment imperialism', *New Left Review*, no. 73, May–June.
—— (1974) 'Myths of development versus myths of underdevelopment', *New Left Review*, no. 85, May–June.
Enayat, Hamid (1982) *Modern Islamic Political Thought*, London: Macmillan.
Erb, Guy F. and Kallab, Valeriana (eds) (1977) *Beyond Dependency: The Developing World Speaks Out*, USA: Overseas Development Council.
FAO (1989) *FAO Production Yearbook 1988*, Rome: Food and Agriculture Organization.
Foster-Carter, Aidan (1973) 'Neo-Marxist approaches to development and underdevelopment', *Journal of Contemporary Asia* 3 (1).
—— (1974) 'Neo-Marxist approach to development', in Emmanuel de Kadt and Gavin Williams (eds) *Sociology and Development*, London: Tavistock Publications.
—— (1976) 'From Rostow to Gunder Frank: conflicting paradigms in the analysis of underdevelopment', *World Development* 4 (3).
—— (1984) 'Theory in development: current trends', *Third World Review*, vol. 1.
—— (1985) *The Sociology of Development*, Ormskirk, Lancs: Causeway Books.
Frank, André Gunder (1966) 'The development of underdevelopment', *Monthly Review* 18 (4).
—— (1969) 'Sociology of development and underdevelopment of sociology', *Catalyst*, no. 3.
—— (1972a) *Capitalism and Underdevelopment in Latin America: Historical Studies of Chile and Brazil*, Harmondsworth: Penguin.
—— (1972b) *Lumpen Bourgeoisie, Lumpen Development: Dependence, Class, and Politics in Latin America*, New York: Monthly Review Press.
—— (1972c) 'Economic dependence, class structure, and underdevelopment policy', in James D. Cockcroft, André Gunder Frank and Dale L. Johnson (eds) *Dependence and Underdevelopment: Latin American Political Economy*, Garden City, NY: Anchor Books, Doubleday & Co.
—— (1978) *World Accumulation*, New York: Monthly Review Press; London: Macmillan.
—— (1982) *Dependent Accumulation and Underdevelopment*, London: Macmillan.
Friberg, Mats, Hettne, Björn and Tamm, Gordon (1979) *Societal Change and Development Thinking: An Inventory of Issues*, 41 pp., Tokyo: United Nations University.
Furtado, Celso (1957) *The Economic Growth of Brazil*, Berkeley: University of California Press.
—— (1964) *Development and Underdevelopment*, trans. by Ricardo W. de Agruiar and Eric Charles Drysdab, Berkeley and Los Angeles: University of California Press.
—— (1976) *Economic Development of Latin America*, Cambridge: Cambridge University Press.
—— (1983) *Accumulation and Development: The Logic of Industrial Civilization*, Oxford: Martin Robertson & Co.
Galbraith, John Kenneth (1983) *The Voice of the Poor: Essays in Economic and Political Persuasion*, London: Harvard University Press.

—— (1985) *The Anatomy of Power*, London: Corgi Books.

Galtung, Johan (1971) 'A structural theory of imperialism', *Journal of Peace Research* 8.

—— (1979) 'Cultural identity, self-reliance and basic needs', Project on Goals, Process, and Indicators of Development – 9 PID, 20 pp., Tokyo: United Nations University.

—— (1980) 'Self-reliance: concepts, practice and rationale', in Johan Galtung, Peter O'Brien and Roy Preiswerk (eds) *Self-reliance: A Strategy for Development*, London: Boghe-L'Ouverture Publications.

—— (n.d.) *Self-reliance and Global Interdependence: Some Reflections on the 'New International Economic Order'*, 31 pp., Oslo.

Galtung, Johan, O'Brien, Peter and Preiswerk, Roy (eds) (1980) *Self-reliance: A Strategy for Development*, London: Boghe-L'Ouverture Publications.

Gerschenkron, Alexander (1962) *Economic Backwardness in Historical Perspective*, Cambridge, Mass.: Harvard University Press.

Goulet, Denis (1975) *The Cruel Choice: A New Concept in the Theory of Development*, New York: Atheneum.

Green, Reginald Herbold (1977) *Toward Socialism and Self-reliance: Tanzania's Striving for Sustained Transition Projected*, Research Report no. 38, 57pp., Uppsala: The Scandinavian Institute of African Studies.

Hagen, Everett, E. (1962) *On the Theory of Social Change: How Economic Growth Begins*, Homewood, Ill.: Dorsey Press.

Ul-Haq, Mahbub (1976) *The Poverty Curtain*, New York: Columbia University Press.

Harris, Nigel (1986) *The End of the Third World: Newly Industrializing Countries and the Decline of an Ideology*, London: T.B. Tauris & Co.

Hayter, Teresa and Watson, Catharine (1985) *Aid: Rhetoric and Reality*, London and Sydney: Pluto Press.

Hettne, Björn (1984) *Development Theory and the Third World*, SAREC Report R2: 1982; Stockholm: Swedish Agency for Research Cooperation with Developing Countries.

Hettne, Björn and Wallensteen, Peter (eds) (1979) *Emerging Trends in Development Theory*, SAREC Report R3: 1978; Stockholm: Swedish Agency for Research Cooperation with Developing Countries.

Hirschman, Albert O. (1977) 'A generalized linkage approach to development with special reference to staples', in Manning Nash (ed.) *Essays on Economic Development and Cultural Change in Honor of Bert F. Hoselitz*, Chicago: University of Chicago Press.

—— (1981) *Essays in Trespassing: Economics to Politics and Beyond*, Cambridge: Cambridge University Press.

Hoselitz, Bert F. (1960) *Sociological Aspects of Economic Growth*, Glencoe, Ill.: Free Press.

Hoselitz, Bert F. and Moore, Wilbert, E. (eds) (1963) *Industrialization and Society*, Paris: UNESCO.

Hunt, Geoffrey (1985) 'Fallacies of "underdevelopment": an epistemological critique of contemporary development theory', *Journal of African Marxists*, no. 7.

Huntington, Samuel P. (1968) *Political Order in Changing Societies*, New Haven and London.

IISS (1983–7) *The Military Balance*, annual issues for the years 1983–4 to 1987–8, London: The International Institute for Strategic Studies.

ILO (1976) *Employment, Growth and Basic Needs: A One-World Problem*, Report of the Director-General of the ILO, Geneva: International Labour Office.

Interregional Seminar on the International Economic Order and UNCTAD IV (1976) *Self-reliance and Countervailing Power: Report*, 31 pp., Colombo: Colombo Catholic Press.

Johnson, Harry G. (1958) *International Trade and Economic Growth*, London: Allen & Unwin.

—— (1962) *Money, Trade and Economic Growth*, London: Allen & Unwin.

De Kadt, Emmanuel and Williams, Gavin (eds) (1974) *Sociology and Development*, London: Tavistock Publications.

Kerr, Clark, Dunlop, John T., Harbison, Frederick and Myers, Charles A. (1960) *Industrialism and Industrial Man: The Problems of Labor and Management in Economic Growth*, Cambridge, Mass.: Harvard University Press.

Keynes, John Maynard (1949) *The General Theory of Employment, Interest and Money*, London: Macmillan.

Kindleberger, Charles P. (1962) *Foreign Trade and the National Economy*, New Haven and London: Yale University Press.

Kitching, Gavin (1985) *Development and Underdevelopment in Historical Perspective: Populism, Nationalism and Industrialization*, London and New York: Methuen.

Kuitenbrouwer, J.B.W. (1975) *Towards Self-reliant Integrated Development*, ISS Occasional Papers, 44 pp., The Hague: Institute of Social Studies.

Lal, Deepak (1984) *The Poverty of 'Development Economics'*, 2nd edn, West Sussex: The Institute of Economic Affairs.

—— (1985) 'The misconceptions of "development economics"', *Finance and Development* 22 (2), June.

Lall, Sanjaya (1975) 'Is "Dependence" a useful concept in analysing underdevelopment?', *World Development* 3 (11, 12).

—— (1985) *Developing Countries in the International Economy*, London: Macmillan.

Lamb, Geoff (1983) 'Rapid capitalist development models: a new politics of dependence?', in Dudley Seers (ed.) (1983) *Dependency Theory: A Critical Reassessment*, London: Frances Pinter.

Lema, Anza A. (n.d.) *Education Self-reliance: A Brief Survey of Self-reliant Activities in some Tanzanian Schools and Colleges*, 110 pp., Dar-es-Salaam: Institute of Education, University of Dar-es-Salaam.

Lenin, V.I. (1948) *Imperialism: The Highest Stage of Capitalism*, London: Lawrence & Wishart.

Lerner, D. (1958) *The Passing of Traditional Society: Modernizing the Middle East*, Glencoe, Ill.: Free Press.

Lord Lever of Manchester *et al.* (1984) *The Debt Crisis and the World Economy*, Report by a Commonwealth Group of Experts, London: Commonwealth Secretariat.

Limqueco, Peter and McFarlane, Bruce (eds) (1984) *Neo-Marxist Theories of Development*, London and Canberra: Croom Helm; New York: St Martin's Press.

Lipton, Michael (1977) *Why Poor People Stay Poor: A Study of Urban Bias in World Development*, London: Temple Smith.

Little, I.M.D. (1982) *Economic Development-Theory, Politics and International Relations*, USA: Twentieth Century Fund.

Little, I.M.D. and Clifford, J.M. (1965) *International Aid*, London: Allen & Unwin.

McClelland, David C. (1961) *The Achieving Society*, Princeton, NJ: D. Van Nostrand & Co.

McMichael, Philip, Petras, James and Rhodes, Robert (1974) 'Imperialism and the contradictions of development', *New Left Review*, no. 85, May–June.

Mandel, Ernest (1970) 'The laws of uneven development', *New Left Review*, no. 49, January–February.

Mansour, Fawzy (1977) 'Third World revolt and self-reliant auto-centered strategy of development', paper read at the Working Group for the Third World Colloquium, Houston: Rothko Chappel.

Marx, Karl and Engels, Friedrich (1888) *Manifesto of The Communist Party*, Authorized translation, London: Reeves.

Mbithi, Philip M. with Rasmus Rasmusson (1977) *Self-reliance in Kenya: The Case of Harambee*, Uppsala: Scandinavian Institute of African Studies.

Meier, Gerald M. (1984) *Emerging from Poverty: The Economics that Really Matters*, New York and Oxford: Oxford University Press.

Mende, T. (1973) *From Aid to Colonization: Lessons of a Failure*, London: Harrap.

Mishan, E.J. (1979) *The Costs of Economic Growth*, Harmondsworth: Penguin.

Moore, Wilbert E. (1963) *Social Change*, Englewood Cliffs, NJ: Prentice Hall.

Mutombo, Kanyana (1980) 'Self-reliance and authenticity: two components of a single problem', in Johan Galtung, Peter O'Brien and Roy Prieswerk (eds) *Self-reliance: A Strategy for Development*, London: Boghe L'Ouverture Publications.

Myrdal, Gunnar (1957) *Economic Theory and Underdeveloped Regions*, London: Duckworth.

Nerfin, Marc (1977) *Another Development: Approaches and Strategies*, Uppsala: The Dag Hammarskjöld Foundation.

Van Nieuwenhuijze, C.A.O., Al-Khatib, M. Fathalla and Azar, Adel (1985) *The Poor Man's Model of Development: Development Potential at Low Levels of Living in Egypt*, Leiden: E.J. Brill.

Nimbark, Ashakant (1984) 'Towards a redefinition of the Third World from development perspectives', *Scandinavian Journal of Development Alternatives* III (2), June.

Nnoli, Okwudiba (1978) *Self-reliance and Foreign Policy in Tanzania: The Dynamics of the Diplomacy of a New State, 1961 to 1971*, New York: NOK Publishers.

Nugent, Jeffrey B. and Yotopoulos, Pan A. (1979) 'What has orthodox development economics learned from recent experience?', *World Development* 7.

Nyerere, Julius K. (1974) *Ujama: Essays on Socialism*, Oxford: Oxford University Press, especially the following essays: 1, 'Ujama – the basis of African socialism'; 2, The Arusha Declaration'; 4, 'Education for self-reliance', and 8, 'After the Arusha Declaration'.

—— (1977) 'The Arusha Declaration ten years after', 51 pp., Dar-es-Salaam: Government Printer, United Republic of Tanzania.

O'Brien, Philip J. (1975) 'A critique of Latin American theories of dependency', in Ivar Oxaal, Tony Barnett and David Booth (eds) *Beyond the Sociology of Development: Economy and Society in Latin America and Africa*, London: Routledge & Kegan Paul.

O'Brien, Rita Cruise (1983a) 'Specialized information and global interdependence: problems of concentration and access', in Dudley Seers (ed.) *Dependency Theory: A Critical Reassessment*, London: Frances Pinter.

OAPEC (1982) *Secretary-General's Eighth Annual Report AH 1400: AD 1981*, Kuwait: Organization of Arab Petroleum Exporting Countries.

OAPEC (1983) *Secretary-General's Eighth Annual Report AH 1401: AD 1982*, Kuwait: Organization of Arab Petroleum Exporting Countries.

OAPEC (1984) *Secretary-General's Eighth Annual Report AH 1402: AD 1983*, Kuwait: Organization of Arab Petroleum Exporting Countries.

OECD (1983) *Aid from OPEC Countries: Efforts and Policies of the Members of OPEC and the Aid Institutions Established by OPEC Countries*, Paris: Organization for Economic Co-operation and Development.

Ohlin, Goran (1966) *Foreign Aid Policies Reconsidered*, Development Centre Studies, Paris: Development Centre of the Organization for Economic Co-operation and Development.

Oxaal, Ivar, Barnett, Tony and Booth, David (eds) (1975) *Beyond the Sociology of Development: Economy and Society in Latin America and Africa*, London and Boston: Routledge & Kegan Paul, especially the following essays: 1, 'Editors' introduction: beyond the sociology of development'; 2, Philip J. O'Brien, 'A critique of Latin American theories of dependency'; 3, Ivar Oxaal, 'The dependency economist as grassroots politician in the Caribbean'; 4, David Booth, 'André Gunder Frank: an introduction and appreciation'; and 10, John Clammer, 'Economic anthropology and the sociology of development'.

Palma, Gabriel (1978) 'Dependency: a formal theory of underdevelopment, or a methodology for the analysis of concrete situations of underdevelopment?', *World Development* 6 (7, 8).

—— (1983a) 'Dependency and development: a critical overview', in Dudley Seers (ed.) *Dependency Theory: A Critical Reassessment*, London: Frances Pinter.

Parsons, Talcott (1951) *The Social System*, New York: Free Press.

Parsons, Talcott and Smelser, Neil J. (1965) *Economy and Society*, New York: Free Press.

Payer, Cheryl (1974) *The Debt Trap: The IMF and the Third World*, Harmondsworth: Penguin.

Perroux, François (1983) *A New Concept of Development: Basic Tenets*, London and Canberra: Croom Helm for UNESCO, Paris.

Pistic, Slobodan (1980) 'The collective self-reliance of developing countries in the fields of science and technology', 23 pp., Tokyo: United Nations University.

Preston, P.W. (1985) *New Trends in Development Theory, Essays in Development and Social Theory*, London, Boston, Melbourne and Henley: Routledge & Kegan Paul.

Pugwash (1975) 'The role of self-reliance in alternative strategies for development, Report of the 24th Pugwash Symposium held at Dar-es-Salaam, Tanzania', 1975, prepared by the Rapporteur, Ashok Parthasarathi, *World Development* 5 (3): 257–65.

Pugwash Symposium (1977) *Pugwash on Self-reliance: Proceedings of the 24th Pugwash Symposium, Dar-es-Salaam, Tanzania, 1975*, edited by W.K. Chagula, B.T. Feld, A. Parthasarathi, Pugwash Monographs, New Delhi: Ankur Publishing House.

Rahman, Anisur (1976) 'Self-reliant mobilization: a conceptual study in development strategy', UN Documents, UNCTAD/RD/123.

Robinson, Joan (1962) *Economic Philosophy*, London: The New Thinker's Library, C.A. Watts & Co.

Rostow, W.W. (1952) *The Process of Economic Growth*, New York: W.W. Norton & Co.

—— (1960) *The Stages of Economic Growth: A Non-Communist Manifesto*, Cambridge: Cambridge University Press.

—— (ed.) (1963) *The Economics of Take-Off into Sustained Growth*, Proceedings of a Conference held by the International Economic Association, London: Macmillan.

—— (1971) *Politics and the Stages of Growth*, Cambridge: Cambridge University Press.

Roxborough, Ian (1976) 'Dependency theory in the sociology of development: some theoretical problems', *West African Journal of Sociology and Political Economy* 1 (2).

—— (1984) *Theories of Underdevelopment*, London: Macmillan.

Sachs, Ignacy (1980) 'Gandhi and development: a European view', in Johan Galtung, Peter O'Brien and Roy Prieswerk (eds) *Self-reliance: A Strategy for Development*, London: Boghe-L'Ouverture Publications.

Sauvant, Karl P. (ed.) (1981) *Changing Priorities on the International Agenda: The New International Economic Order*, New York: Pergamon Press.

Sayigh, Yusif A. (1962) *Entrepreneurs of Lebanon: The Role of the Business Leader in a Developing Economy*, Cambridge, Mass.: Harvard University Press.

—— (1978a) *The Economies of the Arab World: Development Since 1945*, London: Croom Helm.

—— (1978b) *The Determinants of Arab Economic Development*, London: Croom Helm.

—— (1979a) 'A critical assessment of Arab economic development, 1945–1977', *Population Bulletin* of the United Nations Economic Commission for Western Asia, no. 17, December.

—— (1979b) 'The social cost of oil revenues', in Organization of Arab Petroleum Exporting Countries, *Energy in the Arab World*, Proceedings of the First Arab Energy Conference, held in Abu Dhabi, 4–8 March 1979, vol. 1 of 4 vols.

—— (1982) *The Arab Economy: Past Performance and Future Prospects*, Oxford: Oxford University Press.

—— (1983) *Arab Oil Policies in the 1970s: Opportunity and Responsibility*, London: Croom Helm.

Schumacher, E.F. (1984) *Small Is Beautiful: A Study of Economics as if People Mattered*, London: Abacus, Sphere Books.

Schumpeter, Joseph A. (1949) *The Theory of Economic Development*, Cambridge, Mass.: Harvard University Press.

Scitovsky, Tibor (1976) *The Joyless Economy: An Inquiry into Human Satisfaction and Consumer Dissatisfaction*, New York, London and Toronto: Oxford University Press.

Seers, Dudley (1963) 'The limitations of the special case', *Bulletin of the Oxford Institute of Economics and Statistics* 25 (2).

—— (ed.) (1983a) *Dependency Theory: A Critical Reassessment*, London: Frances Pinter.

—— (1983b) 'Dependency options: the strengths and weaknesses of dependency theories in explaining a government's room to manoeuvre', in Dudley Seers (ed.) *Dependency Theory: A Critical Reassessment*, London: Frances Pinter.

—— (1983c) *The Political Economy of Nationalism*, Oxford: Oxford University Press.

Seers, Dudley, Nafziger, E. Wayne, O'Brien, Donald Cruise and Bernstein, Henry (1979) *Development Theory: Four Critical Studies*, edited by David Lehmann, London: Frank Cass.

Sen, Amartya (1978) *On Economic Inequality*, 2nd edn, Oxford: Clarendon Press.

Singer, Hans and Ansari, Javed (1977) *Rich and Poor Countries*, Studies in Economics Series, Policy Studies Institute, No. 12 in Series, George Allen & Unwin.

Smelser, Neil J. (1963) *The Sociology of Economic Life*, Englewood Cliffs, NJ: Prentice-Hall.

Sobhan, Rahman (1982) *The Crisis of External Dependence: The Political Economy of Foreign Aid to Bangladesh*, London: Zed Press.

Stewart, Frances (1985) *Planning to Meet Basic Needs*, London: Macmillan.

Stewart, Frances and Streeten, Paul (1976) 'New strategies for development: poverty, income distribution, and growth', *Oxford Economic Papers*, new series, vol. 28.

Stewart, Michael (1983) *Keynes and After*, Harmondsworth: Penguin.

Stigler, George J. (1982) *The Economist as Preacher*, Oxford: Basil Blackwell.

Streeten, Paul (1972) *The Frontiers of Development Studies*, New York: John Wiley.

—— (1979) 'A basic-needs approach to economic development', in K.P. Jameson and C.K. Wilber (eds) *Directions in Economic Development*, Notre Dame, Ind.: Notre Dame University Press.

Streeten, Paul with Burki, Shahid Javed, Ul Haq, Mahbub, Hicks, Norman and Stewart, Frances (1981) *First Things First: Meeting Basic Human Needs in Developing Countries*, Oxford: Oxford University Press for the World Bank.

Sunkel, Osvaldo (1969) 'National development policy and external dependence in Latin America', *Journal of Development Studies* 6 (1), October.

—— (1979) 'Transnationalization and its national consequences', in J.J. Villamil (ed.) *Transnational Capitalism and National Development: New Perspectives on Dependence*, Hassocks, Sussex: Institute of Development Studies.

Taylor, John G. (1983) *From Modernization to Modes of Production: A*

Critique of the Sociologies of Development and Underdevelopment, London: Macmillan.

Third World Forum (1979) *Economic Integration and Third World Collective Self-Reliance*, Occasional Paper no. 4, Nyon, Switzerland: Third World Forum.

Third World Network (1985) *Third World Development or Crisis?*, Declaration and Conclusions of the Third World Conference, Penang, 9–14 November 1984, Penang: Third World Network.

Thompson, J.H. and Reischauer, R.D. (eds) (1966) *Modernization of the Arab World*, Princeton, NJ: D. Van Nostrand Co.

Tickner, Ann (1980) 'Rousseau's concept of self-reliance compared with that of some contemporary theorists', in Johan Galtung, Peter O'Brien and Roy Preiswerk (eds) *Self-reliance: A Strategy for Development*, London: Boghe-L'Ouverture Publications.

Tinbergen, Jan *et al.* (1976) *Rio: Reshaping the International Order*, New York: E.P. Dulton.

United Nations Conference on Trade and Development (1988) *Handbook of International Trade and Development Statistics, 1987 Supplement*, New York: United Nations.

—— (1989) *Handbook of International Trade and Development Statistics, 1988 Supplement*, New York: United Nations.

United Nations Economic and Social Office in Beirut (1974) *Regional Plan of Action for the Application of Science and Technology in the Middle East*, New York: United Nations.

Vicarelli, Fusto (ed.) (1985) *Keynes's Relevance Today*, London: Macmillan.

Viner, Jacob (1952) *International Trade and Economic Development*, Glencoe, Ill.: Free Press.

von Haberler, Gottfried (1954) *The Theory of International Trade*, London: William Hodge & Co.

—— (1959) 'International trade and economic development', lecture, National Bank of Egypt, Cairo.

Wallerstein, Immanuel (1974) *The Modern World-System: Capitalist Agriculture and the Origins of the European World-Economy in the Sixteenth Century*, New York and London: Academic Press.

—— (1979) *The Capitalist World Economy*, Cambridge: Cambridge University Press.

—— (1980) The World-System II: Mercantilism and the Consolidation of the European World-Economy 1600–1750, New York and London: Academic Press.

—— (1984) *Historical Capitalism*, 2nd edn, London: Verso.

Warren, Bill (1973) 'Imperialism and capitalist industrialization', *New Left Review*, no. 81, September–October.

—— (1985) *Imperialism: Pioneer of Capitalism*, edited by John Sender, London: Verso.

Weiner, Myron (ed.) (1966) *Modernization: The Dynamics of Growth*, Washington, DC: Voice of America.

Wemegah, Monica (1980) 'Self-reliance and the search for an alternative life style in industrial countries' in Johan Galtung, Peter O'Brien and Roy Preiswerk (eds) *Self-Reliance: A Strategy for Development*, London: Boghe-L'Ouverture Publications.

Wiarda, Howard J. (1984) 'Towards a nonethnocentric theory of development: alternative conceptions from the Third World', *Journal of Developing Areas* 17 (4).

Wilber, Charles K. (1979) *The Political Economy of Development and Underdevelopment*, New York: Random House, especially the following essays: 1, Peter J. Henriot, 'Development alternatives: problems, strategies, values'; 6, Keith Griffin, 'Underdevelopment in history'; 10, Thomas E. Weisskopf, 'Imperialism and the economic development of the Third World'; 12, Mahbub Ul Haq, 'The inequities of the old economic order'; 17, John Wong, 'Some aspects of China's agricultural development experience: implications for developing countries in Asia'; 19, Paul Streeten, 'Self-reliant industrialization'; 21, Irma Adelman, 'Growth, income distribution and equity-oriented development strategies'; 22, Celso Furtado, 'The Brazilian "model" of development'; 23, John W. Gurley, 'Maoist economic development: the new man in the new China'; 26, Denis Goulet, 'Development . . . or liberation?'; 28, James H. Weaver, Kenneth P. Jameson and Richard N. Blue, 'A critical analysis of approaches to growth and equity'; 30, Ivan Illich, 'Outwitting the "developed" countries'; and 31, Paulo Freire, 'Pedagogy of the oppressed'.

Woldelsadik, Terrefe (1973) 'Tanzania – the theoretical framework of development: self-reliance and socialism', ISS Occasional Papers, 11 pp., The Hague: Institute of Social Studies.

World Bank (1988) *World Development Report 1988*, Oxford: Oxford University Press.

—— *World Development Report 1989*, Oxford: Oxford University Press.

Worsley, Peter (1982) *Marx and Marxism*, Key Sociologists Series, edited by Peter Hamilton, London and New York: Ellis Horwood.

WORKS IN ARABIC

I have used a simple system of transliteration which reflects the way Arabic words are actually pronounced, without declension. The dots under some letters indicate the 'hardness' of the letters concerned.

Abdallah, Ibrahim Sa'ad ed-Din (1980) 'Ḥawla maqoulat at-taba'iyya wat-tanmiya al iqtiṣadiyya al-'Arabiyya' ('On the paradigm of dependency and Arab economic development) *al-Mustaqbal al-'Arabi* (a monthly published in Beirut by the Centre for Arab Unity Studies, CAUS), no. 17, July.

'Abdul-Fadheel, Mahmoud (1987) 'As-soulouk wal-ada' al-iqtiṣadi li ad-duwal an-nafṭiyya ar-ray'iyya fil-manṭaqa al-'Arabiyya' ('Economic behaviour and performance of the rentier oil states in the Arab region'), *Al-Mustaqbal al-'Arabi*, no. 103, September.

Abdul-Khaleq, Jouda (ed.) (1982) *Al-Infitaḥ: Al-Juthoor, wal-Hiṣad, wal-Mustaqbal* (*Liberalization: The Roots, the Harvest, the Future*), Cairo: Arab Centre for Research and Publication.

Amin, Galal (1983) *Tanmiya am Taba'iyya Iqtiṣadiyya wa-Thaqafiyya? Khurafat Shai'a 'an at-Takhalluf wat-Tanmiya wa 'an ar-Rakha' war-Rafahia* (*Development or Economic and Cultural Dependence? Popular*

Myths on Backwardness and Development and on Opulence and Welfare), Cairo: Cairo Publications.

—— (1984) *Al-Mashreq al-'Arabi wal-Gharb* (*The Arab Mashreq and the West*), 4th edn, Beirut: Centre for Arab Unity Studies.

Amin, Samir (1987a) 'Māhiyyat al-ishtirakiyya wa-ṭabee'at azamaṭiha ar-rahina' ('The essence of socialism and the nature of its current crisis'), *Al-Mustaqbal al-'Arabi*, no. 96, February.

—— (1987b) 'Ṭabee'at nuzum al-ishtirakiyya al-muhaqqaqa wa ma ba'd ar-rasmaliyya' ('The nature of the systems of socialism achieved and post-capitalism'), *Al-Mustaqbal al-'Arabi*, no. 97, March.

—— (1987c) 'Takayyuf am fakk irtibat? Mustawa al-khatt al-istratiji' ('Adjustment [or accommodation] or delinkage? The level of strategy' [literally, the level of the strategic line]), *Al-Mustaqbal al-'Arabi*, no. 98, April.

—— (1987d) 'Mustawa at-takteek: fakk ar-rawabiṭ am iṣlah an-nizam al-'ālami? At-tadhadd ghayr al-muṭlaq' ('The tactical level: delinkage or reform of the world order? Non-absolute [?] antithesis'), *Al-Mustaqbal al-'Arabi*, no. 99, May.

Al-Biblawi, Hazem (1987) 'Ad-dawla ar-ray'iyya fil waṭan al-'Arabi' ('The rentier state in the Arab homeland'), *Al-Mustaqbal al-'Arabi*, no. 103, September.

CAUS (1983) *Dirasat fit-Tanmiya wat-Takamul al-Iqtiṣadi al-'Arabi* (*Studies on Arab Development and Economic Complementarity*) (a collection of several contributions from different economists), 2nd edn, Beirut: Centre for Arab Unity Studies.

—— (1984) *At-Tanmiya al-'Arabiyya: Al-Waqi' al-Rahin wal-Mustaqbal* (*Arab Development: The Present* [*Situation*] *and the Future*) (a collection of several contributions from different economists), Beirut: Centre for Arab Unity Studies.

—— (1987) *At-Tanmiya al-Mustaqilla fil-Waṭan al-'Arabi* (*Independent Development in the Arab Homeland*), papers and proceedings of a seminar conducted by CAUS in Amman, Jordan, 26–9 April 1986, Beirut: Centre of Arab Unity Studies. The following papers were given at the seminar, in the order in which they appear below:

Abdalla, Ismail Sabri, 'Muḥawala li-taḥdid mafhoum mujahhal' ('An attempt to define a mystified concept');

Abdalla, Ibrahim Sa'ad ed-Din, 'An-nizam ad-dawli wa-aaliyyat at-taba'iyya: aaliyyat at-taba'iyya fi iṭar ar-rasmaliyya' ('The world order and the machinery [instruments] of dependence: the machinery of dependence in the framework of capitalism);

Amin, Samir, 'Ḥawla at-taba'iyya wat-tawassu' ar-rasmali' ('On dependence and international capitalist expansion');

Zaki, Ramzi, 'Namouthaj at-tanmiya al-Hindi bayna tanaqudhat an-numou ar-rasmali wa ṭumuhat al-istiqlal al iqtiṣadi wa al-i'timad 'ala ath-that' ('The Indian model of development between the contradictions of capitalist growth and the ambitions for economic independence and self-reliance');

Fergani, Nader, 'Min al-kitab al-aḥmar ila al-kitab al-asfar: 'ardh tajribat as-Ṣeen at-tanmawiyya' ('From the Red Book to the Yellow Book: presentation of the developmental experience of China');

Ḥandousa, Hiba, 'Idarat at-tanmiya al-iqtiṣadiyya fi Kouria al-Junoubia' ('The management [conduct] of economic development in South Korea');

Hussein, Adel, 'Tajribat Miṣr fit-tanmiya al-mustaqilla: at-taqaddum wa at-tarajou' fi at-tajriba al-Miṣriyya' ('The experience of Egypt in independent development: advance and retreat in the Egyptian experience');

Khawajkiyya, Moḥammed Hisham, 'Tajribat at-tanmiya min munṭalaq al-istiqlal wat-taba'iyya fil-mamlaka al-'Arabiyya as-Sa'udia' ('The development experience of the Kingdom of Saudi Arabia from the perspective of independence and dependence');

'Uraybi, Miṣbaḥ, 'Istratijiyyat at-tanmiya al-mustaqilla fi iqtiṣad ṣagheer al-ḥajm maftouḥ: tajribat al-Jamahiriyya' ('The strategy of independent development in a small, open economy: the experience of the Jamahiriyya');

Kan'an Ṭaher, 'Tajribat at-tanmiya al iqtiṣadiyya fil-Urdunn bayna at-taba'iyya wal-istiqlal' ('The developmental experience of Jordan between dependence and independence');

Al-Manoubi, Khalid, 'Ishkaliyyat at-tanmiya al-mustaqilla fi ḍou' at-tajriba at-Tunisiyya' ('The *problématique* of independent development in the light of Tunisian experience');

As-Saqqaf, Abdul-'Aziz, 'Taṭawour fajwat al-mawarid wa shuruṭ at-tanmiya al-mustaqilla fil-Joumhiriyya al-'Arabiyya al-Yamaniyya' ('The evolution of the resources gap and of the conditions [prerequisites] of independent development in Yemen Arab Republic');

Al-Imam, Moḥammed Maḥmoud, 'Dawr al-'amal al-'Arabi al-mushtarak fi taḥeeq at-tanmiya al-mustaqilla' ('The role of joint Arab action in achieving independent development'), and

Sayigh, Yusif, 'Naḥwa tanmiya mustaqilla fil waṭan al-'Arabi' ('Towards independent development in the Arab homeland').

——— (1988), Khait ed-Din Haseb (ed.), *Mustaqbal al-Umma al-'Arabiyya: At-Taḥaddiyat wal-Khayarat – Al-Taqreer al Niha'i li-Mashrou' Mustaqbal al-Waṭan al-'Arabi* (*The Future of the Arab Nation: Challenges and Options – Final Report on the Project for Prospecting the Future of the Arab Homeland*), Beirut: Centre for Arab Unity Studies.

Committee for the Strategy of the Development of Sciences and Technology in the Arab Homeland (1988) *Istratijiyyat Taṭweer al-'Uloum wat-Technologia fil-Waṭan al-'Arabi* (*The Strategy of the Development of Sciences and Technology in the Arab Homeland*), Beirut: Centre for Arab Unity Studies.

Fergani, Nader (1980) *Hadr al-Imkaniyya: Baḥth fi Mada Taqaddum ash-Sha'ab al-'Arabi Naḥwa Ghayatih* (*The Squandering of Potential: Essay on the Extent of the Advance of the Arab People Towards Its Objectives*), Beirut: Centre for Arab Unity Studies.

Al-Ḥamad, Abdelatif Yusif (1987) *Al-I'timad 'ala an-Nafs wal-'Amal al-'Arabi al-Mushtarak* (*Self-reliance and Joint Arab Action*), Kuwait: Arab Planning Institute.

Ḥamza, Sa'ad Maher (1959) *Dirasat fi Iqtiṣadiyyat at-Takhalluf wat-Taba'iyya, ma' al-Ihtimam bish-Sharq al-Awsat* (*Studies in the Economics of Underdevelopment and Dependence, with Emphasis on the Middle East*), Cairo: The Arab Bayan Committee Press.

Ḥilbawi, Yusif (1989) 'Taḥaddi al-mustaqbal wa qadhaya at-technologia al-ḥaditha' ('The challenge of the future and the issues of modern technology'), *Al-Mustaqbal al-'Arabi*, no. 130, December.

Ḥussein, Adel (1981) *Al-Iqtiṣad al-Misri min al-Istiqlal ila at-Taba'iyya 1974–1979* (*The Egyptian Economy from Independence to Dependence 1974–1979*), Parts 1 and 2, Beirut: Dar al-Kalima wa Dar al-Wiḥda.

—— (1985) *Naḥwa Fikr 'Arabi Jadid: An-Nasiriyya wa at-Tanmiya wa ad-Dimoqratia* (*Towards New Arab Thinking: Nasserism, Development and Democracy*), Cairo: Dar al-Mustaqbal al-'Arabi.

Ibrahim, Sa'ad ed-Din (1981) *Ittijahat ar-Ra'y al-'Arabi Naḥwa Mas'alat al-Wiḥda* (*Public Opinion Trends with Regard to the Question of Unity*), 2nd edn, Beirut: Centre for Arab Unity Studies.

Ibrahim, Sa'ad ed-Din (1988) *Al-Mujtama' wad-Dawla* (*Society and State*), Beirut: Centre for Arab Unity Studies.

Sa'ad ed-Din, Ibrahim and Abdul-Fadheel, Mahmoud (eds) (1988) *At-Tanmiya al-Iqtisadiyya* (*Economic Development*), Beirut: Centre for Arab Unity Studies.

Al-'Issawi, Ibrahim (1989) *Qiyas at-Taba'iyya fil-Waṭan al-'Arabi* (*The Measurement of Dependence in the Arab Homeland*), Beirut: Centre for Arab Unity Studies.

Al-Kawari, 'Ali Khalifah (1983) 'Naḥwa fahm afdhal lit-tanmiya bi'tibariha 'amillya ḥadhariyya' ('Towards a better understanding of development as a civilizational process'), *Al-Mustaqbal al-'Arabi*, no. 49, March.

—— (1989) 'Ta'leeq 'ala waraqat ad-Doktor 'Abd-Allah al-Qouwayz hawla "Taharrouk majlis at-ta'awun fi majal al-istithmar" ' ('Comment on Dr Abdallah al-Qouwayz's Paper on "Movement of the Co-operation Council in the field of investment" '), at a Symposium with the theme: 'Tabee'at wa Mustaqbal al-istithmar fi duwal majlis at-ta'awun fi al-khaleej' ('The nature and future of investment in the States of the Gulf Co-operation Council'), held in Dubai, UAE, 12–13 December.

Al-Khauli, Usama and Ḥussein, Mukhtar al-Jammal (1987) *At-Technologia wal-Mawarid al-Bashariyya wal-I'timad 'ala an-Nafs* (*Technology, Human Resources and Self-Reliance*), Kuwait: Arab Planning Institute.

Mas'oud, Majeed (1987) *'Alaqat al-intaj wa al-i'timad ala an-nafs fi al-Waṭan al-'Arabi* (*Relations of Production and Self-reliance in the Arab Homeland*), Kuwait: Arab Planning Institute.

Mas'oud, Samih (1987a) *Al-Mashrou'at al-'Arabiyya al-Mushtaraka wa al-'Amal al-'Arabi al-Iqtiṣadi al-Mushtarak* (*Joint Arab Projects and Joint Arab Economic Action*), Kuwait: Arab Planning Institute.

—— (1987b) 'Al-mashrou'at al-'Arabiyya al-mushtaraka: waqi'uha, ahammiyyatuha, ma'ouqatuha, wa mustaqbaluha' ('Joint Arab projects: their present status, importance, hindrances and future'), *Al-Mustaqbal al-'Arabi*, no. 103, September.

Sa'id, Mohammad as-Sayyid (1984) 'Naẓariyyat at-taba'iyya wa tafseer takhalluf al-iqtiṣadiyyat al-'Arabiyya' ('The theory of dependency and the explanation of the backwardness [underdevelopment] of the Arab economies'), *Al-Mustaqbal al-'Arabi*, no. 62, April.

Sayigh, Yusif (1961) *Al-khubz ma' al-Karama: Al-Muḥtawa al-Iqtiṣadi al-Ijtima'i li al-Mafhoum al-Qawmi al-'Arabi* (*Bread with Dignity: The Economic and Social Content of the Concept of Arab Nationalism*), Beirut: Dar al-Tali'a.

—— (1982) 'At-tanmiya al-'Arabiyya wa al-muthallath al-ḥarij' ('Arab development and the critical triangle'), *Al-Mustaqbal al-'Arabi*, no. 41, July.

—— (1988) 'Fi al-iqtiṣad as-siyasi wa al-ijtima'i li-idarat at-tanmiya al-'Arabiyya' ('On social and political economy and the management of Arab development'), *Al-Mustaqbal al-'Arabi*, no. 114, August.

Secretariat General of the League of Arab States, Arab Monetary Fund, Arab Fund for Economic and Social Development, and the Organization of Arab Petroleum Exporting Countries (1983, 1987, 1989, 1990) *At-Taqreer al-Iqtiṣadi al-'Arabi al-Muwaḥḥad 1982, 1986, 1988* and *1989* (*Unified Arab Economic Report 1982*, etc.).

Secretariat General of the League of Arab States, Directorate of Economic Affairs (1980) *Awraq ar-Ra'isiyya al-'Amma* (*The General Principal Paper*); *araq ar-Ra'isiyya* (*Principal Papers*); and *Awraq al-Musanida li Awraq ar-Ra'isiyya* (*Papers supportive to the Principal Papers*) (in two parts), Beirut. The material has since appeared in two other publications under slightly different titles. The first was published in three volumes by Al-Mu'assasa al-'Arabiyya li ad-Dirasat wa an-Nashr in Beirut in 1985; the second by the League of Arab States, in three volumes, under the overall title, *Nahwa 'Amal Iqtiṣadi 'Arabi Mushtarak* (*Towards Joint Arab Economic Action*); vol. 1: *Awraq ar-Ra'isiyya* (*The Principal Paper*); vol. 2: *Al'Alaqat al-Iqtiṣadiyya al-'Arabiyya ma' al-Kharij* (*Arab Foreign Economic Relations*); vol. 3: *Qadhaya Iqtiṣadiyya 'Arabiyya* (*Arab Economic Issues*).

Zalzalah, 'Abdul-Ḥassan (1987) *Al-'Amal al-'Arabi al-Mushtarak wa al-I'timad 'ala an-Nafs* (*Joint Arab Action and Self-Reliance*), Kuwait: Arab Planning Institute.

Index